MILLER, Wilbur R. **Cops and bobbies: police authority in New York and London, 1830–1870.** Chicago, 1977. 233p bibl index 76-27847. 16.00 ISBN 0-226-52595-3. C.I.P.

Miller focuses on stereotypes identified with the New York and London police departments. Although fears of excessive police authority existed in both cities, there were differing popular expectations that prompted contrasting police methods. In London, where there was concern that policemen might become instruments of aristocratic government, officials insisted that bobbies represent the "rule of law" and act in an "impersonal" and professional manner. In New York, where democracy encouraged confidence in majority rule, there were fears of institutionalized authority and professionalism. The New York police, therefore, were essentially amateurs controlled by partisan politicians. Since there was little legal definition of their authority, policemen exercised broad discretionary power. Miller compares practices of arrest and detention in both cities and shows how social class and ethnicity complicated prevailing views about the police. The book contains an index, bibliographical essay, and documentation but lacks illustrations. Scholars will find it more analytical than traditional works like Augustine E. Costello's *Our police protectors: history of the New York police from the earliest period to the present time* (1885; repr. 1972).

COPS AND
BOBBIES

COPS AND

Police Authority in
New York and London,
1830-1870

Wilbur R. Miller

BOBBIES

**THE UNIVERSITY OF
CHICAGO PRESS**

Chicago and London

WILBUR R. MILLER is assistant professor of history at the State University of New York, Stony Brook.

THE UNIVERSITY OF CHICAGO PRESS, CHICAGO 60637
THE UNIVERSITY OF CHICAGO PRESS, LTD., LONDON

Title page illustrations: New York City policemen, 1864. Reproduced courtesy of the New York City Police Academy Museum. London bobbies, before 1864. Reproduced courtesy of the Metropolitan Police.

Library of Congress Cataloging in Publication Data

Miller, Wilbur R
    Cops and bobbies.

    Bibliography: p.
    Includes index.
    1. New York (City) — Police — History.   2. London — Police — History.   I. Title.
HV8148.N5M54   363.2'09421   76-27847
ISBN 0-226-52595-3

To
Carole
and to the memory of
my parents
Eleanor Roper Miller
Wilbur Redington Miller

CONTENTS

PREFACE

Everybody today can conjure up images of the London bobby and the New York City cop: the one is polite and abstains from deadly weapons; the other might be less polite and is certainly very well armed. These images are obviously stereotypes; but sociologists who study the complex modern reality of British and American police forces have found significant differences in the definition and practice of their authority. To a certain extent these differences make the stereotypes seem not entirely far-fetched after all: the British policeman exercises a sort of impersonal, restrained authority; the American policeman, a more personal and less restrained authority.

This study is an effort to ascertain how the two police forces of London and New York shaped their enduring public images in the formative years of the mid-nineteenth century. During the 1830–70 period crucial decisions were made (or not made) by the heads of the London and New York police forces which created distinctive styles of authority and fostered different public responses to the police image. Though decision-makers exerted personal influence on both forces, the differences between them reflected the broad social trends of two societies which shared a cultural heritage but diverged in the nature of their ideologies, political institutions, and class relationships.

London's Metropolitan Police, created in 1829, was the first modern police force in a nation with representative government. Its modernity rested on its role as "preventive police," which could control crime by preventing it from occurring instead of merely detecting it after the fact. Successful prevention depended on coordination and collective effort—central direction of the police rather than reliance on officers who were more like entrepreneurial private detectives than public officials. Equally important was pervasiveness—full-time day and night patrols with enough men to cover whole districts, men who recognized local residents and could subject them to constant surveillance if necessary. A final element of prevention was visibility—providing the officers with symbols of authority recognizable both by citizens needing assistance and by criminals who would be deterred. Ideally, prevention would replace the old reliance on severity of punishment with certainty of punishment. Such were the elements of London's "New Police," which supplanted a confusion of local forces, policemen attached to the criminal courts, and the ancient night watch.

Americans adopted the general structure of the London force, but chose only the more specific aspects they thought appropriate to a democratic society. Boston may deserve the credit for the first American police organized on the preventive principle, although its beginning in 1837 was very modest. Its small size, only thirty-two men, as well as its retention of the separation between day and night policing, did not allow full implementation of coordination and continual surveillance. New York's Municipal Police of 1845, combining day and night patrols in a force of eight hundred men, was both more ambitious and closer to the preventive ideal.

Although the London and New York police shared the broad principle of prevention, as well as certain structural features, the differences between the forces provide the focus of my study. These differences were apparent in the overall definitions of the policeman's mission, the organization of the two departments, recruitment and discipline, arrest and other practices, the relationship to the legal and judicial systems, and the response of various groups and classes to the police.

The opening date for the period of my study, 1830, marks the first full year of operation of the London police, and the beginning of a decade in New York marked by social disorder and increasing discussion of adopting a London-model police force. The closing date, 1870, is somewhat more arbitrary, although it also roughly marks important events. The arbitrary aspect was dictated by the Public Record Office's hundred-year rule for British police records. However, in 1868 the last of the two original police commissioners died, and 1869 witnessed changes which departed from some of his policies but proved not to alter the general principles established in the early years. In New York, 1870 saw return of the control of the police force to the city government after more than a decade's direction by the state government.

Finally, when I speak of the London police I mean the force of the Metropolitan Police District created in 1829 and later enlarged. This district excluded the square mile in London's heart called "the City," which still retains its distinct police force. Similarly, in the case of New York I will deal with only the police of Manhattan, even though after 1857 New York's Metropolitan Police District covered Brooklyn, Staten Island, and parts of Queens and Westchester as well.

This study is not meant to provide a history of all aspects of the London and New York police during the mid-nineteenth century. British scholars such as Charles Reith, Leon Radzinowicz, and T. A. Critchley, and the American James F. Richardson, have told the story with thoroughness and discernment. Although I will necessarily cover much of the ground broken by these writers, I hope to achieve more than a synthesis. My work is an attempt to examine the two forces in a new light, by comparing their different definitions and practice of police authority, as well as the public responses to their official images in the context of two different societies.

In addition to debts to my predecessors in the field, many people have helped me to refine my thinking on a more personal level. My first acknowledgments are to Sigmund Diamond and Eric McKitrick of Columbia University; I believe I have profited as much from their different general orientations to the study of history as from their specific suggestions. Another primary debt is to Carole Turbin, whose straightforward criticisms led to major improvements and the focusing of some fuzzy thinking. Professors David Rothman, Allan Silver, and R. Jackson Wilson offered constructive criticisms which I have sought to incorporate here. Other people who have been helpful in reading various parts or versions of this study include James M. Banner, Jr., Mark H. Haller, Roger Lane, James M. McPherson, Arno J. Mayer, and James F. Richardson.

Staff members of the Public Record Office; British Museum newspaper division; library of University College, London; and the New York City Municipal Archives eased the dusty work of manuscript and newspaper research. The collections of the British Museum, Guildhall, Columbia University, New York Public, and New-York Historical Society libraries were the indispensable mine for my materials.

Grants for travel, research, and manuscript preparation have made this study possible. I owe thanks to the National Institute of Mental Health, the Woodrow Wilson Foundation, and to Jameson W. Doig, director of the Guggenheim criminal justice research program at Princeton University's Woodrow Wilson School.

The *Journal of Social History* kindly gave permission for reprinting material in chapter 1 originally appearing as an article. Finally, I want to thank Donald E. Meyer, at the time a teaching assistant at Berkeley, who told me as an undergraduate that the image of the cop in America would be a good dissertation topic. Over ten years later, here is something more and less than that.

1 POLICE AND SOCIETY

"Every constitution must first *gain* authority, and then *use* authority," Walter Bagehot observed. "It must first win the loyalty and homage of mankind, and then employ that homage in the work of government." In societies with representative governments, the police must obtain and then utilize voluntary compliance with their authority. Effective law enforcement requires general agreement that the power of the police is legitimate. As Edwin Chadwick said, "A police force . . . must owe its real efficiency to the sympathies and concurrent action of the great body of the people." The experience of the Royal Irish Constabulary, a semimilitary police established in 1822 to bolster English rule in Ireland, proved that police officers were helpless if local citizens did not give them aid and information. The "great body" of Irishmen never accepted the force's legitimacy. Public sympathy and support is by no means automatic; the police must work to achieve and maintain legitimacy. Certainly, as is clear in the case of the Irish constabulary, people's view of the police reflects their general attitude toward the government which policemen represent. Nevertheless, the police have an active role in creating their own public image, and in fact many people's perception of the government derives from their contact with its lowest level of authority, the policeman. Chief William Parker of the Los Angeles police bluntly rephrased Bagehot's idea: "The vital elements of civilized life, including our most sacred institutions, at one time or another have been laboriously *sold* to the people."[1]

The laws which established modern patrol forces in London in 1829 and in New York City in 1845 outlined their basic structure but did not provide a formula for "selling" or legitimating the police. In both cities conscious decisions and historical circumstances shaped

1

the police image. The commanders of the forces were influenced by the ideological, political, and economic contexts of two different societies as reflected in their greatest cities.

ESTABLISHMENT OF THE NEW POLICE

London's Metropolitan Police Act, which Sir Robert Peel finally steered through Parliament in 1829, created a full-time day and night patrol force for a police district which excluded the City and was expanded in later years. The new police, commanded by two commissioners appointed by the home secretary as permanent heads of the force, supplanted most of the old police apparatus. Although the police were an arm of the national government divorced from local control, the parishes, or units of London's local government, had to support them from their tax revenues. The new police were the first force in the world organized to prevent crime by constant patrolling instead of merely apprehending offenders after the fact.

Sir Robert Peel's main contributions to the new institution were synthesizing decades of thought about police reorganization and using his political skill to secure passage of the Metropolitan Police Act. He neither originated the concept of preventive police, nor, except in his insistence that political patronage be excluded from appointments and promotions, did he have much impact on the subsequent organization and practice of the force. The two commissioners whom he appointed played the critical role of fleshing out the skeleton — providing the force's distinctive features and developing its overall image. Charles Rowan, a distinguished military officer, and Richard Mayne, a rising barrister, established the police's military organization and discipline, the system of patrolling fixed beats, the distinctive blue uniform, and numerous important details of structure and practice which added up to the London bobby, or peeler. The organizational history of the mid-nineteenth-century London police is largely the account of the two commissioners' impact on the institution and their response to the social and political milieu. They worked together until Rowan's retirement in 1850, after which, except for an unpleasant but brief colleagueship with William Hay, Mayne held sway alone, with the help of assistants, until his death in 1868. The new commissioner, Sir E. Y. W. Henderson, a military officer and prison official, inherited a well-established police tradition which he modified only slightly.[2]

New York City's Municipal Police Act, put into effect in 1845 after several years of political wrangling, created the first police force modeled on London's precedent outside of the British Empire. The measure spelled out more details of the new institution than did its London forebear. It established a semimilitary day and night patrol force to replace the old system and also specified the qualifications for appointment, fixed the men's terms of office, and established the pay of various ranks. With the mayor's approval, each alderman appointed the police of the ward he represented. Unlike the London police, which remained largely unchanged after the commissioners established its structure and policy, the New York force was altered in various major and minor ways throughout the mid-nineteenth century. The most important of these changes, in 1853, 1857, and 1870, involved control of the police. The 1853 reorganization put the force under the command of a commission of three elected officials, the mayor and two judges. The most drastic change, in 1857, shifted control from city to state authorities, entrusting direction to commissioners appointed by the governor. In 1870 control was returned to the city with a commission appointed by the mayor. In contrast to the London police, the New York force was an evolving and changing institution.[3]

Frequent reorganization of the force resulted in many changes of commanders. None of them even approached Rowan's twenty-year tenure or Mayne's almost forty years in office. Nevertheless, although they operated within a framework set by other officials, men like Chief George W. Matsell, a former justice of the peace who commanded the Municipal Police from 1845 to 1857, and John A. Kennedy, general superintendent of the state-controlled Metropolitan Police from 1860 to 1870, had important impact on the exercise of police authority and the development of the force's image.

In neither London nor New York could daily police work be codified by statutes. The commanders of the forces responded both to common fears of excessive police power and to common demands for order in two heterogeneous, expanding cities. However, they developed structures and practices which reflected the different qualities of London's and New York's political and social conflicts and different public expectations of the police.

The initial task of the police commanders in winning legitimacy for their institutions was alleviation of mid-nineteenth-century Londoners' and New Yorkers' suspicion of expanded governmental power. The old police system which the two cities shared had been casual and sporadic. During the day there was no regular patrol force covering the whole city. Detective officers attached to the criminal courts and elected or appointed constables drawn from the local citizenry served warrants and apprehended offenders for a fee. After dark the night watch, ancient in the sense of both the institution's long history and the age of many of its members, patrolled the streets. However, the watch was not centrally coordinated and in most districts was undermanned and inefficient, the butt of standing jokes like the New Yorkers' quip, "While the city sleeps, the watchmen do too." There was little sense of a police presence: the law was most visible in the public punishment of petty and major offenders.[4]

In contrast, the modern preventive police established in London and New York represented an unprecedented, highly visible increase of the state's power over the lives of ordinary citizens. The new forces patrolled the streets round the clock and could subject citizens to constant surveillance if necessary. To many people the cop on the beat was an ominous intrusion upon civil liberty. Englishmen feared an importation of despotic France's secret political police — "the Continental spy system" — or the creation of a more formidable variety of England's own network of informers and agents provocateurs which had harassed radicals during the Napoleonic Wars. Americans believed that adoption of such an institution was too authoritarian for their democratic society. Citizens of both nations, each with a long tradition of rejection of a professional army in favor of volunteer forces, saw preventive police as a standing army susceptible to the political manipulations of an ambitious despot. The new police were received fearfully by people who, despite differences between their societies, shared a jealous regard for liberty which delayed reorganization of the police until long after the need was felt and articulated.[5]

To overcome public suspicion and fear, the police had to address themselves to different elements of a heterogeneous public. The social and economic position and ideology of various individuals and groups influenced their views of the political order and consequently of the policemen who upheld that order. Because of unequal wealth and power, some people regarded the law and its enforcers as protective while others saw the system as oppressive. Even if "the great body of the people" accepted the police, there were many degrees of acceptance and a substantial minority may have only yielded to superior power without acknowledging any rightfulness of police authority. The police upheld the society which created them; in heterogeneous communities, with unequal distribution of wealth and power, they could not expect a uniform response to their definition of the balance between liberty and authority.

THE GROWING DEMAND FOR CONTROL

Early- and mid-nineteenth-century London and New York were each expanding, complex communities. London's population almost doubled in seventy years (1750–1820) and New York grew even more rapidly, more than quintupling in forty years (1790–1830), with much of the growth spurred by foreign immigration. One of the most important motivations for reorganization of the police systems in both cities was the growing sense that the old informal social controls of hierarchy and neighborhood were breaking down as population expanded and the rich segregated themselves from the poor. Criminal elements found increasing security in isolated slum districts, like London's St. Giles or New York's Five Points, from which they could sally forth into the anonymous urban crowds and to which they could return to escape apprehension. Advocating a preventive police in 1828, Edwin Chadwick described London as a metropolis where "men live for years, often during their whole lives, without knowing their next door neighbours, and an individual may there at his will maintain absolute solitude, or immediately be lost to pursuit amidst the congregated million and a half of inhabitants." In 1837, when New York had "a population . . . rapidly increasing, and a Police the same as it was upwards of twenty years since," public officials asserted that "it is but reasonable to conclude that here crime will seek for means of support, as well as for a place of concealment." In heterogeneous cities, "even distinctions of wealth and rank are almost lost in the crowd; and all that can be relied on are certain external indications and appearances which may be either genuine or counterfeit." The confidence-man, who played upon appearances, and the detective, who disguised himself to deceive his quarry, became familiar urban types.[6]

Whether this picture of the city as a place of isolation and a breeding ground for the breakdown of moral sanctions is accurate matters less than the belief of contemporaries that the quality of urban life was changing for the worse. The well-to-do and middle classes fled from the poor, and as the gulf between the classes grew the poor seemed more threatening and unreachable. The new police, created partly to cope with the crime which seemed to thrive amid urban complexity, could, it was hoped, control symptomatic disorder but clearly could not reverse the social and economic trends

5

which proceeded apace after their establishment. They represented an effort to substitute more formal and efficient social controls for a modest police apparatus which in the past seemed to have been backed up by common moral standards and the direct influence of the wealthy upon their poorer neighbors. "A new Aera in the world seems to have commenced," lamented the police reformer Patrick Colquhoun. "The evil propensities incident to human nature appear no longer restrained by the force of religion, or the influence of moral principle."[7]

Soon after Colquhoun's complaint, however, the growth of evangelical Protestantism in the early nineteenth century spurred many upper- and middle-class Londoners to demand regulation of the manners and morals of the lower classes. "Respectable" citizens grew increasingly intolerant of crime and disorder. They no longer ignored brawling, drunkenness, and petty theft, which the eighteenth century's easier morality and draconian criminal code had encouraged them to overlook. The concern for social control was accompanied by a growing demand for mitigation of severe but capriciously and sporadically administered punishments for major and minor crimes. In both London and New York the movement to replace harsh physical punishments with imprisonment sought to bring about a true moral reformation of the offender which would permanently counteract the influences of his lower-class culture.[8]

Not many criminals were thus regenerated, but legal reform encouraged citizens to prosecute petty criminals since the penalty for stealing a handkerchief was no longer death. Moreover, a stint in the "penitentiary" might prove a young delinquent's salvation. In some neighborhoods of London during the 1820s, when mitigation of punishments was well under way, citizens formed voluntary associations for the prosecution of felons, in which members pooled their resources for the expensive process of apprehension and trial of criminals. During the same decade, justices of the peace increased the number of offenders they committed for jury trial in higher courts. In New York between 1814 and 1834, also a period of legal reform, complaints entered before the city's justices of the peace more than quadrupled, a rate which outstripped population growth during those years. Contemporaries used such figures to prove that crime was increasing, but, as Edwin Chadwick pointed out, rising committal and complaint rates may have indicated that "more crime is now prosecuted and exposed to public view; —not more committed." This is not to say that disorder was a figment of Londoners' and New Yorkers' imaginations, but rather that growing intolerance of crime and willingness to prosecute it were major dimensions of the problem. The growth of evangelicalism and the achievement of legal reform were important preludes to creation of a new police. [9]

Economic developments also prompted the propertied classes' growing intolerance of disorder and demands for its control. As the urban economy became more complex and specialized, it became increasingly sensitive to riots which disrupted its delicate inter-relationships. In eighteenth-century London riots were the only effective avenue of protest for the working classes, which the ruling elite learned to live with as one of the hazards of political life. Major riots which resulted in great property damage and loss of life, such as the anti-Catholic or Gordon riot of 1780, could be violently sup-pressed by troops and the city would return to normal. The Gordon riot inspired William Pitt's comprehensive police reorganization measure, foreshadowing many features of Peel's 1829 act, but nothing was done because of the general belief that the outbreak was "a single instance of a defect in the civil power which, in all probability, would never again occur." New York in the late eighteenth and early nineteenth centuries was much less riotous than London. The only major incident was the Doctor's riot of 1788, in which angry crowds besieged New York Hospital to protest the exhumation of bodies for medical dissection. New Yorkers had less reason for concern than Londoners. [10]

However, with the development of commercial and industrial capitalism during the first half of the nineteenth century, the propertied classes could no longer be complacent about the long-term impact of disorder. The stock market's sensitivity to instability made riots and their violent repression unacceptable: "A shooting affray in the streets of the metropolis might destroy a substantial part of the nominal national capital . . . , stocks collapsed and there was no bottom in prices." In London during the early 1820s a series of political protests and growing doubts about the effectiveness of military riot control prompted demands for police reorganization. In 1823 the duke of Wellington advocated a civilian-controlled police "to preserve the lives and properties of His Majesty's subjects against domestic insurrection and disturbance." At the same time Peel made his first effort to establish a preventive police force, which failed because fears of spies and standing armies still prevailed over the demand for order. At the calmer end of the decade he was able to appeal to Londoners' concern for protection of their property, which was as liable to damage in riots as to theft.*

In New York, the "year of riots," 1834, in which shops were looted and respectable citizens' homes destroyed, was followed by extensive looting during the great fire of the next year. This disorder, new to a people accustomed to policing themselves and proud of America's law-abiding reputation, spurred business-oriented newspapers to campaign for reorganization of the police along London lines. As in London, fears of expanded police power still prevailed, and it took the murder of Mary Rogers (Marie Roget of Edgar Allan Poe's story) in 1841 to revive the demand for order which finally produced a new police. In both London and New York the growing intolerance of riots in a complex economy was an important prod toward police reorganization, although the growth of more ordinary crime and disorder seemed to be the factor which finally caused legislators to subordinate their fears of police power to the need for order. Nevertheless, the economic stability of the city was a vital component of order. As an anonymous New Yorker observed after establishment of the new police, "Men will go with reluctance to make money in a city where pestilence or violence renders life unsafe." Effective police contributed to the city's economic health.[11]

THE IMPACT OF SOCIAL CONFLICT ON POLICE AUTHORITY

Both London and New York were socially, culturally, and economically heterogeneous and complex. Contemporaries' realization that urban growth required new means of social control underlay their demands for police reorganization. Although both cities experienced similar problems and conflicts, and citizens responded in similar ways, the nature of political and social conflict in London and in New York reflected two very different societies in the process of social change. The different forms which conflict took in the

---

*Peel did not mention riot control in his speech proposing the Metropolitan Police bill in 1829. Instead he addressed contemporary concern about protection of property, describing Londoners' possessions as in an "exposed and insecure state" (*PD*, 1828, n.s., vol. 21, cols. 786–87, 791 [quotation]). Elie Halevy dismissed riot control as a motivation for the new police: "Never had the possibility of an insurrection in England seemed more remote than at the time when the New Police Bill was carried" (*A History of the English People in the Nineteenth Century*, 4 vols. [New York, 1949], 2: 288). I should repeat, though, that Peel first devised his police scheme in 1822 when he was home secretary. At this time the fear of insurrection was fresh in people's minds.

two cities influenced each police force's definition of its authority and the public image it developed among various social groups. Michael Banton has argued that the contrasting styles of modern British and American police authority can be explained by Britain's greater social homogeneity. However, it is difficult to maintain that mid-nineteenth-century London was more homogeneous than New York. The "metropolis of the New World" was of course far more ethnically divided than the British metropolis, but the gulf between Disraeli's "two nations, the rich and the poor" made propertied and propertyless Londoners view each other as alien races and political conflict was often more intense than New York's ethnic squabbles. Banton himself recognizes that his thesis may be inapplicable to the nineteenth century. An examination of the quality of conflict in the two cities and its impact on the police seems more promising than an effort to measure their relative degrees of heterogeneity.[12]

The London force took to the streets amid England's constitutional crisis over parliamentary representation for disenfranchised middle-class citizens, whose protests were backed by a reserve of more militant working-class anger. The politically dominant landed aristocracy met the challenge from the industrial, commercial, and professional middle classes by separating them from the working classes and tying them to the existing order through the electoral reform of 1832. The next challenge, fended off rather than coopted, arose from various working-class groups angry at their exclusion and dissatisfied with selecting "one or two wealthy men to carry out the schemes of one or two wealthy associations," the political parties under the new franchise. Culminating in Chartism, which included universal suffrage, annually elected Parliaments, and abolition of the property qualification for M.P.'s among its demands, working-class protest was defeated largely by middle-class commitment to the social order. This commitment was clear in the climactic Kennington Common Chartist demonstration in London in 1848, when shopkeepers turned out as "special constables" to help control the protest. After a lull during the prosperous fifties and early sixties, working-class groups again demanded the franchise in the economically uncertain late sixties. Reflecting the increased economic power of workers organized into trade unions which were more politically moderate than the early protest groups, the reform of 1867 gave urban workers the vote without altering the balance of social and economic power. The "leap in the dark" was another cooptive measure which, as Disraeli said, would "be the means of placing the institutions of this country on a firmer basis" and would "tend to increase the loyalty and contentment of a great portion of her Majesty's subjects."[13]

Recurrent political crises, despite their stable resolution, were of profound importance to the police force charged with upholding the social order and controlling a turbulent population of the national capital, to which people looked with hope or apprehension in difficult times. Since disenfranchised protestors could have impact on Parliament "out of doors" — demonstrations in the streets — policemen inevitably confronted them. Would these confrontations feed the fire of political conflict? Would the police be identified as the cutting edge of the ruling minority's oppression? Since their role was fundamentally political amid challenges to the political order's legitimacy, the commanders of the force had to devise a politic strategy for containing conflict if they expected the new police to survive the Tory government which created them.

The New York police worked within a different context than their London brethren. New York was not a metropolis in the European sense, where a nation's center of culture and commerce was also its political capital. Except in the spectacular draft riots of 1863, Americans did not look to New York for the nation's political fate as Englishmen looked to London. America's mid-nineteenth-century political crisis, the breakup of the Union, was acted out in the corridors of Washington or the plains of Kansas instead of in the streets of the largest city. Sometimes the disorder which New York policemen had to control reflected a national crisis, but usually it was of only local significance.[14]

New York's local disorder was the result of ethnic conflicts which punctuated the era. While not as portentous as London's political disturbances, these conflicts did have consequences for the nature of police authority. The presence of large numbers of immigrants in American cities gave a distinct tone to class conflict. Antagonism between skilled and unskilled urban workers increased with the filling of the unskilled ranks by immigrants, especially Irish, in the mid-nineteenth century. Native-born workers, concerned about the degradation of their trades by industrialization, regarded the unskilled Irishman willing to work for longer hours and lower wages as an economic and social threat. This rivalry between elements of the working classes undercut their sense of common political interest.

10

Moreover, many workers joined the propertied classes in fearing the Irishman's foreign religion and culture, which seemed to contain elements of both a lax morality and political authoritarianism imported from Europe. The native-born workers who dominated American trade unions shared their employers' acceptance of the existing political system of representative democracy, believing that it gave all men an equal chance to rise in the world. The Irishman, who was both rowdy and under the influence of the antidemocratic Catholic church, threatened to disrupt cherished institutions. Organized labor joined the propertied classes in denouncing the Irish draft rioters of 1863. While George T. Strong "would like to see war made on Irish scum as in 1688," the leading labor newspaper pictured them as "thieving rascals . . . who have never done a day's work in their lives." The paper added, "The people have too much at stake to tolerate any action beyond the pale of the law. . . . No improvement can be made by popular outbursts upon the great superstructure created by the wisdom of our fathers."[15] In England workingmen rarely expressed such institutional faith; while skilled workers looked down on the unskilled they had a greater sense of their class's common lot. America's propertied and native working classes alike saw a political order they valued threatened by irresponsible foreigners who did not appreciate democracy.

Since the New York police upheld the political institutions of representative democracy which most Americans valued, there was little pressure for them to transcend social conflict to insure their own survival. Instead of upholding the rule of a small elite which was challenged by the majority of the population, the police supported a political order founded on majority rule which seemed threatened by an alien minority. Along with most New Yorkers, the police were free to treat a large group in the community as outsiders. This group's participation in disorder did not seem to require the sort of sensitivity needed to uphold minority rule without alienating the majority.

What sort of police authority emerged to cope with the different types of social conflict in London and New York? In both cities pure repression was unacceptable because of its past failures, its tendency to promote more violence, and its unpopularity with most citizens. Since the police had to depend on the voluntary compliance of most people with their authority, the commanders of the two forces had to define the institution and develop its practice in ways which would win support or at least tolerance in two heterogeneous

11

communities. They had to develop an image with the broadest possible public appeal, an image aimed at common interests underlying diversity.

The London Police

Taking to the streets amid a serious political crisis, circumstances were not auspicious for the London police. In addition to arousing long-standing fears of military oppression and a secret spy system, the force was created as one of the last acts of the unreformed Parliament. Central control of the police suggested that they would be thoroughly political: "Is it not under the command of one single man, the Secretary of State for the Home Department — and is not he the minion and paid servant of the Government?" This question hinted that the future of the police was as dubious as that of the unreformed Tory government if they became too closely identified with its personnel and policies. Rowan's and Mayne's reply resembled the strategy of the reforming elite of 1832. They would strengthen social order and the authority of the police by crisis management aimed at reducing conflict. Little is known about the two commissioners' political beliefs, but they acted very much like the Whig aristocratic reformers who supplanted the Tories after 1832.[16]

At the center of the commissioners' strategy was their belief that police impartiality was the key to public acceptance. Amid social conflict they "endeavoured to prevent the slightest practical feeling or bias, being shewn or felt by the police." With varying success, during their long terms of office, Rowan and Mayne determined that "the force should not only be, in fact, but be believed to be impartial in action, and should act on principle."[17]

Removal of the police from partisan politics was an important part of this impartiality. Peel's main contribution after establishment of the new police was his insistence on strict exclusion of patronage in appointments and promotions and prohibition of political activity among policemen. Rowan and Mayne gladly sustained his policy of requiring all appointments to be on the basis of merit and promotions to be granted according to merit and seniority, with greater emphasis on merit. The commissioners established strict qualifications for admission to the force, which they maintained with a few minor exceptions throughout the mid-nineteenth century. To keep the men out of politics, the Metropolitan Police Act denied the vote to bobbies. In an era when political patronage was the rule in government departments, the police anticipated civil service reforms which came many years later. Such political neutrality could be sustained because the commissioners, appointed for life and not removable with changes of government, had most of the real power over the police force. By the 1860s a journalist could write that "One great merit in the police is . . . that they know nothing of politics; the man in blue always preserves his neutral tint." Amid political controversy, "the good old cause of order is the only side the policeman supports."[18]

Order may not have been partisan, but whose order it was and the way it was upheld were political issues. In a society with intense class conflict, one man's law and order could be another man's oppression. It was difficult to maintain an image of neutrality and impartiality when one of the police's earliest duties was control of political protest demonstrations. Though the police were sent to maintain order, their presence sometimes provoked disorder. In the early 1830s the mere appearance of "Peel's bloody gang" was sufficient provocation for many demonstrators to reply with stones or occasionally more lethal weapons. Even in more peaceful 1855 an editorial pointed out that the "military array" of the police at the Hyde Park anti-Sunday law demonstration implied a battle, and the threatened crowd responded angrily. The commissioners never fully solved this problem or prevented irritated bobbies from losing control and taking out their anger on demonstrators. Partly this was because of the buildup of tension before the police moved in, and partly because patrolmen who spent most of their time on the beat as individuals with broad personal discretion were often difficult to coordinate in military-style crowd control duties. Nevertheless, Rowan and Mayne sought to maintain order with minimal provocation and violence. If they could not avoid the fundamentally political implications of crowd control, they tried to soften its impact.[19]

The commissioners evolved a technique of restrained power for handling demonstrations. Keeping the military backstage, they first sought to make clear the strength of the police, providing sufficient men so that they "should not on any occasion be worsted." They aimed at making this power a "moral influence" by which the police could minimize overt force. They developed police strength by mobility and coordination in handling crowds; they minimized force by keeping the bobbies in the background until needed and insisting on forbearance under provocation. This emphasis on restraint was critical, for Rowan and Mayne realized that unchecked force would actually weaken police authority. During the Chartist demonstrations of 1842, when some of the radicals were rumored to be armed with knives, the commissioners reminded the men of "the great importance of not using any irritating language or expressions even towards those who may be offending against the laws." Moderation was the best way to win the sympathy and aid of "well-disposed" onlookers. Although violence was never entirely eliminated, crowd control techniques developed over the years by trial and error were more restrained than before establishment of the new police or in areas without the London system. In the early thirties many people acknowledged the superiority of police over military control of demonstrations. Without placating ultraradicals who continued to fear police tyranny, the commissioners won the support of moderate radicals like Francis Place, who shared their concern for peaceful protest from a different perspective.[20]

Aware that Parliament and the press were looking over their shoulders during the thirties, and that "if it is possible to put a sinister construction on anything done by the Police, there are plenty to do it," the commissioners developed what one historian calls "a laudable political discretion." They were particularly sensitive after being burned by sharp criticism of police methods at the Cold Bath Fields demonstration of 1833, and the "Popay incident" of the same year, in which an overzealous bobby acted as an agent provocateur. Rowan's and Mayne's cautiousness and sensitivity prevented the police from being completely identified with the old order which created the force, and enabled the institution to survive a period of recurring conflict virtually unchanged in structure and policy.[21]

The strength the police gained from being an independent agency of the national government lay behind the commissioners' commitment to impartiality and moderation. As a national institution the force could draw from a reservoir of symbolic as well as physical power. "Power derived from Parliament," said a contemporary observer, ". . . carries with it a weight and energy that can never be infused by parish legislation; and in respect of an establishment for general security, it is doubly advantageous, by striking terror into the depredator, and arming the officer with augmented confidence and authority." Similarly, "the mob quails before the simple baton of the police officer, and flies before it, well knowing the moral as well as physical force of the Nation, whose will, as embodied in law, it represents." The commissioners drew from the nation's symbolic and physical power by identifying the police as agents of the legal system who derived both their strength and their restraint from the powers and limitations of the laws of England. Rowan and Mayne expected bobbies to be the impartial representatives of the law, which ideally at least transcended the existing government and social conflicts of the day. The legal and judicial systems were hardly realms of pure justice, and they bore unequally on different social classes, but police subordination to the law aided public acceptance of the force as the law was reformed and political representation of the middle and working classes expanded during the 1830–70 period. The restrained power of the police was the restrained power of the law.[22]

The commissioners' emphasis on impartiality and legality added up to an impersonal image of police authority. An impersonal policeman was somewhat aloof from the local community because of his independence from it; he conducted himself according to, and was limited by, bureaucratic or legal standards which could be influenced by public opinion but were largely independent from immediate political pressures. He resembled, on the whole, one of Max Weber's bureaucratic professionals. Controlled by the national government, London bobbies were a tightly disciplined group. The commanders of the force inculcated loyalty and obedience to the standards they established. To help bobbies carry out their role as impartial agents of the legal system, the commissioners stressed procedural regularity, confinement of police power to legally sanctioned duties, and limitation of patrolmen's personal discretion in exercising their authority. As agents of the law, officers were expected to subordinate their own impulses to the law's requirements and limitations. An observer of the 1850s vividly captured this impersonal image: "Stiff, calm, and inexorable . . . an *institution* rather than a man. We seem to have no more hold of his personality than we could possibly get of his coat buttoned up to the throttling-point."[23] The commissioners deliberately created a stereotype to which they expected their men to conform. Obviously not all did, but Rowan and Mayne were strict disciplinarians who were ready to dismiss men who violated their official impersonality.

London's Metropolitan Police, responsible to the national government for the security of the capital, were thoroughly part of the English political order. Since the police had to forge their public image in a period of crisis and of widespread hostility to the government which created them, the commissioners had to make critical decisions about how to overcome fear and suspicion to insure the new institution's survival. They sought to create an impersonal authority which would transcend the current conflicts by maintaining order impartially and within the law. As early as 1831 the commissioners hoped that "the Police have conciliated the populace and obtained the good will of all respectable persons."[24] As will be developed in chapter 4, impersonal authority generally did satisfy "respectable persons" with a stake in the political and economic system, and, although never entirely acceptable to those who were denied political representation, the police did not provoke further hostility. London's impersonal authority was a response to crisis, a survival mechanism to win the broadest public acceptance or at least tolerance of a new institution which affected all citizens. This image, developed to cope with political conflict, extended outside the political arena into the general maintenance of order and crime control.

The New York Police

The New York policeman was less thoroughly molded than his London brother, but he did embody a distinct image which reflected conscious efforts as well as circumstantial results. New York officials, because the city's social conflict took place within the framework of a widely accepted representative democracy, needed a different sort of political sensitivity than that of the London commissioners. They had to create a force which would conform to preexisting patterns of democratic government. This democratic policeman's authority was personal, resting on closeness to the citizens and their informal expectations of his power more than on formal bureaucratic or legal standards. If London's impersonal policeman was a bureaucratic professional, New York's patrolman was essentially an amateur, viewed as little more than an ordinary citizen delegated with legal power. Technically, the London policeman was also defined in this way, for like his American colleague he could be sued in ordinary courts for false arrest, but the ideology and structure of the force actually made him into a professional public servant. In New York, the policeman was more a man than an institution, arousing public responses more according to his individual conduct than the formal institutional definition of his authority. The personal policeman generally exercised broader discretionary power than his impersonal counterpart; he had a wider choice of when and how to act.[25]

One of the most important of the democratic patterns which shaped the New York policeman's personal authority was the expectation that municipal institutions should be close to the people. The police, as Mayor Isaac Varian said in 1839, should be "but a part of the citizens." The men who established the New York force in the year of Andrew Jackson's death shared his faith in the common man and his belief that "the duties of public officers are, or at least admit of being made, so plain and simple that men of intelligence may readily qualify themselves for their performance." Unlike Peel and the London commissioners, who thought that professional independence and impartiality would avert the danger of a politicized police, New York officials joined Jackson in fearing instead that professional officeholders would "acquire a habit of looking with indifference upon the public interests and of tolerating conduct from which an unpracticed man would revolt." Antiprofessional feeling had already prompted, during the 1820s and 1830s, repeal of eighteenth-century laws licensing doctors and lawyers, thus opening the professions to anybody who took a minimal effort to learn their rudiments. Similar sentiments underlay American distrust of a regular army officered by West Point professionals and preference for a citizen-soldier militia which elected its officers. An important legacy of the Age of Jackson, antiprofessionalism left an enduring mark on the New York and other American police systems.[26]

Partisan control of the police was an immediate consequence of antiprofessional sentiment. Although not themselves elected, policemen were originally appointed by the aldermen of the wards in which they were to serve and had a fixed term of office. Reformers, mainly commercial and professional men concerned with improving the efficiency of municipal services, sought to move the force closer to London's nonpartisanship. Reorganization of the police in 1853 secured good-behavior tenure for the men and gave control of the force to the mayor and two elected judicial officials. This change simply centralized partisan domination of the police. Mayor Fernando Wood, elected as a reformer in 1854, soon became one of America's first urban bosses, controlling the force for his own ends through his power of appointment, promotion, and assignment of the men.

Unable to escape politics, the police became a political issue. Reformers, backed by Republican politicians anxious to break the Democrat Wood's power over the city, transferred control of the police from city to state authorities. The Metropolitan Police Act of 1857, borrowing London's idea of a metropolitan police district, created a force for the separate city of Brooklyn and various villages of Queens, Westchester, and Staten Island, as well as Manhattan. The new police were commanded by commissioners appointed for limited terms by the governor. Wood's stout resistance in the courts and battles between men of the old and new forces on the streets presaged the political controversy which continued to plague the police. The new law improved the force in various ways, including promotion by merit for the first time, but actually involved only a shift of control from Democrats to Republicans. Old forms of corruption and favoritism continued unabated, and establishment of a bipartisan commission in 1864 did little to reduce conflict. The period covered in this study closes with the Tweed Ring era, in which, under the new city charter of 1870, control of the police returned to Democratic municipal authorities, a commission appointed by the mayor.[27] In the midst of serious political crisis the London police would not have survived such partisan wrangling. The New York force did, probably because partisanship was normal in American democracy. There was no other model for municipal government. Reformers' efforts did not really overcome partisanship. Despite the shrill tone of people on different sides of the political battle lines, the police did not face a serious test of their legitimacy. They fit into an established pattern of municipal administration.

Although they did not have to cope with serious political challenges to the authority they represented, New York policemen did not command the legal and symbolic power of their London colleagues. The London bobby exercised a more pervasive presence in citizens' daily lives than did the New York cop. Not only did more officers patrol the London streets in proportion to the population than was the case in New York, but they had greater powers of surveillance over ordinary citizens and particularly over the groups from whom criminals were thought to be recruited. The Police Act of 1839 greatly expanded official power over various urban "nuisances," and the Smoke Nuisances Act of 1855 made the police responsible for control of air pollution. After passage of the Common Lodging Houses Act of 1851 the police could inspect and control the cheap lodging houses of the very poor; the Contagious Diseases Acts of 1866 and later gave the police power to regulate, by a form of licensing, prostitutes in areas near military bases; and the Habitual Criminals Act of 1869 and Prevention of Crimes Act of 1871 greatly expanded police surveillance and control of ex-convicts. Such broad legal powers over the criminal element were unknown in New York. Moreover, the police exercised a political surveillance never felt in

New York except briefly during the Civil War. New York policemen could not draw from a reservoir of national physical and symbolic power. Tied to local officials and embroiled in partisan politics, they lacked much of what Bagehot called the "dignified" aspect of government.[28]

New Yorkers do not seem to have wanted their policemen to have too much formalized institutional power. The *New York Times* and Mayor Fernando Wood agreed in the late 1850s that a somewhat inefficient policeman was one of democracy's necessary prices. The *Times* argued that inefficient policemen were inevitable in America. "The superficial observer who deplores the inefficiency of our peacekeepers, sees in it a sign of incipient decay. There never was a greater mistake; it is in reality one of the consequences of the rudest health, and the most unbounded prosperity." America's distinctive social and economic mobility made the policeman's career appealing only to those without energy or ability to pursue a more lucrative occupation. Before New York could obtain a police as efficient as London's, "we must be content to see in our midst the desperate competition and those impassible [*sic*] distinctions of rank by which society in the Old World is marked." Mayor Wood considered the Londoner more submissive than the New Yorker. The poorer classes from which policemen were recruited in London were "better adapted to military rule," and yielded more readily to discipline than Americans of the same social stratum whose fierce independence could never be absorbed into an organization like the London police.[29]

In addition to democracy's effect on the discipline of the force, the people of New York seemed to be less responsive to police authority than were Londoners. Doubting the applicability of the London force to New York in 1836, the *Journal of Commerce* ascribed its success to "the habit of submitting to authority in which the people are brought up, and which is in England, a principle of their very being." America's "ultra democracy" prevented such submissiveness, making the people "not sufficiently in the habit of respecting the laws and obeying those appointed to enforce them." A. E. Costello, chronicling the New York police in 1885, pointed out that a European policeman could "call on bystanders, in the name of the representatives of law and order, to aid him, and the appeal is seldom disregarded." In America, however, where "our free institutions tend to make men who enforce the law and deprive others of their liberty, objects of contempt," a policeman's request for aid was often "received with a guffaw."[30] The democratic policeman had less symbolic authority than his aristocratic counterpart, which in turn seemed to weaken both his physical and moral force.

If the American democrat was so antiauthoritarian, how could a contemporary remark, "A free government has habituated us to . . . confidence, and possibly a confidence not wholly deserved, in these [police] officers"? Personal, informal authority filled the void created by democratic mistrust of institutional, formal authority. Instead of drawing from his institutional legitimacy, to a great extent each policeman had to establish his own authority among the citizens he patrolled. He would not win much respect if he consistently contradicted local standards and expectations in favor of impersonal bureaucratic ideals. Although this often meant different police behavior in different neighborhoods, the patrolman also worked within broad public views of how to deal with the largely Irish immigrant "dangerous classes," the outsiders of whom many respectable citizens of all classes felt not only contributed most urban crime and disorder but also vaguely threatened cherished political institutions. The police tended to reflect and act out community conflicts instead of trying to establish and maintain standards which transcended the conflicts. Within the context of broad public expectations the patrolman was free to act as he chose. He was less limited by institutional and legal restraints than was the London bobby; he was entrusted with less formal power but with broader personal discretion. Allan Silver has characterized American police authority as "delegated vigilantism"—the patrolman did what most citizens would have done in his position.[31]

Alexis de Tocqueville helps reconcile democratic antiauthoritarianism with trust in policemen's personal discretion. Discussing "magistrates," whom he defines as "all officers to whom the execution of the laws is entrusted," he argued that Americans entrusted their public officials with broad discretionary power because they elected them, being able to remove them if dissatisfied. In aristocracies like England, on the other hand, permanently appointed officials, independent of both rulers and ruled, had to have more formal checks on their discretion to prevent oppression. In democracies, where the majority elected magistrates, "Very frequently the object which they are to accomplish is simply pointed out to them and the choice of means is left to their own discretion." Because they elected their officials Americans had "nothing to fear from arbitrary power."[32]

This argument is very general, and perhaps more applicable to judges than to policemen, who were not elected. Nevertheless, it does help contrast the London and New York police. Fears of both rulers and ruled confined the bobby to the legal boundaries which granted but also limited his power. In New York, patrolmen could be trusted with wide personal discretion because their originally direct and later indirect accountability to elected officials reduced the fear of arbitrary power. Unlike the London police, who were quite separated from the direct influence of public opinion, they looked to public expectations rather than to bureaucratic or legal standards for legitimation of their actions.

Francis Bowen, the American editor of Tocqueville's *Democracy*, objected to his argument: "Magistrates in America do not have so much trusted to their discretion as in England or France. Their modes of action are prescribed beforehand by law, and defined with jealous care." This may be equally true of policemen—surely the United States is a government of laws, not of men? Max Weber helps resolve the conflict between Tocqueville and his editor. Democracy, he said, did indeed require as a guarantee against arbitrary power "formal rational objectivity in administration [the rule of law] in contrast to personal free choice on the basis of grace, as characterized the older type of patrimonial authority." Nevertheless, democracy also called for flexibility in the administration of justice— taking individual circumstances into account when making decisions and rendering substantive rather than strictly formal justice. Weber concluded that for this reason "the democratic ethos" must "emotionally reject what is rationally demanded." In other words, though ambivalent, democracy leaned toward personal authority, and public expectations of the administration of justice were as important as its legal definition. Certainly the same ambivalence could be found in England, but if Weber's theory is correct one would expect to find it to a greater degree in the vastly more democratic mid-nineteenth-century America.[33]

Turning from political theory to local history, it can be seen that the operation of personal discretion was required to make up for the lack of symbolic physical and moral power and public trust in a police force close to the citizenry.

In New York City's ethnic riots, the physical force of military and police weaponry had to compensate for the police's lack of numerical strength and moral force. Many riots became battles in which no quarter was asked or given on either side. The Astor Place riot of

1849, the first serious test of the new police, set the pattern. A dispute between supporters of rival American and English actors became a bloody battle when the mayor called up the militia to reinforce the police. The troops fired over the rioters' heads, hitting many innocent spectators. A contemporary writer saw the episode as a failure of American justice: "We cannot in this consummation recognize any triumph of the laws, nor find any cause to congratulate the friends of order that the arm of the law has been sufficient for the emergency. The bayonet and cartridge are not elements in the administration of the American laws."[34] This was quite a different result from London's handling of the famous Kennington Common Chartist demonstration a year earlier. While London was moving away from violent repression, New York was setting a pattern of violence — the bayonet and cartridge would become familiar instruments of American riot control. Many people continued to see this violence as an institutional failure, but most "respectable" citizens were less particular about the means used to restore order.

Although they had the opportunity to gain experience in crowd control in a number of small riots during the 1850s, the police still had to be supported by troops in large outbreaks, or, if on their own, resorted to revolvers or even light artillery. The greatest challenge was the draft riots of 1863, which had national implications and made London disturbances look quite tame. Since the story of the four-day rioting and looting is familiar, it is sufficient to point out that the Metropolitan Police were generally successful in their battles with groups of rioters in various parts of the city, but lacked manpower and mobility to suppress outbreaks which cropped up elsewhere after they had put down disorder in one location. At best the police, often angry, exhausted, and desperate, drove the rioters from one area to another. Full order was restored only after the military, fresh from the Gettysburg battle, returned to the city. Nevertheless, the police, swinging clubs and firing revolvers, had contained the rioting and became heroes to New Yorkers, who believed they had saved the city from an Irish lumpenproletariat *émeute*. They cheered police toughness as "exemplary punishment" of the rioters. The Metropolitan Police commissioners argued that the experience demanded formation of a specialized, well-armed police riot squad, which they unsuccessfully sought throughout the sixties. Both the advocacy and the failure are significant: there seems to have been little hope or effort to develop London's techniques of restrained power, but at the same time New Yorkers did not give the police the physical strength which might have made restraint possible.[35]

The period covered by this study closes with the Orange riot of 1871, a clash between Protestant and Catholic Irish in which military intervention worsened the violence. Though there was some criticism of the mayor and police commissioners, Walt Whitman, the democratic bard, wrote, "The New-York police looked and behaved splendidly—no fuss, few words, but *action*." Other citizens presented a flag of honor inscribed with the dates of the draft and Orange riots to the police. "Respectable" New Yorkers, though often critical of police inefficiency and corruption, did not press for London's restraint. They seem to have expected and accepted "no fuss, few words, but action" against the immigrant "dangerous classes" who seemed to be a social "volcano under the city."[36]

Unlike London, New York seemed to be growing more violent and disorderly during the mid-nineteenth century. Unable to establish firm physical strength or moral authority, the New York police relied on personal authority responsive to public expectations instead of acting as impersonal agents of the legal system. Like their London brethren, New York policemen were part of the social and political order which created them. A democratic society, which feared institutional authority but originally trusted its policemen because they were accountable to elected officials, continued to accept personal authority even though the police moved away from direct public accountability. Because the police image was not being formed during serious political crises, the creators of the force were not under pressure to rise above conflict with an impersonal image. Though thoroughly enmeshed in partisan politics, the police did not develop a politic way to cope with social conflict by presenting themselves as representatives of the "good old cause of order" above it all. Few people expected that of them.

Although she wrote before the creation of New York's preventive police, Harriet Martineau captured the difference between the London and New York forces. She identified the English police as "agents of a representative government, appointed by responsible rulers for the public good," and the American police as "servants of a self-governing people, chosen by those among whom their work lies."[37] The London policeman represented the "public good" as defined by the governing classes' concern to maintain an unequal social order with a minimum of violence and oppression. The result was impersonal authority. The New York policeman represented "a self-governing people" as a product of that government's conceptions of power and the conflicts which divided that people. The result was personal authority.

Having described the two cities' contrasting general patterns of police authority derived from different social and political circumstances, it is time to explore development of the London and New York police images in detail.

2 SHAPING THE MAN ON THE BEAT

Behind the London and New York police images stood the men who patrolled the streets and performed many other duties. The commanders of the forces sought to mold these heterogeneous groups to their conceptions of how a policeman should present himself to the public. The type of men recruited, where they lived and what they wore, the standards of conduct they were expected to maintain, and the training and discipline given them to inculcate and uphold these standards all contributed to the public image of the police. The combination of these factors into personal and impersonal authority rested on an important question. Where would the balance be struck between the patrolman's ties to the community, which were necessary for effective police work, and his detachment, which was necessary for impartial law enforcement? Both integration and separation were essential elements of police authority, and neither London nor New York stressed one at the entire expense of the other. However, London's impersonal authority placed greater emphasis on detachment from the citizens to maintain professional impartiality, while New York's personal authority originally stressed closeness to the community, although the policeman became more separated from the citizens after 1857.

The Policeman and His Neighbors: Recruitment and Residency

The London commissioners sought to submerge the individual recruit's personality into an institutional personality. They knew just the sort of men they wanted: individuals who were superior physically, intellectually, and temperamentally to most members of the working classes from which recruits were drawn. They required prospective bobbies to be of better than average health and strength, and the minimum height requirement of five feet seven inches exceeded the stature of most Englishmen. Although there was some flexibility in the first years in order to accommodate well-qualified former soldiers and to absorb members of old forces into the new police, the commissioners kept the minimum age requirement of twenty-two and maximum of thirty-five (lowered to thirty in 1839). The education requirement called for the applicant's demonstrated comprehension of what he read and wrote. Finally, candidates had to be even-tempered and reserved, middle-class qualities not often found among the Victorian working classes: "A hot temper would never do; nor any vanity which would lay a man open to arts of flirtation; nor too innocent good-nature; nor a hesitating temper or manner; nor any weakness for drink; nor any degree of stupidity." They had to produce detailed recommendations from "respectable" people, who, as the result of many dishonest references in the early years, were also investigated. Only about one-third of the applicants survived the initial examination and many of the survivors fell by the wayside in subsequent interviews and the final appearance before Rowan and Mayne.[1]

Since the men were to be agents of impersonal authority, the commissioners expected them to be free from local or class ties which would compromise their impartiality. Rowan and Mayne wanted them to be free from "improper connections" with local residents that might create cross-pressures and thus cause the men to be indecisive and unable to do their duty. One important way of avoiding improper local connections was the recruitment of men from outside London, which allowed local residents to become acquainted with bobbies only in their police role and eliminated weakening of their authority because of previous local ties. Historians, relying on a commissioner's statement to a researcher in 1914, have said that from the first days of the force Rowan and Mayne preferred agricultural laborers as recruits. Geoffrey Gorer has assumed that the 40 percent of the Metropolitan Police in 1832 who had formerly been laborers were countrymen, but they were most likely urban because the commissioners limited recruiting to parishes of the Metropolitan District (largely urban and suburban), which supported the force from taxes. In 1837 Rowan said that they "never expressed any preference to one place over another from whence to fill up vacancies in the Police." Countrymen often made good bobbies, but they were troublesome because they soon left the force after finding out how difficult the duty was.[2]

By 1840 Rowan and Mayne seem to have preferred country recruits. Now Rowan believed that countrymen made "the best Police men." Although they took longer to train, they had "not so much to *unlearn*" as urbanites, suggesting a later observer's remark that "your sharp Londoner makes a very bad policeman; he is too volatile and conceited to submit himself to discipline." This commentator asserted that "eight-tenths" of the force came from outside London. I have not found official records to verify his claim, but of forty-one policemen who testified before the Hyde Park disturbances investigation in 1855, only three were natives of the Metropolitan District and even they did not hail from the central city. The rest came from all over England, with a sprinkling of Scots and Irish.[3]

Quite likely most of these men were not agricultural laborers, for our previously quoted observer stated that "the best constables come from the provincial cities and towns. They are both quicker and more 'plucky' than the mere country-man fresh from the village." Agricultural laborers, one of the most depressed social groups of the period, "mere labourers, who require only bodily power, and possess little or no mental development," were not the men the commissioners wanted. Later in the 1860s, however, when police pay increasingly lagged behind skilled workers' wages, they seem to have accepted more agricultural laborers.[4]

Recruitment from outside of London brought strangers into neighborhoods where the inhabitants would come to know them as policemen rather than as private individuals. Once the men were assigned to a division the commissioners required them to live in the area, partly for convenience and as a means for them to gain the necessary local knowledge, but also to enable their superiors to keep an eye on them. The men were expected to lead exemplary private as well as public lives, never forgetting that they were policemen. Single men were quartered in "section houses," or small barracks (a section comprised nine men under a sergeant's command). In the early years Rowan and Mayne believed that the officers should be kept together to avoid conflicts with a hostile public, to aid in assembling them at central points in emergencies, and to prevent them from "associating with others that might be mischievous." If the bachelors were not under their superiors' eyes, "they might perhaps cohabit with women of the town and act in various ways . . . injurious" to the image of the force. This concern was important in the early thirties, when most of the bobbies were single, but by 1834 two-thirds of them were married and that proportion held through the sixties. The commissioners preferred married men because of their stability and allowed them to rent their own quarters but required them to live within their divisions and submit to inspections of their lodgings.[5] Rowan and Mayne expected the men to be a credit to the force off as well as on duty.

Centralization of the force also reduced local influences on the bobbies. Rowan and Mayne frequently transferred men from their divisions. They also required the men to report all gifts they received from citizens; these could be accepted only with the commissioners' consent.[6] The commissioners established a system of small rewards for efficiency and good conduct to reduce the temptation of corruption. This is not to say that the bobby was incorruptible, for patrolmen and superior officers alike seem to have accepted payoffs from the proprietors of high-class gambling dens and whorehouses to ignore the law, and the image of the constable as extorter of small "tips" persists in working-class music-hall songs. Moreover, the police seemed eager to apprehend thieves when large rewards were offered, but dilatory when profits were slight.* Nevertheless, London's police

---

*Some orders on gifts and rewards are included in PO, December 21, 1829, Mepol 7/1, fol. 152; September 17, 1831, ibid., fol. 270; December 13, 1836, Mepol 7/4, fol. 332; February 28, 1838, Mepol 7/5, fol. 308; and January 25, 1844, Mepol 7/9, fol. 234. For the problem of corruption, see charges regarding gambling houses in "Principles of Police, and Their Application to the Metropolis," *Fraser's Magazine* 16 (August 1837): 175n. (which places blame for accepting "hush money" on common informers rather than on the police). Other charges about police acceptance of payoffs from gamblers are in *Illustrated London News* 4 (May 11, 1844): 297. For brothels, see Humanitas, *A Letter to the Right Hon. Sir Robert Peel, Bart. . . . and Facts Demonstrative of His Intention to Subvert Public Liberty and Enslave the Country through the Espionage and Tyranny of the New Police. . . .* (London, [1835]), p. 17; and *Reynolds's Newspaper,* January 5, 1862, p. 4, and January 17, 1869, p. 4. In his documentary novel, *Fanny by Gaslight* (London, 1948), Michael Sadleir asserts that "In the 'sixties of the last century, the police — especially those responsible for the night-areas of London — were not the disciplined and virtually incorruptible force they have since become. Bribes were a matter of course, and the houses paid annual tribute according to their status and size, as well as providing free service on demand" (p. 71; see also pp. 55, 72, for examples). Regarding rewards, Edwin Chadwick's charge in 1830 that the police did not prevent thefts because they sought rewards for apprehension (draft of article, "Thoughts on Municipal Police," 1830, p. 2, in CP, box 2) is echoed in "Perpetual Motion," a music-hall song of the sixties (*Diprose's Music-Hall Song-Book* [London, 1862], p. 29). It is difficult to assess the amount of corruption. The commissioners pointed out that in both gambling and prostitution

force was not riddled with corruption to the degree of the New York police — largely, it seems, because Scotland Yard sought to minimize the opportunities.

New York police officials had a different concern from their London colleagues. Instead of worrying about too intimate ties with local residents, they originally conformed to democratic expectations that the police, in Mayor Varian's words, should be "but a part of the citizens."[7] Although this localism was modified through the years, the New York force remained more closely tied to the community than did the London police.

The heads of the New York force expected applicants to meet physical and mental standards similar to those of the London police, but their democratic viewpoint did not foster strict adherence to them. An alderman was always willing to appoint an able-bodied supporter for a brief stint as a policeman without much concern about his qualifications. Political considerations made democratic antiprofessionalism into "rotation in office," less kindly known as the spoils system. Before the establishment of good-behavior tenure in 1853, a policeman could lose his job if an election did not go the right way or if he had antagonized his patron. Sometimes perseverance, as in the case of George W. Walling, who got himself appointed in another ward after a quarrel with his alderman, could overcome these obstacles.[8]

The three-man commission of 1853, though not as openly partisan as the aldermen, did not seem to have demanded much of prospective policemen. The commissioners were very casual in accepting or rejecting men, and, according to a critic, regulations such as the literacy requirement were "a dead letter," frequently "contemptuously evaded." Sometimes a man with good political connections had only to read a newspaper's title to prove his literacy. Adherence to standards seems to have improved under the state-controlled Metropolitan Police, but the force never shook off partisan politics.

---

the force's legal powers were limited (e.g. Rowan to Rev. Mr. Morris, July 13, 1841, Mepol 1/39, letter 83720; *PP*, 1870, vol. 36, Metro. Police Annual Report 1869, pp. 6, 11–12; *PP*, 1844, vol. 6, Gaming, Report, pp. vi–viii, and test. Mayne, p. 11). Many people must have assumed that police inactivity in these areas involved payoffs. James Grant, in the fourth edition of his *Sketches in London* (London, 1850), let stand a statement he had written in the first edition of 1838: "It is surprising in how few instances charges of corruption have been preferred, far less proved, against any of [the police]. . . . There seems to be a spirit of rivalry as to who shall be the most honest . . . as well as to who shall be the most active and enterprising among the body" (p. 392). Corruption undoubtedly existed, but it probably was not endemic.

The commissioners said in 1858 that "a judicious selection of officers as well as patrolmen, uninfluenced and unbiassed by the prejudices of the day, would tend greatly to remove any hostility that may exist against the department," but charges of political favoritism in appointments persisted. Although concern for upholding standards of admission improved over the years, candidates never underwent anything like London's thorough examination.[9]

The democratic wish to make the police "but a part of the citizens" influenced recruitment and residency policy. Under the laws of 1844 and 1853 policemen were required to have been residents for five years of the wards in which they would serve, and to continue living there while on the force. This provision, which made the patrolman into a local figure probably known to his neighbors before he joined the force, contrasted with the London commissioners' concern to prevent "improper connections" between policemen and local residents. Although some critics complained that "familiarity breeds contempt," most citizens considered the residency requirement perfectly proper and objected to occasional appointments of nonresident policemen. The requirement was generally, but not universally, enforced. In 1850 about two-thirds to three-fourths of the force lived in the ward in which they walked their beat and many of the nonresidents lived close by.[10]

The residency requirement provided policemen from the same ethnic groups as those found in the neighborhoods they patrolled. This was particularly true of the Irish, who entered the police force in large numbers through political patronage. The Germans, many of whom arrived in America with some capital and did not need police jobs to establish themselves, were not as well represented on the force. In 1855, the only year for which both sets of figures are available, 28 percent of New York's population and 27 percent of the policemen were of Irish birth. Only 4 percent of the force represented the city's 15 percent German population.[11] Table 1 reveals a close correlation between the proportion of Irish residents and Irish policemen in most wards, but less of a correspondence between German residents and policemen.

The Metropolitan Police Act of 1857 abolished the local residency requirement, specifying five years' previous residency in the police district instead of the ward in which the patrolman served. Some New Yorkers argued that recruitment of men from Westchester or Staten Island to serve in Manhattan would destroy police efficiency, which had been based on knowledge of local criminals. Although many of these critics were undoubtedly sincere, others lamented the lost local political patronage. However, although the majority of policemen ceased to live in the ward of their beat, the Irish only temporarily lost their important position on the force. In 1857/58 the number of Irish-surname policemen in Irish wards dropped off steeply, but by 1860 the Irish approached former levels. Continued concern about residency may have been the factor that prompted a change in the rules in 1869, requiring policemen to live in the county (e.g., Manhattan) in which they served. It is hard to imagine many officers commuting from Queens or Westchester to serve in Manhattan, but

TABLE 1.
Nativity of Population and Policemen by Ward, 1855, New York City

Ward	Percentage of Irish Population	Percentage of Irish Police	Percentage of German Population	Percentage of German Police
1	46	59	15	8
2	36	39	11	0
3	29	6	9	0
4	47	57	4	5
5	23	19	13	2
6	42	55	15	2
7	34	31	9	2
8	21	13	11	7
9	20	4	6	4
10	13	4	30	4
11	18	14	34	6
12	33	35	12	3
13	19	20	23	6
14	36	56	13	6
15	26	2	5	0
16	39	30	6	0
17	25	20	28	10
18	37	20	9	2
19	35	28	10	0
20	27	25	17	19
21	30	10	5	0
22	25	30	21	7

SOURCES: For the Irish, James F. Richardson, "The History of Police Protection in New York City, 1800–1870" (Ph.D. diss., New York University, 1961), p. 194. For German population, Robert Ernst, *Immigrant Life in New York City, 1825–1865*, (New York, 1949), table 14, p. 193; for policemen, *BAD*, 1855, vol. 22, no. 43, Chief's Report on Police Nativity, p. 2. I rounded percentages to whole numbers in my computations.

there may have been Brooklyn or Staten Island commuters.[12] Although the Metropolitan Police District, or even Manhattan, was much larger than the ward as a source of recruits, the New York force remained more locally oriented than did the London police, which drew from all over the British Isles.

The Irishman who immigrated to New York had more opportunity of becoming a policeman than did his compatriot who settled in London. London's old night watch had been heavily Irish, and people complained that "Charlies" ignored brawls among Irishmen. Perhaps for this reason Mayne objected to stationing Irish bobbies in Irish neighborhoods. He was also concerned that police pay would be inadequate to support the large families which Hibernians tended to have. In 1837 Mayne barred men with more than three children from entering the force. The number was reduced to two by 1860, but there was obviously, considering Victorian attitudes toward contraception, no restriction once a man was recruited. This policy may have been responsible for the declining number of Irishmen in the police: in 1834 they made up about 16 percent of the force; in 1855, about 7 percent. Although both these figures are higher than the 5 percent of Irish in London's population, Irishmen were not an important element of a police which, according to a contemporary, "has done much to purify and pacify the various Irish localities."[13] For London's Irish, in contrast to their New York compatriots, the policeman was definitely not a local figure.

London's recruitment and residency policies reflected the commissioners' concern to preserve professional impartiality by making patrolmen somewhat aloof from the communities in which they served. New York's original democratic concern to make the police close to the citizens was modified by reformers seeking to professionalize the force, but the patrolman never became as detached from the local community as his counterpart in London.

THE MAN IN BLUE

The patrolman's uniform was, of course, the most visible feature of his public image; it clothed the man in an anonymous institutional garb. The uniform not only identified the policeman on sight to citizens seeking his aid and reminded potential criminals of the police presence, but it also controlled policemen's actions by making any irregular activities visible to superior officers and civilians. The type of uniform he wore — or whether he wore one at all — revealed much about the nature of the policeman's authority.

32

The London commissioners uniformed their men to make them easily identifiable, both to help prevent crime by a visible police presence and to alleviate fears that the new police would be a secret "Continental spy system." However, they could not make the uniform too military, for that would arouse fears of the force as a standing army. Peel and the commissioners, in private and unrecorded discussions, decided on a blue uniform modeled on civilian dress. They dropped a proposed red outfit as too military. Bobbies took to the streets in 1829 wearing a blue tailcoat and trousers, a greatcoat for bad weather, boots, and a leather top hat, the crown of which contained supports so the patrolman could use it as a stool for peering over walls. Each man wore an identification letter and number on his coat collar. Reflecting current civilian fashions, the outfit was quite modest compared to gaudy military attire. With some modifications, including adoption of the modern helmet in 1864, the London bobby's uniform remained the same throughout the mid-nineteenth century. Some of the old forces had been partly uniformed, but the appearance of so many uniformed men on the streets was a new experience.[14]

At first many people physically and verbally attacked the uniformed men, confirming a prediction that they would "get marked and hooted at" because the outfit, whatever form it took, would border too much on "military array." The men themselves seemed to share these sentiments, for in the early days many of them wore their greatcoats in all weather to hide the uniform. Rowan and Mayne were "sorry to think that any of the police force can be so ashamed of the uniform of the body into which they have voluntarily entered." By 1834 the men had accepted uniforms, "except some dandies who would always be desirous of wearing plain clothes." Bobbies had to live with the uniform both on and off duty so they could be identified at all times and not be suspected of spying in plain clothes. Men on duty wore armbands so that off-duty men in uniform would not be suspected of negligence when they were on their own time.[15]

The uniform was a key element in Rowan's and Mayne's emphasis on prevention of crime: police visibility was an important deterrent, and the uniform served a "scarecrow function." Clearly, however, visibility hindered much necessary detective work which had to be secret, and the commissioners made exceptions in special cases to their requirement that the uniform be worn at all times. Nevertheless, Rowan and Mayne, particularly Mayne, had persistent doubts about extensive employment of plainclothesmen. They had been burned by the "Popay incident" of 1833, in which an overzealous patrolman in plain clothes joined the radical National Political Union and acted as an agent provocateur. The episode raised fears of the "Continental spy system," and the commissioners seem, with a few lapses, to have heeded the parliamentary investigators' warning that employment of plainclothesmen

> affords no just matter of complaint, while strictly confined to detect breaches of the law and to prevent breaches of the Peace, should these ends appear otherwise unattainable; at the same time the Committee would strongly urge the most cautious maintenance of those limits, and solemnly deprecate any approach to the Employment of Spies, in the ordinary acceptance of the term, as a practice most abhorrent to the feelings of the people, and most alien to the spirit of the constitution.[16]

Subsequently the commissioners, although they created a small specialized detective division in 1842 and expanded detective activity in succeeding years, continued to emphasize the primacy of prevention and to worry about accusations of spying. Mayne sought to make detective duty as temporary as possible, rotating the men to reduce the opportunities for corruption, always a risk because of the dependence on criminal contacts for information. He also insisted that plainclothesmen identify themselves to citizens when making arrests.[17]

Mayne's successor, Henderson, who took office after a crime wave in the later sixties, placed more emphasis on detection. He expanded the central detective force and created permanent divisional detectives, also abolishing the regulation that the men wear their uniforms off duty. Surely Mayne must have at least stirred in his grave, under the handsome monument paid for by police subscription, when in 1877 the three highest officials of the Central Detective Division were exposed as accomplices of an international ring of swindlers.[18]

Until the last years covered in this study, the commissioners made the uniform a vital element of police authority, separating the men from the public both on and off duty, symbolizing the force's emphasis on prevention rather than detection of crime, and helping to alleviate fears of a secret spy network. The uniform became the symbol of impersonal authority, according to an American observer, giving the bobby a "great *moral* power" which "lies in *his coat*."[19]

New Yorkers had little reason to fear that their police force would become a political spy system. Instead, the democratic desire to make the force "but a part of the citizens" originally dictated that policemen dress like citizens. The law establishing the Municipal Police explicitly rejected uniforms and required only a star-shaped copper badge which could be concealed if necessary.[20] Though lawmakers had often spoken of the need for preventive police, they did not fully implement the concept when they created a plainclothes force.

New York had briefly experienced a uniformed police and generally found it distasteful. The short-lived, nativist "Harper's Police" of 1844 had worn a blue uniform with the letters "M.P." (Municipal Police) on the collar, which could be turned down to conceal the officer's identity. The men and the public equally objected to the simple outfit, bystanders booing and stoning the "liveried lackeys" of the nativists when the new force appeared at a fire in the Bowery Theatre. Democratic success in the next election ended the experiment, which left a lingering hatred of uniformed policemen.[21]

Despite the discredit of Harper's Police, proponents of a uniform considered visibility essential if the force were to be truly preventive. They agreed with the London commissioners' emphasis on the uniform's identification, deterrent, and disciplinary functions, which were lacking in the plainclothes force which took to the streets in 1845. Citizens could not identify policemen when they needed aid and sometimes found themselves knocked to the ground or hauled off to jail when they got into altercations with strangers who turned out to be patrolmen. In one case a black woman struggled against a policeman who accosted her because she thought he was a kidnapper seeking to return her to slavery. Such complaints diminished after Chief Matsell ordered the men to wear their "stars" conspicuously when on the beat and the mayor punished violators of the order. Lack of a uniform apparently became more harmful to policemen than to anybody else, for James W. Gerard pointed out that the high number of assaults on policemen in 1852 reflected the lack of moral authority a uniform would provide.[22]

Policemen themselves, however, were the most persistent opponents of a uniform. They invoked a widespread distaste for servants' livery and fears that the uniform would convert the people's police into a tyrannical standing army, all this probably influenced by bad memories of Harper's nativist regime and by anti-English sentiment. One orator thundered, "No man bearing the proud title of an American desire[s] to appear in any dress that should make him conspicuous among his fellows," recalling Tocqueville's remark that democrats resented any visible signs of power or privilege which set men off from the mass.[23]

In the face of such opposition, the uniform was not finally adopted until almost ten years after the force was established. Reformers like James W. Gerard won Chief Matsell's support, and a simple blue uniform was adopted in 1853 over the men's protests. Though the protests were loud, they were unavailing, for the commissioners who were established by the 1853 reorganization dismissed some of the leaders of the antiuniform movement. The commissioners resented being, in their own words, "held up to ridicule and contempt" for "imposing an expensive and fantastical uniform." Chief Matsell credited the uniform with all that its advocates had expected of it: "The uniform dress has proved to be of incalculable benefit to the department in regard to its efficiency and respectability." The men were better disciplined, their moral authority had increased, and their visibility helped prevent crime. As Gerard predicted, assaults on policemen, at least as measured by arrest figures, decreased after the men donned their uniforms.[24]

Even after adoption of a uniform, New York officials did not share Rowan's and Mayne's wariness about plainclothes detectives. Both Municipal and Metropolitan Police regulations repeated the London instructions that "the principal object to be attained is '*the prevention of crime*' " and that police efficiency should be measured by the absence of crime rather than a high number of arrests. However, these instructions were buried in the text instead of appearing at the beginning of the rule book.[25] Consequently the policeman would not have the principle of prevention hammered home to him as his first duty.

The police were free to emphasize detection because, although there was popular suspicion of detectives, no widespread fear of a secret police or spy system was materializing in America. Also, to a certain extent New York officials were forced to rely on detection because of a shortage of manpower. Successful prevention depends greatly on the visibility of many uniformed men, and the New York force, with one officer per 812 people, was small compared to the London police, with one bobby per 351 citizens in 1856. The problem of inadequate strength continued into the sixties under the Metropolitan Police.[26] The importance of detectives in New York seems to have reflected both choice and necessity.

Emphasis on detection in both the Municipal and Metropolitan forces introduced problems. Detailment for detective work, which was generally more profitable as well as more healthy than pounding the beat, became a means of rewarding political fidelity. Metropolitan Police captains selected their favorites to "work up" all reported robberies, but if these cases produced no leads or involved only small amounts of property they were "loftily refused and turned over to a patrolman." Such favoritism bred rivalry and destroyed incentive. Moreover, detectives revived an evil of the old police system: recovery of property by collusion with the thief. A journalist urged that "In some way the attention of the police officer must be diverted from the property stolen to the person stealing it." The detective force seems to have been a little empire of its own within the police, one which retained the entrepreneurial competitiveness that had been typical of the old police forces attached to the courts.[27]

The New York police, originally concerned with integration into the local community and unsuspected of secret political spying, at first rejected a uniform as incompatible with democratic authority. But the growing need for visibility and deterrence, combined with reformers' efforts to professionalize the force, finally led to adoption of a uniform. The change, however, did not fully implement Rowan's and Mayne's emphasis on prevention over detection of crime. Their concern depended greatly on the uniform as a symbol of police power, which was national instead of merely local as in New York. The bobby's uniform invoked more of the "dignified" or symbolic aspect of government than did that of the New York cop. The uniformed patrolman had more symbolic power than his plainclothes predecessor, but impersonal dignity took second place to personal efficiency as embodied in the plainclothes detective.

BEHAVIOR AND DISCIPLINE

Recruitment and residency policies and the uniform contributed to the police image, but more important for public response was how policemen behaved and how effectively their commanders upheld the standards of conduct they set for the force. Official ideals of behavior were important, but they could be meaningless without discipline directed at maintaining them.

So far I have emphasized the London commissioners' concern to prevent local ties from interfering with police impartiality. Would this separation increase public hostility by causing the force to become ingrown, isolated from the public with its own subculture? It was quite possible that the bobbies, facing intense hostility in the early years, would regard citizens as antagonists and become hostile to them in turn. An early critic warned that "by taking their whole time, and appointing them to reside together in Station-houses, the individuals composing the force are as completely separated from the rest of the community as are the soldiers; and, in the course of a little time, will become a band of men having a strong *esprit du corps*, with nothing to link them to the rest of their fellow citizens."[28] Rowan and Mayne, though they wanted to develop solidarity among the men, were aware of this danger.

One way to prevent social isolation from turning into mutual hostility was the commissioners' insistence that policemen be models of restraint and politeness. They scrutinized the bobbies' smallest actions in order to minimize friction with the public. In the early days of the force they reiterated orders against rude answers to citizens' questions, shouldering people aside when walking through crowds, provocation into physical or verbal abuse, failure to show an identification number on request, and a host of minor irritants such as loud conversations when two men were patrolling together or noisy behavior in the section houses. These orders suggest that policemen indeed committed the offenses mentioned, but the commissioners' continuing vigilance is indicated by incorporation of some of them into the permanent standing orders and repetition of them when infractions cropped up in later years.[29] By monitoring the men's behavior in large and small matters the commissioners hoped to prevent a force separated from the community from becoming an irritating and hostile presence. They seem to have expected good behavior to compensate for distance from local residents and to win respect if not friendship.

Enunciating standards of conduct and drumming them into the ears of the men was one thing; maintenance of them in practice was another, more difficult task. A contemporary remarked, "As is the case with all large communities, the police force must include in its number men malicious, prejudiced, wrong-headed and foolish." Such men had to be controlled by more than exhortation; the answer was strict military discipline, which would have been frightening if it were not directed toward minimizing friction with the public. Discipline, which created sort of an automatic policeman, was a key element of impersonal authority: "The policeman, 'too clever by half,' is generally an instrument of injustice, and an impediment in the way of the law's impartial acting. So long as the common constable remains a well-regulated machine, and fulfils his functions without jarring or unnecessary noise, we will ask no more." Rowan and Mayne would have agreed with the journalist who said, "The police, like soldiers, when they know they are strictly watched by their officers, will acquire good conduct and regularity; they are at first raw, like soldiers, but by drilling them, and acquainting them with the manner in which they are to perform their duty, and having intelligent men to instruct them, the effect on the body generally will be highly beneficial."[30]

Making the policeman into "a well-regulated machine" was important because the commissioners presided over a very transitory body of men. In 1860 the average length of service was only four years, hardly enough time to allow thorough absorption of the commissioners' ideals of conduct. The principal cause of high turnover in the early years was dismissal for misconduct—mainly drunkenness, toward which the commissioners showed no mercy. Later the principal problem was voluntary resignations of good men because of low pay. The Home Office rather stingily controlled police salaries and, although Rowan and Mayne pressed for raises, the pay of entering patrolmen remained at nineteen shillings per week. This was better than the pay of unskilled urban and rural workers but was not competitive with artisans' wages. Experience in the police was an avenue of mobility for many able men who had no skills when they entered the force. If they received a favorable "character" from the commissioners they had good chances of moving into skilled occupations. Many skilled recruits joined the force in bad times as a temporary refuge until they could return to their usual occupations. A bobby said in 1830, "If I had not been miserably reduced, you would not have seen me in such a situation as this"; in 1868 "the most intelligent" policemen saw their job "as a mere resource against want, to be retained only till something better presents itself." By 1839, bobbies who did stay on were eventually eligible for a pension and for raises according to merit and length of service, but low pay caused discontent and prompted a small strike in 1872. Mayne pointed out that, as in the Dublin police, higher salaries encouraged the men to value their positions, and their concern to retain them made them perform their duties more conscientiously.[31] Low pay and consequent turnover did not foster a tightly knit organization which would develop loyalty to ideals of conduct. Strict discipline was necessary to maintain them.

Sir Robert Peel had appointed Col. Charles Rowan on the strength of Wellington's recommendation of him as having brought his

39

regiment "to a high state of discipline." Mayne increasingly adopted Rowan's views as the best way to control the force, and in his last years a subordinate said "there never was a stricter disciplinarian." His successor, Henderson, an army officer and prison official, seems to have carried discipline even further, giving the force "a greater military smartness throughout" and appointing assistant commissioners "whose ideas savour more of the barrack than of the police station." The commissioners' discipline rested on thorough centralization of the force, reliance on a nucleus of committed superior officers promoted from the ranks, and responsiveness to public complaints of police misconduct. The result may have been too much discipline — the men "were kept in such a state of subordination that they hardly dare say a word of their own" — but strictness was apparently necessary to maintain the standards of conduct the commissioners demanded.[32]

Rowan organized the new police along military lines, from the home secretary at the top, who rarely interfered with police policy, through the commissioners, who were the chief executive officers of the force, and then to the superintendents in charge of divisions containing thousands of inhabitants, inspectors in command of individual station houses, and sergeants heading sections of nine patrolmen each. In the early years the commissioners liked to appoint former noncommissioned military officers to the higher ranks of the police because of their ability to maintain discipline. Subsequently, however, there were very few former military men, because superior officers were promoted from police ranks. Rowan and Mayne required superior officers to consider themselves loyal primarily to Scotland Yard rather than to the men under their command. While they warned against too strict discipline, the commissioners expected officers to maintain enough distance from their men so that their authority would not be weakened by personal ties — this was analogous to the impartiality they expected patrolmen to maintain toward the public. They prohibited business relations between officers and men, and favoritism in assigning duties.[33]

As for the men, they had to obey all orders "readily and punctually" and could hope for promotion only by following the maxim that "he who has been accustomed to submit to discipline will be considered best qualified to command." They could complain to the commissioners if they thought any orders illegal or improper, but only after they had obeyed them: "Any refusal to perform the commands of his superiors, or negligence in doing so, will not be suffered." Inspectors and sergeants kept their eyes on bobbies for any infractions of the rules or neglect of duty; discipline extended to minor forms of protocol such as saluting.[34]

Training before entering upon police duties was an important part of discipline, but it was very slight by modern standards. In the early years bobbies received instruction in military drill for riot duty and some examination on the rules and regulations before they went out on patrol. Most of their knowledge, however, had to be picked up from experienced policemen or learned by trial and error. By the 1850s the commissioners increased the amount of drill and thoroughly examined the men on the instruction book, also requiring them to attend the police courts to learn the art of presenting evidence. By 1870 bobbies had to spend a week in the station house reserve and another week patrolling the streets with an experienced officer before going on duty alone.[35]

Rowan said that fear of dismissal and hope of promotion con-stituted the basis of discipline. Dismissals were highest in the first two decades, averaging annually some 10 percent of the force from 1834 to 1848. Reflecting declining police drunkenness, fewer public charges of police misconduct, and introduction of fines for minor infractions, dismissals for all causes remained between 4 and 5 percent of a much larger police force in the 1850s and 1860s.[36]

All of the various methods of discipline described so far sought to make a force that was distant from the local community and that consisted of many sojourners conform to standards laid down by the commissioners. Rowan and Mayne also helped bridge the gap between policeman and public by their procedure in handling civilian complaints. They were grateful to "all respectable persons" who sought redress of police misconduct, offering complainants the choice of a private hearing at Scotland Yard or an appearance before a magistrate. Most people chose the private hearing, which involved less time and expense, although the commissioners referred all serious cases of improper arrest or violence to a magistrate. Charles Reith has found their handling of complaints fair and impartial, but it should be pointed out that the burden of proof was squarely on the complainant. Many people received the reply that was given to a boy clubbed at a Chartist meeting, "the polite intimation that if the man could be identified, every assistance should be rendered." Rowan and Mayne ran a tight ship, and the complaint procedure probably was of most benefit to "respectable" people with time and energy to have their grievances redressed.[37] Nevertheless, the commissioners' willingness to hear complaints with a minimum of red tape allowed them to punish improper behavior which otherwise might have escaped notice.

The London commissioners had insisted on strict standards of behavior to counteract any antagonism arising from the policeman's isolation from the public. In New York, with the force integrated into the community until 1857 and still not as separate afterward as the police in London, a need to overcome the potential dangers of police isolation was not an incentive for behavioral standards maintained by strict discipline.

Both the Municipal and Metropolitan Police instruction books repeated Rowan's and Mayne's insistence on coolness and impartiality in performing police duties, but discipline does not seem to have been strong enough to maintain the ideals consistently. Mayor Mickle warned that "Every policeman . . . must possess civility and a proper control of temper, or he will bring himself into disgrace and the whole department into disrepute," but Municipal Police officials seem to have tolerated a more rough-and-ready style than would have been acceptable in London. Mayors, who performed the London commissioners' disciplinary functions until 1853, tended to impose lighter punishments on policemen against whom charges of brutality or illegal arrest were proved than did the London commissioners, favoring suspension from pay rather than dismissal. Except for their strict attitude toward drunkenness, they seem to have been more willing than Rowan and Mayne to overlook minor indiscretions. In one case a patrolman clubbed a man for insulting his wife, which in his own words "caused me to forget for the moment my position as a guardian of the public peace, and without reflection[,] being keenly impressed with the unprovoked outrage I had received in the person of my wife[,] I inflicted summary punishment upon him, and left him immediately." Mayor Kingsland dismissed the charge of brutality, observing that the policeman did not do "anything which a man should not do under such circumstances." Such loss of temper, even under provocation, would probably have received at least a reprimand from Rowan and Mayne.[38]

Under the Metropolitan Police, newspapers increasingly complained of police brutality. The problem may reflect a decline in the quality of recruits. During the Civil War years, a period of rising wages and prices, police pay for the first time fell below the wages of skilled workers. Previously, skilled workers made up most of the recruits, but in the sixties they began resigning and replacements could be obtained only from the unskilled labor force. The commissioners asserted that a pay increase was necessary to prevent "a fatal deterioration in the character of the force," and a journalist said, "We have no right to look for saintliness in blue uniforms and pewter badges when their wearers receive but $25 to $30 a week." London had compensated for low pay and consequent turnover by strict discipline, but New York officials do not seem to have adopted their method. Although the Metropolitan commissioners were strict with departmental infractions such as neglect of duty, policemen themselves called the procedure for dealing with civilian complaints "trying the complainant." The previously quoted journalist said in 1869 that policemen "are compelled to associate with vulgarians and scoundrels of all grades; are exposed to every species of temptation; act unfavorably on each other, and have no restraining influence beyond their own intelligence, which is not very great, and their fear of exposure, which is not probable." Apparently policemen were not well-regulated machines like their London brethren, who were fairly certain of exposure and punishment if they stepped out of line.[39]

An important reason for the discrepancy between ideals and practice, in addition to public expectations of the police (which will be discussed in chapter 6), was the force's involvement in partisan politics. Decentralization and political favoritism weakened discipline. Before 1853 patrolmen looked to local politicians for appointment and promotion. Consequently they were less amenable to their superior officers' orders, and friction developed which "soon ripened into the bitterest hatred and enmity, and which were carried out of the department into the private walks of life." Policemen participated in political clubs, often resigning to work for reelection of their aldermen, who left the positions vacant until they won the election and could reappoint the loyal patrolmen. Chief Matsell said that this politicking kept the department in "constant excitement." Discipline improved somewhat under the 1853 commission, which cut the tie to local aldermen and prohibited participation in political clubs. However, the commission had little chance to improve its effectiveness, for favoritism was rife under Mayor Fernando Wood, elected in 1854. Captains were not promoted from the ranks but "taken from the citizens, and placed over Lieutenants and Sergeants of ten years' experience, depressing the energies of the men." According to a critic of the Municipal Police, discipline depended on the individual captain's "attention, or skill and tact." Patrolmen's only training was on the street after a stint of military drill.[40]

The Metropolitan Police commissioners improved the force's discipline, and the law enacted in 1857 introduced the principle of promotion according to merit. Improved discipline and coordination in the early sixties aided police success in the draft riots. The commissioners believed that "the marked fidelity, vigilance, and efficiency of the police, in ordinary as well as extraordinary occasions, is the legitimate fruit of the system. Instead of fearing or despising the policeman, the public have learned to trust him as the protector and defender of social order." General Superintendent John A. Kennedy, who took office in 1860, introduced the rank of inspector to check on patrolmen's behavior. One contemporary thought that this surveillance made the force "attentive and efficient, as if by magic," so that New York had "the best police force in the world."[41]

However, problems caused by decentralization persisted, and grew worse by the end of the sixties when the force was caught up in Tweed Ring politics. Early superintendents complained that they had too little power over the men, that the commissioners made policy and the captains had a firm grip on the station houses. Superintendent Kennedy gained somewhat more autonomy but the captains continued to be independent, autocrats "who could, and many of them did, destroy whatever of efficiency headquarters had left."[42] Personal authority seemed to reign in the department, the captain's personality and ability still being the most important factors in discipline.

Despite improvements of discipline, the New York force was never as closely controlled as the London police. Ideals of behavior were not as effectively bolstered by discipline to insure that they were carried out. The New York patrolman, with less institutional constraint, had more personal freedom than the London bobby. Far more than his London colleague, he was still "but a part of the citizens" despite modifications of the force's original democratic structure.

Recruitment, residency, the uniform, behavior, and discipline were fundamental aspects of the police image. It is now time to turn to the policeman in his active role as peacekeeper and law enforcer to see how the personal and impersonal images worked out in practice.

3 POLICE AND THE RULE OF LAW: FROM ARREST TO BOOKING

The policeman is the initial element in a complex system of criminal justice. The relationship of the police to other agencies of the system influences how patrolmen carry out their function and how the public perceives them. Much of the police image derives from the image of the larger system, but the police themselves are a crucial element in how the whole process of criminal justice is regarded.

Policemen initiate operation of the criminal justice system and are much more than mechanical agents of the law. The patrolman's crime prevention function includes discretionary power — decisions when or whether to invoke the law under specific circumstances, and how to act in carrying out his duty. He is constantly called on to act according to his personal experience, informal departmental patterns, and what the general public seems to expect of him. Police discretion is necessary, but because discretionary decisions are immediate and personal they amount to a police interpretation of the law not openly acknowledged in the criminal justice system.[1]

Although policemen often say that they merely enforce the law without judging its merit, their exercise of discretion actually defines who is deviant in any social context and how deviance should be controlled. Although such definitions often take purely individual circumstances into account, they also involve categorization of entire classes or ethnic groups. The police may enforce some laws more strictly against some groups than against others; they may adopt different techniques of maintaining order with different groups; and they may be more likely to follow up their suspicions when one group rather than another is involved. Discretion thus involves discrimination in the form of selective law enforcement and

45

order maintenance. Police definition of a group's collective character is part of the informal lore of patrol work. The discriminatory aspect of discretion introduces the need for controls to prevent undue favoritism or unnecessary arbitrariness. What sorts of checks are applied to discretionary power influence how the police cope with conflicting classes or groups in heterogeneous communities.[2]

In addition to internal departmental regulations, other criminal justice agencies, particularly the judiciary, control police discretion. Judges in lower as well as higher courts often reach decisions reflecting their views of the propriety of police behavior, the adequacy or legality of their evidence, or the constitutionality of their interrogation practices. The judiciary can encourage or discourage many discretionary powers. Policemen's awareness of judicial decisions, often reached only by hearsay, may not alter their determination to arrest a suspect, but it may affect the methods used and the law they will invoke.[3]

The police have been limited by the "rule of law," a framework which has grown out of both individual judicial decisions and long-standing traditions of representative governments and defines how far individual rights may be infringed to maintain public order. Law is not only something the police enforce; it is also a sanction which can be enforced against the police. Legal checks on police methods range from the basic right of suit for false arrest to complicated judicial determinations of the legality of police practices. In both England and America protection against false arrest has been a traditional civil liberty, but precisely spelled-out and codified limitations on the police are mostly a product of the twentieth century. The English Judges' Rules, regulating admissibility of confessions as evidence and interrogation practices generally, were first promulgated in 1912 when police officials requested the Court of King's Bench to clear up conflicting judicial opinions. These were supplemented in 1918 and revised in 1930 and 1964. The United States Supreme Court first ruled on admissibility of evidence in 1914, but the decision applied only to federal law enforcement agencies. After public exposure of brutal "third degree" interrogation practices in local police forces in the late 1920s and early 1930s, the Court made generally applicable restrictive rulings, although the most important decisions are those of the 1960s.[4] Many of the issues which became prominent in the twentieth century were raised and sometimes contested in the nineteenth century, but the London and New York police of a hundred years ago did not have many external directives except the often conflicting decisions of local courts. How the police would operate within the rule of law was mostly up to the heads of the police forces and the pressures generated by public opinion.

Nevertheless, questions raised by modern police practices can be asked of nineteenth-century forces. Are the police to be granted broad and unchecked discretion in the interest of public order, even at the expense of individual rights? Or are they to be checked by the rule of law in the interest of individual rights, even at the expense of public order?[5] Neither London nor New York gave simple answers to these questions, but in many areas of police work they gave different responses which influenced relations with other agencies of criminal justice and the reactions of different social groups to the police.

How much the rule of law limited police practices was a key element of the London and New York forces' style of authority and public reception. The degree of discretion which the patrolman was allowed to exercise was critical in the definition of his authority as impersonal and institutional (narrow discretion) or personal and individual (wide discretion).

In London, early fears of police tyranny did not prevent parliamentary grants of wide responsibilities and powers to the force after the initial worry had subsided. However, lingering public suspicion prompted the commissioners to limit patrolmen's discretion to powers clearly specified by law. They discouraged any police assumption of authority not justified by statute. Rowan believed that a centralized force free from public pressures was the best guarantee of the "liberty of the subject," because it could be regulated by clear, impartial principles, and any increases of its power would be through legal grants instead of extralegal responses to demands for order. The German-American Francis Lieber praised the London policeman as the embodiment of legality. He was impressed by an officer who chose not to act in a certain case because he was not sure of his legal powers. That bobby's reaction may have been extreme, but it represented the commissioners' rejection of unregulated discretionary power. Although never perfectly achieved, subordination to the law proved a firm foundation of growing public acceptance of the police during the mid-nineteenth century.[6]

Contemporary New York was much more democratic than London, but the rule of the people seemed to place less emphasis on the rule of law. Subordination to the law and concern for individual rights were important ideals legitimating the police and other criminal justice agencies, but when they conflicted with popular demands for order and police efficiency they often yielded to immediate, personal retribution against offenders. Lingering democratic fears of tyranny, perhaps reinforced by the rise of the urban political boss, made upper- and middle-class New Yorkers reluctant to legislate police powers as broad as those of the London force. However, their growing fears of the lower classes — who were their political equals and often outvoted them — prevented careful scrutiny of discretionary practices. They tolerated extralegal methods which they were unwilling to write into the statute book. The patrolman's personal discretion was much broader than in London. Though the English were willing to widen police powers in the conflict with the "dangerous classes," legalization of these powers made them visible. As Lieber said, the police were "strictly under the public law, and that implies publicity."[7] In New York, many police practices were invisible until critics called attention to them. Exposure, however, did not lead to limitation or legalization of them. New Yorkers remained ambivalent toward their police, continuing to hold conflicting expectations of limited formal institutional power but unchecked informal discretionary power.

THE ULTIMATE DISCRETION: POLICE WEAPONRY AND THE USE OF FORCE

In London, control of police violence was essential to winning public support of the force. Especially in the early years, the commissioners had to cope with the problem of patrolmen responding to provocation with violence or using force to frighten recalcitrant citizens into respect for their authority. Not only were the commissioners concerned with inculcating reserve and self-restraint in their men, but they minimized violence by limiting bobbies' weapons to the truncheon or "baton" carried concealed in the tail pockets of their uniform coats, to be drawn only in self-defense. Not until 1863, after most antagonism to the police had simmered down, was the truncheon made visible for the first time, in a leather case suspended from the policeman's belt. The truncheon was a constable's traditional symbol of authority, which the commissioners retained as a reminder of the police force's civilian character. Denial of lethal force emphasized the bobby's moral authority and his role as an agent of the law; punishment was left to the judiciary. Unlike a soldier armed with a musket, who, if using his weapon at all, generally inflicted death, the policeman could "safely be entrusted with the right of interference, and by a moderate application of force at an early period, may *prevent* the growth and progress of crime, which the soldier could only *punish.*" The soldier acted on an officer's orders, not on his own discretion. The policeman, patrolling his beat alone, was entrusted with discretionary use of force, but reliance on the club minimized the damage he could inflict if he were indiscreet. His discretion was limited to using or not using the truncheon; he did not have a choice of weapons.[8]

The truncheon can inflict a nasty wound, as anybody who has felt its effects can testify. In the early years of the force policemen had to be cautioned against unnecessary clubbing, for it threatened the moral basis of police authority and aroused public antagonism. Sometimes an angry crowd would rescue an officer's prisoner, outraged by his bad treatment. The truncheon was supposed to be a last resort, not to be used in response to insulting language or actions which did not endanger the policeman. The commissioners' warnings had some effect, for complaints of police violence diminished after the early 1830s.[9]

Although the great majority of bobbies carried only the truncheon, there were some exceptions. Inspectors were provided with pocket pistols, and men on dangerous assignments, such as ferreting out notorious criminals from their slum hideouts, probably carried firearms. Another important exception was the provision of cutlasses to bobbies patrolling isolated rural areas of the sprawling Metropolitan Police District. The commissioners acted on numerous petitions from inhabitants of lonely areas who sought better protection for both themselves and the policemen against "some of the daring characters who frequent such places." They had a precedent, for the old Bow Street Mounted Patrol had carried cutlasses in rural districts. Rowan and Mayne were very careful about this, following Home Secretary Lord Melbourne's injunction to carry "it into effect carefully, both with respect to the place and to the person to whom the weapon is entrusted." They warned the policeman that "the sword is put into his hand merely as a *defensive* weapon in case his life should be in danger, and that if he shall use or even draw it, for any less weighty cause, he will be called to strict account and probably dismissed." By the 1850s policemen in the rural divisions, who were now mounted, added pistols to their cutlasses, which suggests that rural peace and quiet may have been more dangerous than urban congestion. They, and the country police forces generally, had to deal with armed and desperate gangs of poachers, while urban constables were spared having to enforce the detested game laws. There do not seem to have been complaints of the reckless use of firearms, possibly because the mounted men were an elite corps carefully selected on the basis of experience and skill.[10]

Political crises sometimes prompted the commissioners to strengthen police armament temporarily. During the Chartist tensions of 1842 and the great scare of 1848, bobbies patrolled urban streets at night armed with cutlasses, but only men who had never been reported for drunkenness or any "intemperate conduct" were so armed. Any man who drew his sword on duty had to report the circumstances to his sergeant and to the desk officer when he returned to the station house. The talk of violence by the "physical force" Chartists prompted this temporary armament; after the crises passed, policemen resumed their normal truncheons. The Fenian scare of 1867–68 prompted an updating of police armament to cope with the revolver-packing Irish terrorists. Each division received a supply of thirty or forty revolvers to be distributed among the station houses as a replacement for the old-fashioned single-shot pistols the police stocked up till that time. They do not seem to have ever carried revolvers on patrol, however. Even "the wild Irish" did not provoke that step.[11]

Under ordinary circumstances the bobby relied on his truncheon. Even when dealing with hardened criminals, the police seem to have prided themselves on their muscle and intelligence. A detective in an 1860s melodrama, armed with a pistol, says, "I always feel rather ashamed to burn powder. Any fool can blow a man's brains out." This character, Hawkshaw, seems well on the road to the Sherlock Holmes tradition. In dealing with criminals, as with political protestors, the police developed a combination of power and restraint. On the one hand, "Better organised, composed of younger and stronger men, they soon proved themselves more than a match for any combination, even of the most desperate and determined characters." On the other hand, police success also "required not a little humoring of the rules tacitly established among the thieves themselves." If a bobby entered a thieves' hangout to make an arrest, he had little difficulty "provided he did not venture into their penetralia or show his staff. Woe to the policeman who should be so incautious or so foolhardy as to disregard this latter condition." One patrolman who did was severely beaten; upon recovery he returned to apprehend his man according to the rules and was successful. English criminals apparently disdained violence. According to a writer of 1833, an experienced worker in prisons, "The generality of thieves have even an abhorrence of any violence committed on the person," and often gave the cold shoulder to any of their brethren who had assaulted their victims. English criminals were not exactly peaceful; the "garroters" or muggers of thirty years later had no qualms about violence, but they were only briefly active and may have been exceptional, although complaints of criminal violence increased during the sixties. Perhaps more significantly, when the English bruiser picked up a weapon, he usually reached for a bludgeon, brickbat, paving stone, or at worst a knife—rarely a gun. Even in some of their most desperate battles with hardened criminals the London police were able to rely on muscle and the club. English criminals were thus less deadly than their American brethren, who were armed with revolvers. The carrying of any concealed weapon in London invited immediate arrest, while laws against concealed weapons remained lax throughout the mid-nineteenth century in New York. Guns were generally the sporting aristocracy's prerogative; anybody else carrying them was a likely object of police suspicion. All things considered, the police did not feel threatened enough in their ordinary duties to abandon the truncheon for more lethal weapons.[12]

New York policemen were armed with only a truncheon, like their London brethren, until 1857, when the state government took control of the force out of the hands of municipal officials. Some members of the old Municipal Police apparently carried pistols on dangerous assignments but never on routine patrol. Men who had served on the force said that Chief Matsell had "made it a standing rule to look upon every man as a coward and unfit to be put a second time on duty, where he had descended to the use of a pistol."[13] Matsell's idea of a tough cop stressed muscle over lethal force.

In the troubled year of 1857, which witnessed numerous riots and much resistance to the state-controlled Metropolitan Police, there does not seem to have been much deliberation about arming patrolmen with revolvers, a new departure which permanently influenced the character of American police work. The practice seems to have resulted from a series of individual captains' decisions in response to disorder and increasing attacks upon lone policemen. The commissioners acquiesced in the use of revolvers, but they never officially authorized the weapons and in fact denied that they purchased them for the men's use. However, the guns were provided with cardboard holsters to fit in the uniform pockets labeled

"Metropolitan Police Patrol." The commissioners admitted that by July 1857 "pretty much all the men" were armed. By the later sixties a journalist reported that revolvers were standard equipment.[14]

Not all the captains in 1857 relished arming their men with guns. Captains Speight, Turnbull, and Dilks, who had served in the Municipal Police, rejected the innovation and went unarmed, discouraging their men from adopting revolvers. Captain Hartt, however, believed in guns. One of his men boasted of the "custom at this station house" and asked a reporter "to feel in his pocket, where accordingly, one of Colt's Patent Revolvers was ready for instant use."[15] As in many other areas of police discipline, individual captains' attitudes influenced what arms their men carried.

Apparently the commissioners saw fit to leave matters at that. In November 1857 Superintendent Frederick A. Tallmadge sought their authorization for "the arming of ten prudent and discreet patrolmen in each precinct, with revolvers, that a sufficient force may, in any emergency, be called upon to suppress any riots or unlawful assemblages without the necessity of invoking the aid of the military." His argument for revolvers suggested that the blue policeman's uniform, hailed in 1853 as a guarantee of the officer's moral authority, was no longer sufficient: "The mere exhibition of firearms in the hands of those who can legally use them produces a most instantaneous revulsion in the courage of the blustering violators of the law. Its efficiency has been tested, and its further application I trust will be approved."[16] The commissioners did not act on Tallmadge's request, apparently opting for unregulated, unofficial armament over his plan for a limited, officially armed riot squad. If the *Herald*'s reports were correct, many more than ten policemen were armed in each precinct.

Armed policemen aroused some apprehensions, but protests were tempered by the belief that the police had to protect themselves in a war in which criminals gave no quarter, carrying lethal weapons and not hesitating to attack policemen. The *Times* remarked on the prevalence of armed individuals in 1855, and argued that "it would seem quite as necessary to legislate on this subject, as it has been found to be among the impulsive populations of the South and West." The Metropolitan Police commissioners urged four years later that, except for policemen, the carrying of concealed weapons should be made punishable by fine and imprisonment. After the Civil War, during which "the practice of carrying concealed deadly weapons by the violent and vicious classes of the city, has become common," they repeated their demands for strict controls.[17]

The state legislature passed a law against carrying concealed weapons without a police permit in 1865, but it proved difficult to enforce. Scruples about the "right to bear arms" apparently caused the lawmakers to include slungshots and other blunt weapons, but not knives and pistols. Roughs simply abandoned their old favorite, the slungshot, for more deadly weapons. Violence seemed endemic by 1870. Armed ruffians were seen as "simply the natural products of a civilization that fires its recklessness with rum, then arms it with a pistol, and turning it into the street to see what will become of it, pretends to be horrified when blood comes of it." An English visitor in 1865 asserted that "Generally speaking, human life is held at a very cheap rate in this land of freedom, and as a consequence disputes of the most trivial nature are often settled by the use of the most deadly weapons." He had hard words for American conceptions of liberty: "The idea attached to personal liberty ... by many of the people is of the most selfish character. They esteem liberty so long as it squares with their feelings or interests; but an equality of social liberty is a thing which they either cannot or will not understand." This was not entirely John Bull's prejudice against uncivilized Brother Jonathan, for the Metropolitan Police commissioners used similar language. After the Civil War, which they called "a school of violence and crime," they asserted that "probably in no city in the civilized world, not the theatre of actual war, is human life so lightly prized and subject to as great hazards from violence as in New York and Brooklyn."[18]

The general climate of violence encouraged the police to respond in kind for their own protection. There seemed to be no rules of the game which could reduce violence. In 1857 the *Times* accepted arming of the police as the lesser of two evils:

> As nearly every ruffian carries a concealed weapon of destruction about his person, the single-handed policeman goes on his beat at a great disadvantage to encounter the villains he will be called on to arrest. . . . It may not be prudent to put revolvers into the hands of the policemen, but something must be done to render them effective or even safe. . . .
>
> The objections to an armed police are patent to every one; the danger of placing deadly weapons in the hands of men who may use them with impunity at their own discretion, is too great to be lightly incurred; and it is only as the choice of a lesser evil that such a measure could be recommended.[19]

The paper's wariness was justified during the next decade, when complaints of police violence increased apace with complaints of criminal violence. Shooting seemed to be a growing substitute for arrest. Believing that use of revolvers was a "most perilous power to put in the hands of . . . men no more discreet in the use of power than the mass of our policemen are apt to be," the *Times* demanded strict regulation of police weaponry.[20] However, a society careless in its control of civilians' weapons was not likely to be too stringent with its policemen. The broadest possible discretion, the power to inflict death, remained unregulated and a vicious cycle of criminal and police violence became part of American life.

ARREST AND DETENTION ON SUSPICION

London patrolmen possessed a broad power of arrest on suspicion of criminal intent without witnessing an overt act. This power, accepted by the Home Office, Parliament, and "respectable" people generally, posed special problems of control. Generally the commissioners considered the power of arrest on suspicion an important aid to crime prevention, especially burglaries. They encouraged policemen to watch for felonious-looking individuals on their beats. However, they were also aware that such broad police power presented a delicate issue of how to prevent arbitrary or ill-considered arrests with consequent public anger. Besides realizing that uncontrolled arrests on suspicion would reinforce fears of police tyranny, Rowan and Mayne probably would have agreed with a magistrate who said that too many such arrests would make innocent people dangerously familiar with courts and jails.[21] The commissioners had to educate bobbies in the proper exercise of their power, seeking to refine their discretion so that suspicions would be based on concrete actions rather than vague hunches.

Under the Metropolitan Police Act of 1829 (section 7), officers had the power to "apprehend all loose, idle, and disorderly persons, whom he shall find disturbing the public peace, or whom he shall have just cause to suspect of any evil designs" as well as to arrest all loiterers at night. These powers ultimately derived from ancient statutes against vagrants—"rogues and vagabonds"—as potential criminals, but more immediately from the Vagrancy Act of 1824, which defined "many acts characteristic of criminals though not actually criminal," such as being armed "with intent to commit a felony," loitering in private property without being able to give a satisfactory account of oneself, practically any visible activity of "reputed thieves," and a wide range of offenses against "the public decency." As Sir James F. Stephen remarked, these and later provisions made it practically certain "that any person of bad character who prowls about, apparently for an unlawful purpose, is liable to be treated as a rogue and vagabond." Though the 1824 law gave precise definitions of suspicious activity, police powers under it and the later Metropolitan Police Act were very broad. To define a man as a suspected thief it was "sufficient for a police-officer to have seen a person at the police-office, complained of as a thief or a felon, to say that a person is a reputed thief, though discharged and perhaps perfectly innocent of the complaint."[22] How would bobbies exercise such broad responsibility?

Experience and knowledge of his beat would reveal what sorts of people and behavior the policeman should consider suspicious. The problem was to make quick but discriminating judgments. Given the nature of English society, it was the poor who most often came under police scrutiny, but in the early years of the Metropolitan Police "respectable" people complained that bobbies were too impartial in stopping and questioning "suspicious" persons. They apparently believed that their external respectability was sufficient shield against police curiosity, and made their complaints heard at Scotland Yard.

"Respectable" complaints centered on policemen stopping and searching people suspected of carrying stolen goods. Bobbies indiscriminately stopped carriages or pedestrians no matter how respectable they were. In the case of carriages, this occurred because the men acted on an imprecise description of a suspected vehicle or because their newness on the job prevented familiarity with local residents' equipages. In these instances the commissioners warned the men that they must "not ... cause delay or impediment to respectable people on their lawful business, and that the distinction necessary to be made, will call for a careful exercise of their individual judgment." They would be held strictly accountable if they stopped anybody, such as a "gentleman's servant carrying a bag," without "good cause to suspect the goods were stolen." Superintendents were not to recommend men for rewards for stopping and searching suspicious persons unless they could satisfy the commissioners that the men acted with good cause and handled the matter discreetly. Such warnings, combined with the bobbies' increasing familiarity with local residents, decreased "respectable" people's complaints. However, such attention to outward respectability did not ease the burden of police scrutiny on poorly dressed laborers walking through well-to-do neighborhoods, and it may have reinforced the tendency of police activity to be "as much directed to who a person is as to what he does."[23]

Rowan and Mayne were satisfied that arrests on suspicion disrupted what was formerly a nightly traffic in stolen goods. The Home Office and Parliament seem to have been equally satisfied, for section 66 of the 1839 police act specified that patrolmen might "stop, search, and detain . . . any person who may be reasonably suspected of having or conveying in any manner anything stolen or unlawfully obtained," and required that all arrested persons be taken before a magistrate. This provision, still retained in London, seems to have been designed to allow arrest without warrant for the misdemeanor of possessing stolen goods when the person was not himself the thief, but it has sometimes been used for on-the-street questioning of generally suspicious persons. Like earlier provisions, this one aroused complaints of excessive police interference, but the commissioners considered it a useful preventive power and urged their men to take advantage of it.[24]

Perhaps more important than internal regulation was the magistrates' wariness of arrest on suspicion. On one occasion a man arrested on an apparently unfounded suspicion was released even though he had assaulted the bobby. Even in 1870, when the provisions of the 1829 and 1839 police acts were reinforced by the Habitual Criminals Act of 1869, magistrates viewed the power of arrest on suspicion cautiously. In some divisions they would not convict for "loitering with intent" unless an overt criminal act could be proved.[25]

Although prisoners brought before magistrates on suspicion did not have counsel present and often only the prosecution witnesses were heard in the preliminary examination, higher courts strictly enjoined magistrates from grilling prisoners to prove their guilt. Also, the courts directed that individuals could be detained for investigation without formal charges and trial for only five days in normal circumstances or a maximum of two weeks in unusual cases. Although the statute allowed magistrates to postpone examination "to such future time as may be necessary," the court rulings seem to have been an effective limitation of detention on suspicion.[26]

Generally, magistrates' committals of suspects for jury trial did not keep pace with London's population growth during the 1830-70 period. This lag may have reflected declining crime (the favorite contemporary explanation) or the shift of many petty offenses to magistrates' summary jurisdiction between 1847 and 1861. However, since the conviction rate in jury trials increased in proportion to magistrates' committals during this period, and higher court convictions also increased in proportion to policemen's arrests, it is likely that bobbies, magistrates, and juries were moving toward a common definition of what constituted "reasonable cause" for suspicion of criminal intent. Internal and external regulation of arrest on suspicion seem to have prevented flagrant abuses, but enough public fears lingered to prevent the stop-and-search provisions of the 1839 police act from ever being adopted outside of London.[27]

Like their London brethren, New York patrolmen had full power "to arrest any person who, from his acts, conduct, situation and character" they had "*just cause to suspect* is about to commit a *felony,*" including loiterers around buildings. The 1846 regulations directed policemen to be cautious, since they had to prove the reasonableness of their suspicion to the magistrate. Later regulations, clearly modeled on the stop-and-search powers granted by London's 1839 police act, spelled out the power of searching persons suspected of the misdemeanor of conveying stolen goods:

> If a Police officer see any one carrying, or in any manner conveying goods, under circumstances which lead to a *strong suspicion* that they have been stolen, he should, *particularly in the night,* stop and examine the person; and if the appearance and manner of the party, his account of himself and of the goods, and all the circumstances of the case, should leave no doubt that the goods have been stolen, he should arrest the person, and take possession of the goods. But if the suspicion of the Police officer *be slight,* he should not stop the person, but watch him to discover where the goods may be deposited; and if he then become *fully convinced* that the property be stolen, he will make the arrest, and take charge of the goods.[28]

These directives inculcated even more specific cautions than the London police orders, although as in London they placed great emphasis on the patrolman's ability to judge suspicious activity from manner and appearance.

However, in practice New York policemen seem to have had greater leeway in making such judgments and broader discretion in making arrests on suspicion. George W. Walling, a police officer whose experience went back to 1847, was enough struck by cautious use of the London patrolman's power of arrest on suspicion that he mistakenly thought that bobbies dared not "lay a finger on a man unless he is engaged in the very act of violating the law." In New York, however, criminals did not "experience such forbearance. A New York police officer knows he has been sworn in to 'keep the peace,' and he keeps it. There's no 'shilly-shallying' with him; he doesn't consider himself half patrolman and half Supreme Court Judge." He did not hesitate to act on his suspicions even if it were "often a case of 'giving a dog a bad name and then hanging him,' — men being arrested merely because they are known to have been law-breakers or persons of bad character," and sometimes even people of entirely respectable reputations were caught in the net of police suspiciousness.[29]

Police powers were vaguely defined in the statutes, so that as the eminent lawyer Robert Livingston said, "officers of justice, often uneducated and overbearing men, either do not know, or designedly exceed the bounds of their authority. The accused sometimes submits to illegal acts; at others, resists those to which he ought to submit." Important powers like arrest on suspicion may have been detailed in the policemen's rule books, but they did not appear in the publicly accessible Session Laws (containing the original police acts) or in the complete collections of state statutes. Indeed, these collections are silent on the vital area of arrests without a warrant throughout the period of this study, despite the recommendation of a commission for codification of the criminal law that the powers and limitations of arrest without warrant be spelled out alongside those of arrest under a warrant. "When obedience is exacted . . . ," Livingston complained, "the least the people can require, is to be clearly and explicitly told what it is they are to obey." Although resistance to an unlawful arrest was legally justifiable, the statutes "cruelly and wantonly refuse to explain what is a lawful and which an unlawful arrest." Under such circumstances much power was left in the hands of the police to exercise as they saw fit.[30]

Police discretion was unchecked by judicial cautiousness. Justices of the peace in the overcrowded police courts did not take time to investigate cases fully, tacitly encouraging hasty arrests on suspicion by accepting police testimony without oath, giving the accused no opportunity for refutation, failing to inform prisoners of their rights, and sometimes frightening ignorant people into confessions. The whole process of preliminary examination, designed to determine simply whether the prisoner should be committed for jury trial in a higher court, resembled the grilling by French magistrates who presumed the prisoner's guilt until his innocence was proved. Although the examination was intended, "in the humane and benign spirit of the common law," to give the defendant an opportunity to exculpate himself by a voluntary statement, the procedure became an ordeal for prisoners, who were often unaware of their right to counsel. Instead of being informed that the examination "is furnished to him as a shield and is not to be used against him as a sword, he is by a loose course of practice, if no other motive be imputable," subjected to an interrogation aimed at establishing his guilt. The confused prisoner had little choice but to offer equivocal testimony or to refuse to answer the questions put to him. Although refusal was the defendant's legal right, silence, as much as contradictory testimony, was taken as a presumption of guilt.[31]

New York's criminal code commissioners recommended in 1850 that the whole examination process be eliminated. The legislature did not go this far, but did enact some reforms which improved the defendant's lot. The Revised Statutes of 1862 specified that the prisoner be allowed "a reasonable time to send for and advise with counsel," who could be present during the whole proceeding at the prisoner's request. The new laws also gave the defendant the opportunity to see the magistrate's written version of his testimony for the purpose of addition or correction. He had lacked this right previously, and the change was apparently modeled on a British statute. Further reforms provided that the prosecution and defense witnesses could not be present during each other's testimony, and that the magistrate could exclude witnesses on the same side from hearing the testimony of others on their side. All the witnesses' testimony was to be put into writing and signed by them.[32] These reforms improved the situation, but they did not change the nature of the examination from a trial to its original purpose as a preliminary inquiry.

Prisoners brought before the magistrates by suspicious policemen faced further difficulties. When testimony was not sufficient to establish guilt, police justices would allow incarceration of prisoners until further evidence could be obtained. Such prisoners could not be released on bail, which would have been permitted if they had been committed to jail for full jury trial. Some people were imprisoned in this manner for up to two months, sometimes only to be discharged "in what is termed the *discretion* of the magistrate." Other prisoners, even less fortunate, would be committed as vagrants as the only way to provide time for obtaining testimony against them. These practices were sanctioned under the loose wording of the law, which provided only that the examination should be completed "as soon as may be" practical.[33]

In the late forties and early fifties both the New York Prison Association and the criminal code commissioners attacked detention on suspicion as a flagrant violation of civil liberties. The prison reformers were especially vehement:

> The doctrine that the King can do no wrong, has been here
> exploded, while its counterpart, that the public can do no
> wrong, is still suffered to exist to the manifest injury of the poor.
> How so flagrant an outrage upon the rights of individuals and
> the condition of society should have continued to exist up to this
> moment almost without comment seems astonishing. The object
> of government, which is to protect individual rights, has in this
> instance been perverted to destroying those rights and harassing
> and oppressing the individual.[34]

Later these critics were even more emphatic: "If our government was monarchical instead of republican; if the supreme power was vested in the hands of one instead of many," imprisonment on suspicion "would be a just cause for revolution."[35]

The reformers did achieve court rulings which limited the detention period of people arrested on suspicion. The criminal code commissioners in 1850 had recommended that examinations be postponed for a maximum of six days unless at the prisoner's request. Justice J. W. Edmonds of the state supreme court ruled that prisoners could be detained only five days without full examination, following the British precedent. As in Britain, the provisions of the statutes remained unchanged, continuing to specify examination "as soon as may be" possible. The legislature and the prison association seem to have been content to let the change remain in the realm of case law instead of formalizing it in the statute books.[36]

Court rulings limiting the detention period do not seem to have changed police practices regarding suspected criminals. The state legislature's investigation of the Municipal Police in 1855 revealed that the police informally held prisoners in the station house while evidence was gathered against them, a sub rosa form of detention on suspicion. Police justices cooperated by hearing only the officer's statements and allowing return of the prisoner to the station house so the same man could "work up the case." Such prisoners were usually suspected robbers, burglars, or pickpockets, who would be held until the police could prove they had stolen the property found on them or a civilian complainant came forth. With the permission of the mayor and police chief, prisoners were sometimes held up to a week while the evidence was being sought. Interrogation was part of this investigation, and the police had no scruples about obtaining confessions and implications of other persons by trickery or "stratagem." The captains at their discretion could grant prisoners' lawyers permission to see them. One testified that he gave permission when he was satisfied that the lawyer was the prisoner's regular counsel. Clearly a prisoner in such circumstances had little recourse but cooperation with the police.[37]

Public attention was again focused on station-house detention when the legislature investigated the state-controlled Metropolitan Police in 1860. Superintendent Kennedy described practices similar to those of the 1850s, asserting that they were "nothing new" and had "always been done." He said he did not know of any law authorizing detention of suspects while evidence was being sought and did not mention judicial sanction of the practice. A police justice charged the force with excessive prosecutorial zeal; the *Herald* accused "Mr. Fouché Kennedy" of heading a secret police system "at variance with the spirit of our government and the sentiments of our people." The paper warned that the police, "saddled upon us by the Albany Legislature, is fast assuming an aspect so odious, and insufferable that the people will be compelled at last to revolt against it and overthrow it altogether" unless the new force were abolished. Kennedy was unpopular in New York because of his determination to enforce the detested liquor laws and because his later emergence from near death in the draft riots left him with few scruples in handling evildoers.[38]

The unpopularity of Kennedy and his force made the time ripe for legislative restriction of police powers, but no such laws were enacted. Though generally hostile to the Metropolitan Police, the Democratic-dominated state senate investigating committee believed that existing laws were sufficient to limit abuses and concentrated its criticisms on some of Kennedy's other practices. A clue to this inaction may be found in a journalist's later comment that, although he was called "King Kennedy" among "the masses," the tough superintendent was better regarded by the upper and middle classes: "He has often exceeded his power, and has committed acts that smack strongly of petty tyranny; but there can be no doubt of the fact that he has earnestly and faithfully labored for the cause of law and order." A few extralegal practices in the name of law and order did not seem inconsistent to Kennedy or his admirers. Lack of internal and external checks gave New York patrolmen a much freer hand to act upon their suspicions than was possible for their London brethren.[39]

"Blanket" or "Cover" Charges

Sometimes policemen, in an effort to assert their authority over unruly or uncooperative citizens, will arrest them for offenses such as obstruction of an officer or disorderly conduct. The officers are less concerned with obtaining a conviction than with exacting a form of street-corner punishment. Indiscreet use of police power in such cases can feed public fears of oppression and tyranny.

Some Londoners complained of police use of cover charges. A journalist in 1838 charged that people of "correct morals" were arrested "simply because they had refused, in going home, to submit obsequiously to the behests of a capricious policeman." One of *Punch*'s "Maxims for the Police" in 1854 was "Necessity is the mother of invention; so when you find it necessary to make a charge against somebody you have locked up, invent one."[40]

The commissioners knew that such complaints would foster an image of the policeman as an arbitrary petty tyrant. During the early years of the force, when bobbies were often overzealous, the commissioners were particularly concerned to prevent the invention of cover charges. They urged the men to "understand, that their interests and safety are best consulted by a check being . . . given to unnecessary or vexatious prosecutions," assuring them that they would "at all times be efficiently protected by every legal means in cases that require prosecution." Having found many instances of policemen exceeding their authority by improper arrests for obstruction of an officer in his duty, they stated that they wished

> to discourage this practice, and expressly state that the P. Constable is not authorized to take any one into custody without being able to prove some specific act by which the law has been broken. No Constable is justified in depriving any one of his liberty for words only and language however violent towards the P.C. himself is not to be noticed . . . ; a Constable who allows himself to be irritated by any language whatsoever shows that he has not a command of his temper which is absolutely necessary in an officer invested with such extensive powers by the law.[41]

They demanded that inspectors on duty at the station house refuse to accept policemen's charges of assault or obstruction unless satisfied by their precise statement of the circumstances. Toward the end of his career Mayne required a full report of all such charges, including any "blame attached to the police," at his office the morning after the incident.[42]

"Disorderly conduct" was another vague charge. Sometimes inspectors dismissed these charges at the station house when the prisoner promised to be orderly in the future. Thus a policeman could scare a person into respect for his authority without having to bring a weak case before the magistrate. The commissioners objected to station-house discharge because they could not determine whether the bobby had made a proper arrest. They required inspectors to accept all charges for examination by a magistrate unless they believed the policeman had made an improper arrest. The inspectors had to report all discharges and the reasons for them to Scotland Yard.[43]

The problem of false arrests recurred despite the commissioners' early efforts. In 1845 they demanded that superintendents carefully investigate patrolmen's charges of prisoners' misconduct. Rowan and Mayne would not allow prosecution of such charges unless the superintendent were satisfied that "the evidence is accurate and sufficient for a conviction." As a magistrate pointed out, people could rarely recover damages for false arrests, and the victim who was poor suffered most of all: "What damages could a police constable give to a man so imprisoned, or what kind of action could a poor labourer, who has been locked up all night and got his head broken, bring against the police?" Arbitrary arrests for assault or obstruction of an officer cropped up in the mid-sixties, and Mayne ordered that the rules on the subject be read monthly; he demoted men who made false arrests and praised a sergeant who was known for his cautiousness in assault and disorderly conduct charges. Abuses seem to have recurred, but the commissioners made an effort to check them.[44]

The commanders of New York's forces were as careful as the London commissioners in regulating arrests for assault or obstruction of an officer. In fact, parts of both the Municipal and the Metropolitan regulations were copied from a London police order of 1830. Policemen had to receive permission from the heads of the force before they could apply for warrants on assault or obstruction charges.[45]

However, patrolmen had a free hand to arrest for disorderly

conduct. Although Metropolitan Commissioner Acton said that this offense was covered by "a good many rules," a police justice charged that there were "frequent instances of parties being arrested for 'disorderly conduct' merely because they took the number of the policeman," and a journalist contended that arrest for disorderly conduct usually depended "exclusively upon the fancy of the policeman," who had "a discretionary power that few use discreetly." Whatever their motives, New York policemen made many more disorderly conduct arrests than did London bobbies. In 1851 they made one such arrest for each 109 people, while London officers made one for each 380 people. In 1868–69 New York's absolute number of disorderly conduct arrests was greater than London's: 14,935 compared to only 2,616 in the much larger British metropolis. There is evidence that New York was more rowdy than London, but the great discrepancy probably reflects London's discouragement of disorderly conduct charges. The heads of the New York force left disposition of patrolmen's charges, without any special checks on disorderly conduct arrests, up to station-house desk officers. Disorderly conduct seems to have been a blanket charge, used to search people for weapons or perhaps, as in modern practice, to bring them to the station house for interrogation about more serious crimes.[46]

Cover charges were never entirely eliminated in either London or New York, but London police officials seem to have made more efforts to prevent their men from abusing arrest powers.

Arrests for Assault: Problems Caused by Restriction of Police Discretion

In one area of arrest practices the London commissioners sought to broaden police discretionary power. Their efforts reveal their determination to seek legal rather than extralegal means of increasing police powers. Bobbies were not allowed to arrest without a warrant a person charged with assault unless they had witnessed the incident. This was the law's normal definition of a misdemeanor. A victim could not point out the assailant to a patrolman and expect to have him arrested. The rationale for this restriction was prevention of false or malicious assault charges. In the first years of the force officers often acted on their natural impulses and did arrest for assaults they had not seen. The magistrates gave different opinions in these cases; many people complained of the police, threatening to sue for false arrest. The commissioners found that "much embarrassment is in consequence caused in regulating the conduct of the Police

Force," and reminded the men that they had to see an assault to make a legal arrest, and could not take a person charged with assault into custody unless charged by another policeman. The commissioners approached the law officers of the crown about modifying the restriction, but they were adamant: bobbies had to see the assault committed.[47]

By 1833 criticism of police nonintervention in assault cases outnumbered complaints of false arrest. A parish official pictured "a respectable man . . . left weltering in his blood at his own door, and although 12 respectable inhabitants, his neighbours, might see the transactions, they were not to be believed or taken any notice of, if the policeman did not see it." After a magistrate strongly disapproved of the assaults policy, charging that it allowed the "greatest criminals to escape," Rowan and Mayne warned Home Secretary Melbourne that "such observations are calculated—if unnoticed—to destroy their authority over the police, and to fix upon the police themselves a most undeserved stigma, as if they were culpably ignorant and remiss in the performance of services which the public are entitled to expect." They requested him to make some public statement on the assaults controversy.[48]

Melbourne replied instead with a loosely worded revision of the police orders, allowing bobbies to arrest in assault cases if "the person making the charge has received some manifest wound or bodily harm." The commissioners scrupulously pointed out their objections. Since the policeman decided what constituted bodily harm, his discretion in accepting or rejecting assault complaints was unduly increased. Moreover, the revision entailed certain legal complications since the law of assault, placing the offense in the misdemeanor category, remained unchanged. Finally, Melbourne drew up an order which Rowan and Mayne accepted. Policemen were not to arrest in assaults not personally witnessed unless the victim "has been cut or wounded, and gives into custody the party charged with having given the cut or wound." Specification of cutting and wounding was meant to distinguish between simple and aggravated assault and serve as a clear guide to police action.[49]

Problems persisted, however. It was not always easy to tell whether a victim had been wounded if he did not point out his injury to the officer. Another difficulty arose when "a fellow struck a gentleman in the street" without wounding him, and the victim pointed out the attacker to a policeman who came up after the affray. The officer, though he desired to make the arrest, patiently explained that he was

65

not authorized to act, whereupon the "gentleman" declared that he would take the law into his own hands and then struck his assailant. He was promptly arrested because he had committed an assault in the bobby's presence, and the original attacker went his way. This was an extreme example of police nonintervention in assaults, the greatest source of public complaint in the later thirties. Rowan and Mayne pressed for full arrest powers, but the parliamentary Select Committee of 1834, generally favorable to the new police, did not endorse their recommendations. Finally, the 1839 police act's section 65 granted full powers of arrest in all assaults which policemen had "good reason to believe" were committed. The commissioners opted for broader discretion, but discretion which was clearly granted by law.[50]

New York policemen never obtained full arrest powers in assault cases. Municipal policemen could not arrest without a warrant in assaults they had not witnessed unless either the assailant were arrested by a witness to the affray or "a person has been severely cut or wounded, and gives into custody the party charged with having cut or wounded him."[51] This was more restrictive than Melbourne's similar order of 1833, which did not require the victim to be "severely" wounded. Metropolitan policemen apparently had no greater power than Municipal policemen. With the tacit consent of their superior officers, patrolmen may have made up for this lack of legal power by exercising personal discretion. They may have charged people with disorderly conduct who had actually committed assaults for which the police lacked power of immediate arrest. There is no way to verify this, but such a discretionary practice may have swelled the disorderly conduct arrest figures. At any rate, New Yorkers do not seem to have complained about limited police powers in assault cases. Instead of obtaining a legal grant of increased power, the police may have broadened personal discretion to fill the void. Restricted discretion in one area may have expanded it in another area.

STATION-HOUSE BOOKING
The patrolman having made his arrest, the desk officer's decision to accept or reject his charge was the next step in the process of criminal justice. Desk officers' discretionary power was controversial in both cities, but generally the London commissioners resolved the issue with clear policy guidelines, while the heads of the New York force left much more up to individual desk officers without centralized direction.

In London, superintendents and inspectors on duty at the station house had the power to accept or dismiss bobbies' charges, to lock up the prisoner or release him. Rowan and Mayne stated that they introduced this practice over Whig Home Secretary Melbourne's disapproval, although he eventually acquiesced. Public complaints and doubts raised in a court case prompted Melbourne to eliminate discretionary acceptance of felony charges in early 1832. He pressured the commissioners to submit a proposed police order that all persons charged with a felony must be locked up until they could be brought before a magistrate, "whatever rank, condition, or under whatever circumstances." They submitted the proposal, but added a persuasive list of objections. Mandatory lockup would be hard on "persons ... who, from station and circumstances in life, and the nature of the felony of which they are accused, appear to be perfectly innocent" of the charges perhaps made by "persons themselves utterly undeserving of credit; — or it may be from malice or mistake, and where it is fairly to be presumed, the party preferring the charge at the Police Station, will never appear before a magistrate." Moreover, such charges were "frequently" made by "low women of the town, by dismissed servants, and workmen, against their employers, and others of known bad character, whose only object would be gained by gratifying their revenge, and having the party locked up." Mandatory incarceration would be especially hard on weekends, when justices were not sitting; twelve or fourteen hours might have to be spent in a cell. Supporting discretionary release, the commissioners contended that a strict policy would "be felt a very serious grievance by the public, and will excite great odium against the police." Apparently, Melbourne had his way, but he soon gave in, agreeing that existing discretionary power should stand but be limited to superintendents and inspectors, who must report all such discharges to the Home Office. Earlier the commissioners had required reporting of all discharges to them for determination of their propriety. Discretionary release in felony cases continued, but under careful controls.[52]

A related area of station-house discretion was police power to release misdemeanor suspects on bail. This practice, established by the Metropolitan Police Act of 1829, has never existed in America but remains an important feature of English criminal justice. Originally the power to release on bail applied only to petty offenders arrested at night. The decision to grant bail was up to the desk officer "when he shall deem it prudent," presumably with the arresting officer's advice. Bail does not seem to have been granted indiscriminately, for the commissioners could say in 1838 that "there has been no instance in which any party admitted to bail by the police has not been forthcoming when required at the Magistrates' offices."[53]

Rowan and Mayne complained that police bail-taking powers were too limited, not because of excessive restriction on the police, but because of hardship on people arrested during the day after the magistrates had left their offices or on Sunday. They had to remain locked up until the justices were available. This was especially hard on "really respectable" people able to provide bail. As it did in many other areas, the Police Act of 1839 extended bail-taking powers, section 70 authorizing the police to take bail in all offenses subject to magistrates' summary jurisdiction whenever the Police Offices (J.P.'s courts) were closed. The number of these summary offenses increased substantially in the 1850s because many petty crimes no longer required jury trial, consequently extending police bail-taking powers. In felonies and serious misdemeanors policemen were given the power to require persons making the charge to post bail for their appearance in court as prosecutors. If they refused, policemen were authorized by the 1839 act's section 71 to discharge the accused on his own recognizance, with or without sureties as they deemed proper. The modern English law of bail is substantially the same, except that now the taking of bail is required rather than discretionary if the accused cannot be brought to court within twenty-four hours.[54]

Another station-house discretionary power was originally broad but subsequently was limited by the Home Office. Actually, discretionary decisions were moved from the station house to the street. During the early 1830s the commissioners and the home secretary agreed that policemen could "take up" drunks incapable of getting home and confine them in the station house for their own protection until sober. After signing a receipt for property the police had taken from them for security, they would be released without being brought before a magistrate. They were given the option of going to court if they felt themselves unjustly arrested. Though the commissioners had "rather gone beyond the law, in releasing so many who have been taken up by the police, without carrying them before the magistrates," most of the individuals involved "generally have been grateful for having been so dealt with."[55]

In 1833, however, Melbourne became concerned over the practice's extralegality. He decided that it would be more proper to require all drunkenness cases to be charged before a magistrate. Rowan and Mayne objected that "it would cause an unnecessary exposure of some respectable persons; and to the working classes it would occasion very serious mischief, from the loss of so much additional time, and the evil effects in many cases, of confinement with dissolute characters, after they had become sober." Moreover, bringing all drunks before justices would interfere with policemen's more important duties. Typically the commissioners agreed with Melbourne's objection to extralegality, but sought legal authorization to continue the policy. This time Melbourne prevailed, and after August 1833 bobbies were directed to bring all persons arrested for drunkenness before a magistrate. However, they could still release drunks on bail even if they had not sobered up, provided their sureties took them home.[56]

The result of the new policy was that patrolmen usually arrested only disorderly drunks, preferring to help quiet inebriates home instead of arresting them. Arrest now involved more than a night at the station house, and the bobby had to decide who should suffer the consequences. This discretionary power may have discriminated against the working classes, whom policemen were more likely to consider disorderly. The Chartist leader Feargus O'Connor complained that the new policy reflected prejudice against working-class inebriates while falsely concealing "their betters' " vices. Insensible drunks were sometimes still arrested to protect them from robbery, but some magistrates considered this a waste of time and manpower. In 1832, 25,702 drunks had been discharged from the station house when sober; in 1860, 9,365 individuals were arrested as intoxicated and incapable of taking care of themselves. The drop may have reflected declining drunkenness as well as police practice, for only about half the number of *disorderly* drunks were arrested in 1867 as in 1840. Under both the old and the new policies the police seem to have been rather tolerant of at least "respectable" intoxication, preferring not to treat it as a crime unless it created disorder. This was a more easygoing attitude than conventional Victorian morality dictated.[57]

In New York, station-house discharge was never officially entrusted to the police, although they often exercised the power, and was the focus of continuing controversy. The issue was only partly resolved by legal changes; generally the police exercised extralegally a power they deemed necessary.

Under the Municipal Police, conflict over station-house discharge centered on the privilege of city aldermen (who were ex officio magistrates) and police justices to bail or discharge prisoners at night after a brief examination in the station house. The rationale of this power, granted in 1813, was prevention of inconvenient all-night lockups. In New York the power of bail or discharge at night was not entrusted to the police, as was the case in London, but to elected officials who frequently abused it by releasing their political supporters without any investigation of the charges.[58]

Conflict became especially acute when the judiciary and police commanders were of different political persuasions, as after 1857, but even under the city-controlled Municipal Police judicial intervention after arrest lowered police morale. Aldermen could even discharge prisoners committed by the police justices, until revision of the city charter in 1853 eliminated this power. However, they could still release a prisoner between arrest and committal on the strength of a note to the police captain. These powers provoked ill-feeling between policemen and some aldermen. In 1856 Mayor Fernando Wood allowed only the recorder and city judge (at that time presiding over the court of special sessions), his fellow police commissioners, the power to discharge on a note. Other magistrates had to hold a hearing in the station house. This change only slightly improved matters.[59]

Soon after taking office the state-appointed Metropolitan commissioners urged complete elimination of magisterial power to bail or discharge prisoners at night, but the amended Police Act of 1860 still permitted the practice. Superintendent Kennedy got around the law by ordering the captains to refuse judicial discharge of prisoners unless the district attorney were present. He and the district attorney agreed that police justices could hold station-house hearings only if prisoners were not allowed to choose their own judge as they had in the past. Kennedy's order did not recognize aldermen's magisterial powers and thus eliminated the worst abuses.[60]

The police attack on judicial intervention aroused opposition. The state senate investigating committee of 1860 recommended full restoration of discharge powers. Nevertheless in 1864 the law vindicated Kennedy, the revised police act directing that if an arrest were made when the justices were not holding court, "such offender shall be *detained* in a station-house, or precinct thereof, until the next *public* sitting of the magistrate." The law did not grant discharge powers to station-house desk officers. Technically all people arrested had to be detained until court appearance.[61]

Metropolitan Police regulations specified that "Captains, sergeants, policemen or doormen are not authorized by law to discharge any prisoner from custody." The regulation and the law upon which it was based were ignored; desk officers did discharge prisoners in the station house. Commissioner Acton said that the police board reviewed all discharges, but that he did not believe that such discretionary decisions should be written into the law. When asked, "Is it good policy to do that which is not permitted by law?" he replied, "It is absolutely necessary to exercise discretion sometimes."[62]

The 1860 investigation castigated station-house discharges as a usurpation "dangerous to the rights of the community" and "pernicious to the public interests." The senators demanded strict adherence to the letter of the law requiring all prisoners to be taken before a magistrate. They suspected that station-house discharges were a way of covering up arrests which the police knew would not hold up in court. Arbitrary arrests do seem to have been a problem, and discharge before court appearance may have been a frequent method of dealing with them. A police justice charged that patrolmen "arrogate to themselves the right to construe the law." A journalist who was no friend of the justices concurred:

> Not a day passes that patrolmen do not take prisoners into nearly every one of the thirty station houses of the city, the charges against whom dissolve under the first examination, and the accused are discharged by the officer in charge. But all these cases go upon the record, and do duty in the annual reports as so many offenses, when, in fact, they may be nothing more than proofs of the malice of accusers or the stupidity of patrolmen.[63]

If such discharges covered mistaken or arbitrary arrests, they may also have been an unofficial compensation to people so arrested. Since the police lacked bail-taking powers and magistrates had been prohibited from releasing prisoners at the station houses, the only alternative to station-house discharge was locking the prisoner up all night or taking him to court. Although it is impossible to know, many people may have been glad to get out of the station house as quickly as possible. Of course they may also have left with bad memories of police harassment which they could do nothing about.

Oddly, considering the easygoing attitude toward station-house discharge, police commanders required adherence to the letter of the law which denied desk officers the power to release drunks after they had sobered up. We have seen that the London police could still release drunks on bail after the abolition of discretionary release. Under the Municipal Police the prisoner could send for his alderman to hold court in the station house and take bail, but only if he could put up the money or had political pull. The poor and friendless remained locked up all night. Equality prevailed under the Metropolitan force: the captain had "to throw those of whose innocence he is satisfied, into the company of the most abandoned wretches for the entire night." Many New Yorkers, tolerant of broad police discretion in other areas, thought that intoxication deserved punishment — fines rose from three dollars in 1850 to ten dollars in 1857 — and mistrusted discretionary release of people charged with drunkenness. The New York Prison Association condemned discharge of "drunkards" by magistrates even after a hearing, and complained that though usually done for charitable motives, "its use is so liable to abuse that it should be strictly prohibited." Metropolitan Police Superintendent Kennedy was ambivalent about granting more discretion to his men. At first he said he favored release of drunks after they had sobered up, but then warned that generally "it is of questionable propriety to give to any officer the exercise of such discretion." Commissioner Acton, remarking that justices convicted in 70 percent of intoxication charges, thought that 90 percent should bring conviction. The Metropolitan commissioners did not share their London counterparts' attitudes toward drunkenness. They were more disposed to view even harmless intoxication as a crime against which the law should be strictly enforced.[64]

Municipal Police instructions specified a policy similar to London's: policemen must "arrest any person they may find intoxicated under such circumstances as amounts to a violation of public decency." Even after temperance reformers tightened the laws in the later fifties, Captain Daniel Carpenter testified that drunks were arrested only when there was "a violation of public decency, as for instance a man staggering up against parties," although the law now required arrest of all inebriates found in public places. However, high arrest figures for mere drunkenness suggest that policemen in Chief Matsell's day had a very strict interpretation of what violated public decency. The police made 14,705 arrests for ordinary intoxication in New York in 1855, compared to 9,756 in London in 1858. Moreover, arrests for simple intoxication in New York outnumbered drunk and disorderly arrests, while the reverse was true in London. Apparently the police justices cooperated by fining or imprisoning a large proportion of those arrested both on intoxication and on drunk and disorderly charges.[65]

This pattern continued under the Metropolitan Police. Superintendent Kennedy said that only disorderly drunks were arrested, but a police justice pointed out that in 1859 some 19,000 arrests had been made for mere intoxication. In 1869 the London police made only 9,538 arrests for intoxication, compared to New York's 24,023 in 1868-69. Arrests on drunk and disorderly charges were slightly higher in London (10,853) than for ordinary drunkenness; in New York they were considerably lower (8,698). London's general non-interference with harmless drunks except for their own protection may have occasioned George W. Walling's remark that "The London police do not arrest for gross intoxication and disturbance in the street." That is precisely what they did arrest for, instead of simple drunkenness as in New York. Perhaps they had different notions of what was gross and disturbing.[66]

Why was New York's policy toward intoxication an exception to the force's general reliance on broad, even extralegal, police discretion? Perhaps this toughness was a concession to temperance reformers and nativists who viewed intoxication as one of the vices of the Irish immigrant "dangerous classes." Respectable citizens expected toughness in dealing with this group, whether calling for broad discretion as in the use of firearms or narrow discretion as in drunkenness arrests. New Yorkers may have been less willing than Londoners to distinguish between respectable and disreputable intoxication. In this area, though not in other vices, the "double standard" may have been less acceptable.[67]

Except in the case of drunkenness, the London commissioners allowed discretionary station-house discharges with either specific legal justification or careful internal and external controls. Again, with the exception of drunkenness, the heads of the New York force accepted station-house release by the police as an extralegal, often unregulated, discretionary power. When dealing with intoxication the two forces reversed their attitudes, the London commissioners being more charitable than the law, the New York commanders enforcing it strictly.

4 POLICE AND THE RULE OF LAW: FROM INTERROGATION TO TRIAL

For more serious offenders the next step after arrest and station-house booking was police interrogation. In the twentieth century, British and American courts have been especially concerned with regulating police practices in this area. In the mid-nineteenth century, however, there was a marked contrast between the attitudes of London police and judicial officials and their counterparts in New York.

INTERROGATION AND EVIDENCE-GATHERING

In London all levels of the criminal justice system scrutinized police interrogation and evidence-gathering practices. Such scrutiny was especially important because in England the police acted as public prosecutors in all criminal cases, major and minor alike. Since the English system lacked, and still does, a public prosecutor comparable to the American district attorney or the Scottish procurator fiscal, policemen prepared and presented their cases in court. Since 1829 magistrates had bound over policemen to prosecute cases they committed for jury trial in higher courts. Bobbies largely replaced private citizens as prosecutors.[1] They not only apprehended an offender but prepared a case against him if the magistrate committed him for trial. All policemen present a case against the offender when a magistrate first hears the charge, but in Scotland or the United States the public prosecutor takes over the case after committal for jury trial and decides not only how to conduct the prosecution but whether to prosecute at all. In these systems the policeman appears as a prosecution witness; in England he is the prosecutor. In the nineteenth century bobbies actually presented their own case. Today police barristers present the prosecution arguments.

74

One of the most delicate police problems in the mid-nineteenth century occurred immediately after arrest, when prisoners made statements which could be used against them or gave outright confessions. The attorney general of England pointed out the need for careful control of police handling of prisoners' statements. He urged precise recording of prisoners' remarks made during the stress of arrest and lockup, as these often were the only evidence upon which a conviction could be obtained. "But if you have a policeman who is already overzealous in the cause," he observed, "the slightest difference in a word or two, a little more colour, a little more complexion, given to the prisoner's statement, makes the difference between the man's being convicted or not." J. P. Cobbett, a barrister, catalogued several police abuses which he had encountered. He asserted that despite their knowledge of judicial disapproval of questioning of prisoners, policemen persisted because they knew that once the facts were obtained they could not be ignored in court. They sometimes privately interrogated prisoners in the courtroom awaiting the magistrate's preliminary examination. Some policemen, if they could not support their charges in any other way, industriously sought people implicated in a crime who would turn "King's evidence." Sometimes the police would deliberately put prisoners together in jail and listen in on their conversations for incriminating evidence. Cobbett remarked, "As things now unfortunately are, there is necessarily a strong inducement with this modern species of peace-officer to make stretches in his duty to the public for his own personal advancement and gain; that one whose highest praise is sounded in the phrase of 'active officer,' will occasionally, if not very often, allow his activity to go beyond the control of his conscience." Even if abuses were not widespread, it was clear that somebody had to monitor the gathering and presentation of evidence.[2]

Until the 1850s English courts were extremely sensitive about confessions and statements which could be used against prisoners. They held that the policeman's familiar warning, "Anything you say will be used as evidence against you," was an inducement or threat which would pressure the prisoner into making damaging admissions. The underlying concern was that an innocent person would be intimidated by the official warning and falsely incriminate himself. This interpretation of the warning is exactly the opposite of the United States Supreme Court's *Miranda* decision of the 1960s, which requires the warning as a *protection* of the prisoner's right to remain silent under official interrogation. The nineteenth-century English judicial sensitivity about induced confessions may have been a carry-over from the days of a harsh penal code when confession invited death or transportation for life.[3]

The police commissioners' directives to their men reflected this sensitivity:

> Whenever a person is brought to the station on a charge of felony, the Inspector or other officer on duty, will not on any account suffer any statement in the nature of a confession, to be extracted from the person charged, either by the Police Constables concerned in the case, or by any other person. Should any private individuals attempt such a course at the station, they will be immediately turned out, and the circumstances reported to the Commissioners.[4]

Bobbies sometimes took Rowan's and Mayne's caution too much to heart, advising prisoners "not to say anything about the charge against them." In 1844 the commissioners had to warn their men that such advice often "defeated the ends of justice" by squelching voluntary confessions. The lord chief justice complained that the courts' position on confessions, "that the arresting officer shall apprise his prisoner of the cause of his arrest, and leave him free to speak or keep silence," had been misunderstood by policemen, "who fancy themselves bound to stop the prisoner's mouth by a caution against criminating himself, or by the use of language which leads to the invention of falsehoods and the suppression of truth." Bobbies were overcautious because judges and defense counsel sharply criticized confessions in which the "slightest inducement either of fear or hope [was] held out to an accused party by any one whose position of authority may be supposed to exercise an influence over his mind." One policeman, when asked whether his prisoner had made any sort of confession while in custody, replied, "Oh no; he began to say something about it, but I knew my duty better, so I stopped him." He was reprimanded, but his caution was understandable, "for he had so often heard his brethren assailed, and had been so often assailed himself, for deposing to confessions, that he was determined to be on the safe side for once." Instead of inducement to confession, the "safe side" seems to have been discouragement of confessions.[5]

In 1852, the courts reversed themselves, holding in the case of *Regina* v. *Baldry* that the policeman's warning was not an intimidation or inducement of the prisoner. Courts increasingly admitted confessions made after arrest as evidence against defendants.[6] This change of position may have reflected the complaints against police overcautiousness and the culmination of a period of legal reform which drastically reduced punishments for most major and minor offenses.

Whatever the judges thought, the commissioners remained cautious, warning policemen not to carry judicial acceptance of confessions too far. They pointed out that bobbies' treatment of the confused and ambiguous statements of prisoners as confessions occasioned "frequent complaint" and "reprehension." Judicial rulings on this area of police power were sometimes confusing and subject to subtle interpretations. For example, while confessions under threat or inducement were not themselves admissible, material facts so obtained were acceptable as evidence against the prisoner. Also, confessions made under threat or promise by a private citizen rather than the police were acceptable. These exceptions could have been used as loopholes in the general restrictive rulings, but Mayne seems to have preferred more cautiousness in interrogation practices than the judges demanded. He closely monitored police practices. In 1865 he cautioned bobbies against making a prisoner's statement seem more like a confession than it actually was. The next year he directed that "Prisoners are not to be cautioned by Police that any statement they make will be given in evidence against them," and they were "not to endeavour to extract any statement or confession" from a prisoner, referring to the order of 1837 quoted earlier. He advised, in fact, that the best procedure was to avoid any questioning of arrestees. He apparently believed that the safest course was the most cautious interrogation procedure.[7]

Mayne's attitudes have left their mark on modern English interrogation practices. Today all questioning must cease after arrest; any information from a suspect must be obtained before arrest.[8]

Previous discussion of broad police discretion in New York revealed lower-court toleration of arrest and interrogation practices. Higher courts followed this pattern and were very liberal in admitting prisoners' confessions despite the techniques by which they were obtained. They seem to have shared the attitude of a prestigious commission for codification of New York criminal law, which asserted in 1850 that existing restrictions on the admissibility of confessions, following British precedents, were "too tender" toward suspected criminals. The Court of Appeals ruled in one case that a visibly frightened prisoner's statement in a mixture of English and German was admissible as a confession, even though the arresting officer did not understand German. In another case the supreme court (New York's second highest, below Appeals) ruled that a policeman's promise of leniency, which induced a prisoner to tell him the location of a stolen watch, did not rule out the confession. Since the watch was found, what mattered was not the technique of obtaining the confession but its truth. Most remarkable, however, was another important state supreme court ruling in 1862. The court held that a confession was admissible even though the prisoner was drunk from liquor obtained for him by a disguised detective seeking to win his confidence. Here also the standard was the confession's truth, not police techniques, which the court did not hesitate to describe as "deception." The high court's view reflected that of the judge in the original trial, who charged the jury to keep in mind that police techniques were matters of morality, not law:

> Some men think that no means necessary to detect and punish a criminal are dishonorable, no matter what they are; others think that criminals should be handled with gloves; that they should only be pursued by the most honorable, open and upright means. . . . It is of no possible consequence which view I entertain, nor what your views may be upon that mere question of morals.

The jury had only to ask itself if it thought the confession was true. Such rulings would seem to give a free hand to all manner of police "stratagems" to induce confessions, as long as they netted the guilty.[9]

These interpretations of the law of evidence were based on a very early British precedent, which specified that while induced confessions were not admissible, any material facts thereby obtained could be used as prosecution evidence. This provided a loophole in the control of police practices. However, though it was cited in later British decisions, the courts there seem to have kept the loophole quite small. New York courts, on the other hand, made it into a very large breach which seems to have allowed broad leeway to the police.[10]

Why should democratic Americans accept such institutionally unchecked police power? One explanation may lie in the existence of the popularly elected district attorney, which gave the police much less independence and responsibility within the criminal justice system. Since this official conducted the prosecution in higher-court jury trials, and decided whether to prosecute at all, incentives for regulation of police practices were not as great as in London, where the police acted as public prosecutors. Presumably the district attorney judged the merits of police charges before deciding to prosecute. Police loss of control over the case after the police justice's first hearing also meant loss of responsibility for its final outcome. The police were accountable to an elected official, illustrating Tocqueville's argument that electoral accountability prompted democratic societies to trust their officials with broad discretion. The police had broad discretion in their realm, the district attorney broad discretion in his. Since the police did not have ultimate responsibility for conviction, judges and juries often accepted their evidence with little question. [11] Unfortunately the system of balanced power between the police and the district attorney produced conflict instead of mutually accepted standards of interrogation and evidence-gathering practices.

The district attorney was the most powerful officer in the American system of criminal justice. His zeal or laxity decided the fate of hundreds of people accused of serious crimes. He presented all magistrates' committals to the grand jury, which then decided whether to issue an indictment, and subsequently took charge of the prosecution of all indicted offenders. Required to be an experienced lawyer, the district attorney, whose office was created in 1777 as appointive, became an elected official, serving a three-year term, under the democratized constitution of 1846. [12]

Unfortunately, like many elected officials, the district attorney was usually a politician "indebted for his election to the exertions of many individuals who are not enrolled among the saints." Desiring to continue in office, he had to remain on good terms with his political friends, a requirement "not altogether propitious to the stern and impartial administration of justice." Reformers charged that candidates for the office pledged themselves in advance to be lenient on certain offenders, especially violators of the unpopular liquor control laws. They asserted that "a really active and influential politician cannot be convicted in some counties of any crime, by any amount of proof that can be adduced." The *Times* gave irony full rein regarding indicted offenders whom the district attorney never prosecuted:

> The District Attorney ... hoping they will reform, refrains from bringing them, and waits year after year for the benign influences of our Christian civilization to soften their hearts. They naturally feel grateful for this forbearance, and depraved though they may be, appreciating the purity of his motives, testify their gratitude by working for him at elections.

Corruption was difficult to detect, for the district attorney could easily make a technical mistake in drawing up an indictment which would let the offender go free, or leave loopholes in his presentation of evidence easily spotted by defense counsel, or demand the appearance of witnesses whom he knew to be out of town. Official laxity frustrated the police, who did not hesitate to protest. Superintendent Kennedy charged in 1869 that 10,000 grand jury indictments had been pigeon-holed in the district attorney's office.[13]

"Plea bargaining," or the district attorney's encouragement of a guilty plea for a lesser offense than that for which the accused was originally indicted, became common in the mid-nineteenth century. The bargains were always under the table and depended entirely on the district attorney's discretion. Critics complained that plea bargaining too often allowed short prison terms for offenders who deserved stricter punishment. A murderer allowed to plead guilty to manslaughter might undergo "a brief confinement for his homicide, and is then released to shoot or dirk the next man that crosses his path." With this route of escape open to hardened criminals, the police were powerless to stop the increase of crime, which seemed to be reaching the proportions of a "wave" in the later sixties. Ultimately it was the judge's prerogative to accept or reject negotiated pleas, and some courts consistently rejected them; but usually judges accepted the district attorney's explanation of the plea. He was thus allowed a power which, if not always abused, in reformers' eyes was at least subject to abuse.[14]

Whether the district attorney was lenient on political supporters or bargained for briefer sentences than an offender deserved, legal standards of argument and evidence were replaced by personal discretion. The district attorney's honesty or dishonesty was more important than the rule of law. Refusal to prosecute or to properly conduct a prosecution was one way of informing the police about the quality of the case against their prisoner, but such regulation produced conflict and frustration instead of coordination. The district attorney's role as public prosecutor prompted less scrutiny of police evidence than in London, giving patrolmen greater leeway in their practices along with less responsibility for the outcome of the case. Unlike their London brethren, the New York police could exercise many powers freely but irresponsibly.

POLICE-JUDICIAL RELATIONS

The trial is the last stage of direct police participation in the system of criminal justice. Police-judicial relations are important for understanding patrolmen's attitudes toward discretionary power and procedural regularity. Police views of the rule of law reflected their opinions of the principal external agency which evaluated their practices through legal directives, convictions or lack of them in lower courts, or instructions to juries.

One of the most difficult of the London police's initial tasks was winning acceptance from the courts in which the people and policemen most often appeared, the metropolitan police offices. The police offices or courts, for trial and sentencing of petty misdemeanors by the magistrates and for preliminary examination in felony cases, were established in 1792 by Home Office appointment of salaried justices of the peace. Previously, metropolitan area justices had been unpaid, like country J.P.'s, but since no public-spirited gentry were willing to take on the immense task of presiding over the London police offices the job fell to corruptionists, who made the most of it. These "trading justices" sometimes directed the police officers under their command to "take up all the poor devils in the street," making a small fortune from the fees collected for bailing prisoners or pocketing fines. Appointment of salaried justices was a major reform, although they were not required to be experienced lawyers until 1839.[15]

Handling sometimes up to three hundred major and minor cases a day, the mid-nineteenth-century police office was often a grim introduction to English justice. A journalist described the courts as

> Dingy, fetid, close-smelling rooms, for the most part, places
> like a cross betwixt a bare, neglected, decaying school room, and
> a squalid sponging house, approached by low-browed, intricate
> passages; the walls greased and stained by the ceaseless friction
> of the forlorn, ragged groups of witnesses, and prosecutors, and
> the friends of prisoners, who lounge about in every avenue and
> approach which winds and crosses betwixt the Justice Room and
> the loathsome box-like cells — the headquarters and general
> garrison of legions of policemen, who cluster around the outer
> door, and speak dictatorially to the swarms of poverty-stricken,
> squalid men and women who come for summonses, or with
> complaints, or who make distracted enquiries about missing
> friends or strayed children.[16]

The only tribunals readily available to the poor, the police offices lacked the pomp and circumstance of higher courts like Old Bailey. Contemporaries worried that in a crowded and noisy chamber the law, "by losing most of its impressiveness," would lose its "moral power over delinquents." The magistrates missed the great opportunity of becoming teachers of valuable moral lessons to the people. While most were competent men, some of the justices, like Allen Stewart Laing (prototype of Dickens's Mr. Fang), were harsh and punitive. Working-class spokesmen often complained of "Justices' justice" as one aspect of "one law for the rich, another law for the poor," although they most often directed their fire at the unpaid country magistrates.[17]

Despite their courts' unimpressiveness, the police magistrates were jealous of their authority and resented the Metropolitan Police during the 1830s. Part of their animus can be traced to general popular dislike of the new police, especially their novelty as public prosecutors, but the new force also threatened magistrates' control of the detective officers attached to their courts. According to the ancient pattern of local justices of the peace, police as well as judicial functions were magisterial prerogatives. Although the magistrates and police commissioners were both appointed by the home secretary, continued judicial control of some police officers and the justices' determination to retain law enforcement functions prevented coordination with the new police.

Rowan and Mayne were appointed justices of the peace to establish their social status and official power, but also because of earlier precedent. The old police forces, such as the Bow Street Runners and the Thames police, had been controlled by magistrates, and it was logical that creation of a new police force involved appointment of new magistrates. However, the Metropolitan Police's great departure was that the commissioners were barred from exercising any judicial functions. This was a new principle of law enforcement, unquestioned and essential today, but apparently it was originally adopted simply to allow the commissioners time to develop a police force free from judicial duties.[18] Unfortunately, the police act did not define how the commissioners and their force would relate to the magistrates and the officers under their command.

Rowan and Mayne soon realized the problems caused by loose definition of their authority. Sometimes officers of the magistrates' courts and Metropolitan policemen worked on the same case unknown to each other. Sometimes, if aware of each other's efforts, jealousy prevented coordination of their work. The police magistrates always granted warrants to their own men rather than to the Metropolitan constables, even when a peeler's efforts had led to the warrant's issue. The policemen were demoralized because credit for the arrest went to the magistrate's man. Sometimes an offender would escape because the justice's officer, through ignorance or neglect, would fail to execute the warrant for his arrest. Metropolitan constables were thus tempted to exceed their powers of arrest without warrant. In addition to these jurisdictional problems, magistrates often hired men whom the commissioners had dismissed from their force for misconduct.[19]

On the justices' side, Sir F. A. Roe, chief magistrate at Bow Street (commanding the important Bow Street forces and considered head of the police magistrates), argued that judicial and police functions could not be separated. He believed that many police duties were so delicate that they could be carried out only by an officer whom the magistrate knew and could direct without any other authority attempting to control his actions. The issue was control over police detective work; Roe praised the preventive duties of the Metropolitan Police and generally approved of their conduct.[20]

The commissioners urged that the magistrates be limited to judicial functions, with the police performing all law enforcement and detective as well as preventive duties. The parliamentary Select Committee of 1834 seconded their recommendation, but it was not put into effect until passage of the comprehensive Police Act of 1839, after an investigation of the police offices had resulted in the same proposal. With a few exceptions, institutional conflict between police and magistrates was removed. Bobbies took over all the duties of the old magistrates' forces.[21]

In the Metropolitan force's early days, policemen were frequent targets of magistrates' criticism. When the bobby left the catcalls and occasional stones of the street, in the courtroom he often met a lecture or brief but pointed observations on his conduct. Charles Reith exaggeratedly portrays the magistrates as Messrs. Fang when they dealt with the police and describes their criticisms as an "astonishing record of mean and unscrupulous intrigue." Nevertheless, he correctly points out that light (if any) punishments were meted out to individuals guilty of assaulting policemen, and that sometimes police evidence would be rejected out of hand because of judicial hostility to the force.[22]

However, policemen themselves added to the conflict, sometimes because of ignorance of proper procedure, overzealousness, or intemperate outbursts in the courtroom. The commissioners recognized the problem and insisted on proper presentation of evidence in court; they also sought to instill a sense of deference toward the magistrates, making the bobbies into examples of courtroom decorum in their language and conduct.

In their effort to inculcate respect for the magistrates, Rowan and Mayne had to cope with the bobbies' frustration caused by judicial decisions and attitudes. Judicial demands for proof of actual begging in vagrancy arrests and the strict standards of evidence required in arrests for violation of the Sunday liquor laws caused the commissioners as well as their men to grumble. An inspector lamented that "it seems the thieves have as good a right to walk the streets as the police themselves. This has been said to the police by the magistrates at the public office in the presence of thieves." Even in the later sixties, when police-judicial relations had improved, a sympathetic journalist complained that

> A Judge who makes up his mind that policemen are always to be disbelieved, and that every prisoner who represents himself as an artisan seeking work and his plunder-bag as a tool-chest, is to be implicitly believed, does more for the encouragement of crime than can be neutralized by a hundred constables. Indeed, when we see how the police may be badgered by rogues' advocates on and below the bench, we do not wonder at the apathy and inertness with which they are often charged.[23]

Such feelings would not breed respect for the rule of law.

The commissioners were strict with policemen who publicly expressed anger and frustration. Accompanying a warning that all constables must "treat every Police Magistrate with every attention and respect," they stated that they would have dismissed a particular bobby who made an "improper observation" on a magistrate's decision if the judge in the case had not made a request for leniency. Their general policy was to "discourage . . . any opinions upon the decisions of the Magistrates," requiring "the police to continue to do their duty, without expressing any opinion to us on the subject."[24]

Rowan and Mayne also sought to improve police-judicial relations in more concrete ways, trying to develop the impartiality essential to police legitimacy in the courtroom as well as on the street. They worked to insure careful and objective police testimony in court. This was especially important because some people suspected that the police as public prosecutors would distort the evidence to obtain a conviction. Charging in 1869 that "People say [the police] are addicted to lying, and support the assertion by facts," a working-class newspaper pointed out, "It must be recollected that sometimes the lives, and far more frequently the liberties, of men depend upon the evidence given by the police. And it should also be borne in mind that such evidence, generally speaking, carries much greater weight than what is given by private persons." "Establishment" critics did not accuse the police of deliberate falsification but feared that their responsibility for both arrest and prosecution introduced bias in presentation of the case even though the evidence had been honestly obtained. The government at least was satisfied with police impartiality. A high Home Office official agreed that in principle police prosecutions invited "marshalling the evidence" to insure conviction, but that the system actually worked well in practice despite some exceptions. What success the police did have owed much to the commissioners' watchfulness over their men.[25]

Because an arresting officer did not wish to appear arbitrary or foolish, he sometimes lost his objectivity in his efforts to secure conviction. The commissioners had to reiterate their warning that strict impartiality in presentation of evidence was required for "the safety of the administration of justice." In giving evidence the policeman should not "suppress or overstate the slightest circumstance" to bolster his case. He should "endeavour as far as possible to feel indifferent as to the results of the case & that he performs his duty best by stating accurately & without malice or favor the whole of the matter." This caution was especially important when the policeman had been injured, as judges and juries would be skeptical of his evidence unless he stated the case "fully & without passion." It was also essential that the officer state all the facts of a case in his first presentation of the evidence. If he added facts later, "his evidence is naturally looked on with mistrust & is open to suspicion either as to his accuracy or veracity." Moreover, when policemen introduced facts not mentioned in their initial statements, they were subject to sharp questioning which often made them bewildered and "consequently fit prey for the *gibes* of the Prisoner's Counsel." All these cautions were even more important in jury trials, when the policeman was under pressure of defense counsel's cross-examination: the bobby was expected to reply to questions, no matter how insolent, with "the same readiness and civility as . . . when giving . . . evidence in proof of the charge." The commissioners were trying to improve the policeman's public image as well as his efficiency.[26]

The commissioners also watched over policemen's courtroom behavior in many lesser but still important matters. Before passage of a law in 1837 which prohibited mention of a defendant's previous convictions at the trial, policemen were warned not to reveal them unless the judge asked for the prisoner's record. After enactment of the law and a subsequent measure of 1851, the commissioners still found it "no uncommon thing for the Police to render that merciful statute a complete nullity" by mentioning previous convictions, often in reply to a juror's "injudicious question" when the case was in a higher court. They warned that any such appearance of "an overdesire to convict" would encourage acquittals which might "frustrate the ends of justice." The commissioners were concerned not only with what policemen said in court, but also with how they said it. They warned bobbies to "stand in an upright and respectful manner and not lean over the bar . . . in a lazy and slovenly way," and to speak clearly and loudly when presenting their case. They should be precise in describing stolen property taken from prisoners after arrest. They should never "use any low or cant language when speaking of the occupation of any person." The men should never refer to a fellow officer as their "mate." Mayne was dismayed that many policemen in court "shew by their conversation that they are conversant with the 'vulgar tongue' and unobservant of the *Third Commandment*. It would be well if they left out of their vocabulary an offensive word commencing with the letter B — which the mind of a proper thinking person induces him to believe the utterer to be a blackguard." From the early days of the force the commissioners directed superintendents to report immediately all constables whom the magistrates criticized for improper presentation of evidence or any other reason. Reports had to be in by the following morning, so that Rowan and Mayne would not first learn of the incident when reading the morning newspaper.[27]

Despite the persistence of problems of police conduct in court, grand juries and the higher courts early expressed approval of how bobbies handled themselves. The commissioners communicated this praise to the men and encouraged them to continue the good work.[28] Police magistrates took longer to accept the peelers, but after settlement of the jurisdictional dispute over detective officers in 1839 relations improved. An important indication of improvement was the increasing proportion of misdemeanor convictions to arrests in the magistrates' courts, as well as a similar increase of felony convictions in jury trials in higher courts.

Ideally a policeman's decisions whether to make an arrest are so careful and intelligent that all his prisoners are convicted. Such a condition has never existed and never will. Policemen make mistakes or act too hastily, arresting persons subsequently proven innocent.

Sometimes magistrates and juries, not satisfied with the policeman's evidence, will inadvertently let a guilty person off. Police grumbling over judicial decisions is probably inevitable because winning a conviction is a vital element of the policeman's psychology. Convictions make him feel that his job is worthwhile and that he is competent; they give meaning to his work by validating the judgment he made in arresting a person. Having acted quickly, according to his discretion, he finds it hard to admit later that he is wrong.[29]

A great disparity between arrests and convictions, whether due to police carelessness or arbitrariness, or to judicial leniency or strict standards of evidence, can lead to poor police-judicial relations and tempt policemen to use arrest as punishment when they know they cannot obtain a conviction. Police complaints about the judiciary undoubtedly occurred, but the increasing proportion of convictions to arrests must have reduced the problem, especially when combined with the commissioners' concern for proper arrest practices.

Tables 2 to 6 reveal important aspects of the relationship of convictions to arrests. Table 2 covers the disposition of cases by justices of the peace during roughly the first decade of the police force. Magistrates summarily convicted for misdemeanors, required bail, or committed felony cases for trial in higher courts on the average of just under half the time, with a few years showing a little higher rate. Tables 4 and 5 cover magistrates' disposition of indictable offenses and offenses tried summarily from 1856 to 1870. A policeman who brought in a person on a felony charge had the satisfaction, on the average, of seeing him committed for trial almost three-fourths of the time. He was rewarded less by summary convictions for misdemeanors, on the average just a little more than half the time. Comparing the figures in table 2 with those of tables 4 and 5, we see a distinct increase in magisterial decisions favorable to the police. From 1831 to 1841, the justice convicted, held to bail, or committed for jury trial 49 percent, on the average, of the arrestees brought before him. From 1856 to 1870, he summarily convicted or committed for trial an average of about 65 percent of the felony and misdemeanor cases brought before him. Table 3, which compares magistrates' decisions *and* higher court convictions in proportion to arrests between 1842-48 and 1860-70, reveals a somewhat less dramatic increase, from an average of 47 percent bails and convictions in all courts to an average of 56 percent. Finally, table 6 gives the results of jury trials for the most frequently committed indictable offenses against property, between 1860 and 1870. Clearly, conviction rates varied according to crime, but only in the difficult to prove

87

crime of receiving stolen goods were they predominantly below 50 percent. Robbery, which shows a marked decline of convictions in 1862 (from 98 percent to 79 percent) and again in 1868 (from 67 percent to 53 percent), raises some speculation about police practices. There were robbery "crime waves" in 1862–63 and 1867–68, which will be discussed in detail in chapter 5. Public pressure on the police could have induced them to make poorer-quality robbery arrests, ones which did not stand up in court. It is difficult to tell, but, as we have seen, arbitrary arrests did crop up in the sixties. Overall, though, as time went by policemen had an increasing likelihood of having their arrests rewarded with convictions.

TABLE 2
Arrests, Convictions, Bails, Committals, 1831–41, Metropolitan Police District, London

Year	Arrests	Summarily Convicted, Held to Bail	Committed for Trial	Convictions, Bails, and Committals as Percentage of Arrests
1831[a]	49,037[b]	21,843	2,955	51
1832[a]	51,841	23,468	3,656	52
1833[a]	51,472	20,791	3,672	48
1834	64,269	26,302	3,468	46
1835	63,474	27,817	3,113	49
1836	63,384	30,433	3,175	53
1837	64,416	28,345	3,028	49
1838	63,936	29,685	3,295	52
1839	65,965	28,488	3,595	49
1840[c]	70,717	29,076	4,082	47
1841	68,961	28,235	4,018	47
Average percentage				49

SOURCE: Cols. 1–4, "Criminal Returns of the Metropolitan Police for the Year 1850," *Edinburgh Review* 96 (July 1852): 22, in anon. article, "The Police System of London." Col. 5 is my computation from cols. 2 to 4, rounded to the nearest hundred.

[a] Does not include drunks discharged at station houses, a policy abandoned in August 1833.

[b] Corrected from original source, which gave 59,037. The *Annual Register* for 1832 gives 72,824 total arrests, less its figure of 23, 787 drunks discharged at the station houses, leaving 49,037 (*Ann. Reg.* 74 [1832], Chronicle, p. 1).

[c] Metropolitan District extended over an additional population of 267,266 in January 1840 (note in original source).

TABLE 3
Arrests, Convictions, Bails, 1842–48, 1860–70, Metropolitan Police District, London

Year	Arrests	Summarily Convicted, Held to Bail[a]	Higher Court Convictions	Bails and Convictions as Percentage of Arrests
1842	65,704	27,664	3,316	47
1843	62,477	26,171	3,455	47
1844	62,522	26,871	3,126	48
1845	59,123	23,890	3,548	46
1846	62,834	26,333	3,828	48
1847	62,181	23,689	4,551	45
1848	64,480	27,274	4,364	49
Average percentage 1842–48				47
1860[b]	62,937	30,407	2,286	52
1861	63,244	30,101	2,468	51
1862	68,287	32,894	2,936	52
1863	64,760	32,676	2,911	55
1864	65,827	32,387	3,052	54
1865	70,224	35,164	3,099	54
1866	65,806	33,179	3,192	55
1867	63,042	31,698	3,018	55
1868	66,870	34,727	3,297	57
1869	72,951	40,408	3,291	60
1870	71,269	43,338	2,855	65
Average percentage 1860–70				55

SOURCES: Cols. 1–4, 1842–48, Joseph Fletcher, "Statistical Account of the Police of the Metropolis," *Journal of the Statistical Society* 13 (1850): 258; 1860–70, *PP,* 1871, vol. 28, Metro. Police Annual Report 1870, p. 21. Col. 5 is my computation, division of col. 2 into the sum of 3 and 4 (rounded to nearest hundred).

[a] Getting out on bail was infrequent in both lower and higher courts, amounting to only a small proportion of the cases (see "Judicial Statistics," *PP,* 1856–57 to 1869–70).

[b] During the 1850s many petty larcenies, juvenile offenses, and assaults on women and children were transferred to the police magistrates' summary jurisdiction. Thus conviction figures in the higher courts for those years are lower than those for the 1840s.

TABLE 4
Magistrates' Disposition of Indictable Offenses, 1856–70, Metropolitan Police District, London

Year[a]	Total Arrests	Discharged[b]	Committed[b] for Trial	Committals as Percentage of Arrests
1856/57	5,679	2,451	3,176	56
1857/58	4,200	1,533	2,636	63
1858/59	4,216	1,235	2,935	70
1859/60	3,746	957	2,782	74
1860/61	3,972	982	2,972	75
1861/62	4,725	1,392	3,291	70
1862/63	4,984	1,220	3,748	75
1863/64	5,088	1,207	3,835	75
1864/65	4,993	1,058	3,882	78
1865/66	5,179	1,042	4,074	79
1866/67	5,195	1,168	3,949	76
1867/68	5,448	1,265	4,148	76
1868/69	5,546	1,264	4,216	76
1869/70	5,003	1,084	3,869	77
Average percentage				73

SOURCE: My compilations are from "Judicial Statistics," *PP,* for the year following each one given.

NOTE: Indictable offenses include murder, assaults of more serious nature, rape, burglary, robbery, larceny to value of £5 from dwellings, larceny from the person (pocket-picking), simple larceny, receiving stolen goods, frauds and forgeries, arson, keeping a disorderly house (a brothel), and others of less common occurrence. Justices of the peace conducted the preliminary hearing of persons charged with indictable offenses, and decided if evidence was sufficient to commit them for jury trial.

[a] The dates given are from October of the preceding year to September of the following year.

[b] The discharge and committal figures do not add up to the total arrests because I have not included the original source's "bailed," "bailed for trial," and "committed for want of bail" categories. The largest year total for all three of these is 78 arrests.

TABLE 5
Magistrates' Disposition of Offenses Tried Summarily,
1856–70, Metropolitan Police District, London

Year[a]	Total Proceeded Against[b]	Discharged	Convicted	Convictions as Percentage of Total
1856/57	98,217	46,293	51,924	53
1857/58	98,037	45,038	52,999	54
1858/59	84,399	39,382	45,017	53
1859/60	80,477	37,169	43,308	54
1860/61	79,337	37,698	41,639	52
1861/62	84,356	39,404	44,952	53
1862/63	83,373	36,672	46,701	56
1863/64	84,551	37,731	46,820	55
1864/65	91,579	41,979	49,600	54
1865/66	89,980	38,737	51,243	57
1866/67	89,628	39,482	50,146	56
1867/68	86,136	37,084	49,052	57
1868/69	99,036	39,581	59,455	60
1869/70	91,756	32,579	59,177	64
Average percentage				56

SOURCE: My compilations are from "Judicial Statistics," *PP*, for the year following each one given.

NOTE: Offenses tried summarily include lesser assaults, intoxication, drunk and disorderly, lesser larcenies, vagrancy, prostitution, loitering with intent to commit felony, unlawful possession of goods, violations of the liquor control laws, various obstructive nuisances, violations of Sunday laws, offenses under the poor laws. The magistrate decided these cases without a jury.

[a] The dates given are from October of the preceding year to September of the following year.

[b] Not all of these arrests were by the police. Many were by parish officials, poor law officials, or private individuals. Comparing these totals with the totals of police arrests for indictable *and* summary offenses in table 3, and subtracting the totals for indictable offenses only in table 4, gives a rough estimate that the police made the arrest in about two-thirds of the summary offenses. There is no way of knowing if magistrates were any more or less hard on police than other prosecutors. My impression is that magistrates were more skeptical of the police in the early years but had clearly accepted them by the fifties.

TABLE 6
Arrests (A), Convictions (C), and Convictions
as Percentages of Arrests (%), for Important Indictable Offenses,
1860–70, Metropolitan Police District, London

	Burglary, House- breaking	Robbery	Larceny to Value of £5 in Dwelling	Larceny from Person (Pocket- Picking)	Simple Larceny	Receiving Stolen Goods
1860						
A	172	44	86	412	988	197
C	141	43	78	327	778	78
%	82	98	91	79	79	40
1861						
A	179	62	73	376	1,004	188
C	179	61	46	288	780	73
%	100	98	63	77	78	39
1862						
A	265	121	71	366	1,168	209
C	218	96	66	308	890	88
%	82	79	93	84	76	42
1863						
A	231	77	92	435	1,156	218
C	156	54	79	335	876	97
%	67	70	86	77	76	44
1864						
A	252	111	92	498	1,237	189
C	187	72	74	375	970	82
%	74	65	80	75	78	43
1865						
A	240	133	105	523	1,272	147
C	157	89	90	391	975	97
%	65	67	86	75	77	66
1866						
A	231	120	122	554	1,455	188
C	165	74	39	404	1,141	93
%	71	62	32	73	78	49
1867						
A	244	124	149	556	1,423	175
C	161	83	89	405	1,071	90
%	66	67	60	73	75	51

(Table 6 continued)

	Burglary, House-breaking	Robbery	Larceny to Value of £5 in Dwelling	Larceny from Person (Pocket-Picking)	Simple Larceny	Receiving Stolen Goods
1868						
A	286	122	39	594	1,503	285
C	197	65	32	429	1,094	117
%	69	53	82	72	73	41
1869						
A	274	160	101	540	1,409	342
C	207	86	72	400	1,099	146
%	75	54	71	74	78	43
1870						
A	208	116	126	476	1,251	230
C	148	62	104	331	991	118
%	71	53	83	69	79	51

SOURCE: *PP*, 1871, vol. 27, Metro. Police Annual Report 1870, table 11, p. 22, my compilation.

The commissioners' concern with police practices, judicial insistence on the careful presentation of evidence, and reduction of penalties for many crimes during the mid-nineteenth century, which made juries more likely to convict, all helped increase convictions in proportion to arrests. Measured by this partial standard, police-judicial relations seemed to be improving.

Increasing conviction-arrest ratios do not of course mean that the police were satisfied with the punishments judges handed down after conviction. The commissioners themselves complained of the short sentences for vagrancy and for juvenile offenders. Juvenile delinquents returned to the streets after incarceration, making policemen "quite discouraged." Bobbies responded by sacrificing prevention for detection. They were reluctant to arrest for *attempted* pocket-picking, preferring to wait for the boys to actually get hold of their loot; thus a felony, which carried a long prison term, was committed instead of the misdemeanor of attempted larceny, which resulted in only a short incarceration. Rowan and Mayne discouraged this tactic, insisting that policemen arrest as soon as they spotted an attempt. Also, the mildness of punishments for assaults on policemen compared to those for crimes against property must have been especially galling, although by 1834 magistrates were beginning to hand down stiff, exemplary sentences. After the abolition of minimum punishments for particular offenses in 1846, magistrates were free to act on their own discretion, according to the circumstances. Some magistrates might have had a less punitive attitude than the police, but others were satisfactorily tough. Police dissatisfaction with the judiciary certainly existed, but overall it does not seem to have encouraged widespread disrespect for procedural regularity and the rule of law.[30]

Tracing the London bobby's actions from arrest to presentation of his case in court has not revealed a policeman perfectly subordinated to the law or always on good terms with the judiciary. However, it is clear that the commissioners sought, on the whole successfully, to commit their men to the cautious exercise of their powers within the framework of legal protections of civil liberties. This principle was a foundation of police impartiality and a key element in securing public acceptance of the force.

Across the Atlantic in New York the broad discretion of the police was tolerated by the judiciary in many areas; however, paradoxically, their relations were initially poor and grew worse over the years. Conflict was especially acute after 1857, when the state-controlled police and municipally elected judges represented different "constituencies."

As in London the police courts were the first stop for all offenders, from vagrants to murderers. The police justices could summarily dispose of vagrancy, disorderly conduct, and intoxication cases, and they determined whether other offenders should be committed for trial in higher courts: the court of special sessions for misdemeanors and the court of general sessions for felonies. The justices' powers were increased by reorganization of the court of special sessions in 1857. Formerly held by the recorder or city judge (without a jury), it was then held by the police justices on a rotating basis, also without a jury because of the petty nature of the offenses tried there.[31]

While the English magistrates were sometimes viewed as acerbic, authoritarian old men, New York police justices were frequently seen as venal corruptionists. Like the old London "trading justices," who were replaced by salaried magistrates, the police justices were accused by critics of pocketing fines and letting off known thieves for a price. "I am aware that some of the English Justice Shallows occasionally gain unenviable notoriety by their decisions," remarked an English visitor, "but however far they may go astray in the discharge of their duties, it is a rare thing for any one of them to be charged with mercenary motives." Creation of an elective judiciary by the state constitution of 1846 did not influence the justices' character, probably because they had originally been appointed by the politically minded Common Council. Little respected before they were popularly elected, their image declined during the mid-nineteenth century. Reformers depicted the police justices, who were rarely lawyers, as "coarse, profane, uneducated men," usually "excessively conceited and overbearing, and in some cases positively brutal in their demeanor." Because "the large mass of offenders" could vote, and their votes were "as good as anybody's and sometimes very desirable," judicial corruption became an accustomed practice. According to one critic, a judge's dishonesty in the sixties excited "no more surprise than the untruthfulness of a servant-girl or the uncleanliness of a coal-heaver." "Oh, the pain and shame of the police court!" lamented another critic. "It is a tribunal without dignity, and a sentence without sympathy. It seems to rob justice of all beauty by its coarseness, and to strike humanity into the dust with a brutal hand."[32]

The police agreed with the critics who saw the justices as too lenient rather than those who accused them of harshness. Relations with the justices recall those of the London police with the magistrates during the 1830s, but in New York they worsened instead of improving over the years. Under the Municipal Police, officers complained that the justices "don't ask our advice or co-operation, and we don't feel like offering it," and that some magistrates were too willing to let offenders out on bail in assault and disorderly conduct cases. Chief Matsell, disturbed by the murder of four policemen in 1852, attacked what he saw as judicial leniency:

> Policemen are called upon to encounter dangers in every form, and if they are not fully sustained by a strict execution of the law against those who unlawfully resist their authority, they are shorn of their power to protect peaceful citizens in the exercise of their rights and privileges. This subject forcibly commends itself to the attention of those who have the power to punish offenders against the law.[33]

Since this appeared in an annual report, it is clear that New York police officials did not have the London commissioners' compunctions about complaining in public.

The police justices had their complaints as well. Recalling criticisms of the London police, some magistrates said that many patrolmen were "not intelligent enough to take care of their cases," making imprecise statements and introducing new facts while the examination was in progress. Recalling London magistrates' objection to the employment of bobbies in their courts, they complained that the police department's detailment of officers to the courts prevented close cooperation between justices and policemen. Indeed, some of the detailed men refused to serve magistrates' warrants.[34] Even when the city controlled both the police and the judges, relations were strained.

Bad relations became open warfare after the establishment of the Metropolitan Police. Charges of judicial leniency increased during the sixties. In 1861 the commissioners, though crediting the justices with "strict regard to the interests of the public, and for the repression of crime and licentiousness," complained that their "ill-judged clemency" toward drunks, vagrants, and rowdies only encouraged these offenders to become hardened criminals. Five years later they pointed out that only about a third of the arrested murderers, arsonists, burglars, robbers, and receivers of stolen goods were convicted. While allowing that "either the arrests are too numerous or the convictions too few," they asserted that most of those let off did not "escape because they are innocent, but by reason of defects in the administration of the criminal law." The heads of the police force were among the judiciary's leading critics.[35]

We have seen that the Metropolitan commissioners successfully curtailed judicial intervention at the station house. Sometimes the police grappled with individual judges in their efforts to circumvent judicial leniency. Under the Municipal Police a justice had been "told by the Captains of police that they wanted to arrest certain parties and . . . they did not wish to do it until a certain magistrate was on the bench," who presumably was disposed to convict.[36]

The most spectacular police revolt against a judge with whom they were dissatisfied was Metropolitan Superintendent Kennedy's 1867 war against Police Justice Michael Connolly. Opposed to the unpopular excise (liquor control) law of 1866, Connolly had imprisoned two policemen charged with assault and battery by the saloonkeeper they had arrested. Kennedy ordered his men to stop taking prisoners to Connolly's court:

> When it becomes unsafe for a member of the police force to
> faithfully perform his duty; lest by doing so he should incur the
> displeasure of a judicial incumbent, and expose himself to insult

and degradation: it also becomes the duty of the executive officer of the Department to exercise his authority for the protection of the men under his command.

The Big Judge, as Connolly was affectionately known, asked in reply, "Are the magistrates elected by the people to be coerced and intimidated by impudent underlings in the discharge of those sworn and solemn duties, for the faithful performance of which they are responsible, not only to the law, but to their constituents, their conscience, and their God?" The feud had been simmering for many years, and Connolly's attitude toward excise enforcement was only the immediate cause of Kennedy's action. To support his low opinion of Connolly, Kennedy submitted thirty policemen's affidavits, going back to 1860, testifying to the justice's leniency and antipolice attitudes. On one occasion Connolly had released a man charged with assault and battery, telling the policeman that he was sorry the accused "did not take your club from you and break it over your head." Connolly replied to each of the affidavits and issued a crusading denunciation of police brutality:

> As a magistrate, I have ever denounced violence by officers, believing that the club should be their last resort, justifiable only by emergency, and that the wanton use of it should be peremptorily put down. That this view of the subject is not entertained by the present heads of our Police Department I am well aware, from the fact that the frequent and indiscriminate practice of that species of discipline in the hands of their patrolmen goes unchecked and unpunished.

If Connolly were trying to regulate police practices, it reveals much about police views of the judiciary that his efforts were a source of conflict instead of changed police attitudes.[37]

The quarrel raised important issues, but politics and one's opinions of liquor control laws generally dictated reactions to the controversy. The other police justices backed Connolly, demanding that patrolmen take prisoners to the *nearest* police court. The commissioners supported Kennedy, arguing that although the 1862 police law had specified "nearest magistrate," the amended law of 1864 allowed patrolmen to choose the judge before whom they charged their prisoners.[38] The police had their way, but the Metropolitan force did not last much longer to enjoy the fruits of their minor victory.

How well-founded were police charges of judicial leniency? We have seen that the London force witnessed an increasing number of magistrates' committals and convictions in higher courts for most crimes. Unfortunately the New York courts and police did not publish the detailed figures on which the conclusions for London are based. However, it is possible to compare arrests with magistrates' committals for trial in the court of special sessions and convictions in this court for two common misdemeanors, assault and battery and petty larceny.

Tables 7 and 8 reveal lower conviction-arrest ratios for assault and battery and petty larceny in New York than for all crimes in London. Beyond that, a consistent pattern does not emerge. Assault and battery committals and convictions were both less under the Metropolitan force (1858-67 figures) than under the Municipal Police (1851-55 figures), but petty larceny committals increased and average convictions were the same number under the two police regimes. The increase of petty larceny committals might be explained by the police justices' taking over the court of special sessions in 1857. By committing offenders for trial in special sessions, they saved themselves work in their own overcrowded courtrooms, and in the higher court their colleagues had a better opportunity to assess the evidence. However, this practice seems to have committed more persons ultimately found innocent than when the recorder and city judge presided over special sessions. There was a greater disparity between convictions and committals in 1858-67 than in 1851-55.

The assault and battery figures are more difficult to explain. Committals to special sessions averaged 51 percent of arrests (raised by two high figures, 1853 and 1855) in 1851-55; 36 percent in 1858-67.[39] Thus it would appear that the police justices were dismissing more assault and battery charges on first examination under the Metropolitan Police than under the Municipal Police. Average convictions in proportion to arrests were also less under the Metropolitan force. It is impossible to know whether the declining ratios reflected dubious arrest practices, station-house discharges, or judicial leniency. While the police could point to these assault and battery figures as revealing something wrong with police-judicial relations, they could not say the same of petty larceny convictions, which remained at the 41 percent average during both the Municipal and Metropolitan Police regimes.

Unfortunately, data which would allow exact comparison of London and New York conviction-arrest ratios do not exist except

TABLE 7
Arrests, Committals, Convictions in Court of Special
Sessions, Assault and Battery, 1851–55, 1858–67, New York City

Year	Arrests	Committals (Total Cases Tried)	Con- victions	Committals as Percentage of Arrests	Convictions as Percentage of Arrests
1851	4,877	1,899	662	39	14
1852	4,984	2,196	978	44	20
1853	3,127	2,417	1,230	77	39
1854	6,287	2,402	1,152	38	18
1855	3,350	2,077	929	62	28
Average percentage 1851–55				52	24
1858[a]	8,606	3,825	1,697	44	20
1859	9,219	3,897	1,699	42	18
1860	9,419	3,834	1,919	41	20
1861	9,489	3,432	1,606	36	17
1862	8,226	3,064	1,475	37	18
1863	7,303	2,466	1,191	34	16
1864	6,591	2,118	1,067	32	16
1865	7,744	2,476	1,239	32	16
1866	7,222	2,205	1,110	31	15
1867	6,927	1,953	957	28	14
Average percentage 1858–67				36	17

SOURCES: Col. 2, Arrests, from *BAD*, 1851–55, Municipal Police Semi-Annual Reports, and *AD*, 1858–67, Metropolitan Police Annual Reports. Col. 3, Committals, is the sum of the convictions, acquittal, and discharge (i.e., without trial) figures in the court statistics printed in Shannon, comp., *Manual of the Corporation of the City of New York 1868*, p. 178. Col. 4, Convictions, is from the same source. Cols. 5–6 are my computations, kept at two places as a reminder that the figures are only rough guides.

[a] Beginning in 1858, arrest and committal/conviction figures do not exactly correspond, for the Metropolitan Police arrest figures cover the year November 1–October 31 (e.g., November 1, 1857–October 31, 1858), whereas the court figures are for full years (e.g., 1858). For 1851–55, arrest and court figures exactly correspond. I have compared police and court figures for 1857/58 to 1866/67 (arrests and convictions only) as published in the Secretary of State's Annual Criminal Statistics Report (*AD* and *SD* for the various years) and found that the figures for convictions in this table are roughly comparable to those adjusted to correspond to the police year.

TABLE 8
Arrests, Committals, Convictions in Court of Special
Sessions, Petty Larceny, 1851–55, 1858–67, New York City

Year	Arrests	Committals (Total Cases Tried)	Convictions	Committals as Percentage of Arrests	Convictions as Percentage of Arrests
1851	3,335	1,630	1,453	49	43
1852	3,293	1,689	1,475	51	45
1853	3,216	1,594	1,415	50	44
1854	4,630	1,519	1,411	33	30
1855	4,902	2,237	2,047	46	42
Average percentage 1851–55				46	41
1858[a]	4,410	2,772	1,919	63	44
1859	4,535	2,723	1,953	60	43
1860	3,946	2,823	2,082	72	53
1861	4,187	2,490	1,747	59	42
1862	3,856	2,007	1,397	52	36
1863	3,497	2,377	1,512	68	43
1864	4,866	2,258	1,411	46	29
1865	5,240	2,870	1,963	55	37
1866	5,269	3,082	2,184	58	41
1867	4,785	2,587	1,824	54	38
Average percentage 1858–67				59	41

SOURCES: See table 7.

[a]See table 7.

for petty larceny. In this case, London is significantly higher: an average of 77 percent of arrests for "simple larceny" resulted in conviction between 1860 and 1870, compared to New York's 41 percent between 1858 and 1867. London police statistics for specific crimes, which do not appear until 1869, list "common assault" but not "assault and battery." Comparison may be dubious here, but in 1869 convictions for common assault were 55 percent of arrests in London, and in New York assault and battery convictions during 1868–69 were even lower than the figures in table 7, amounting to 8 percent. In cases of petty larceny at least, it is clear that conviction was less likely in New York than in London; the same may have been true for assault, although the comparison may be undependable.[40]

Turning to trials in higher courts, table 9 reveals declining

TABLE 9
Number of Indictments Tried and Convictions,
Courts of General Sessions and Oyer and Terminer,
1845–70, New York City

Year	Total Indictments	Convictions	Convictions as Percentage of Indictments
1845	351	208	59
1846	269	189	70
1847	250	172	69
1848	303	196	65
1849	292	197	67
1850	308	205	67
1851	292	195	67
1852	338	233	69
1853	487	324	66
1854	410	244	59
1855	369	227	62
1856	298	220	74
1857	339	241	71
1858	367	241	66
1859	409	246	60
1860	433	216	50
1861	370	215	58
1862	204	115	56
1863	149	103	69
1864	178	104	58
1865	362	194	54
1866	302	159	53
1867	321	167	52
1868	240	121	50
1869	309	149	48
1870	445	194	44

SOURCE: Table H, New York Secretary of State's Annual Report on Criminal Statistics, in *AD* or *SD*, for the year following each one given.

convictions in indictments tried in general sessions and in oyer and terminer (a superior criminal court) from the mid-sixties on. Excluding convictions obtained by guilty pleas or indictments discharged without a trial, these figures measure cases in which the jury had an opportunity to weigh the testimony and reach a verdict. Under the Metropolitan Police, convictions were about as high in proportion to cases tried as under the Municipal Police until 1864, when they begin a steady decline to under half the cases in 1869. In the later sixties the public relations of the Metropolitan Police were at their lowest

101

point since 1857; juries may not have trusted police testimony. In 1866 the state legislature passed a tough liquor control act which was very unpopular with city officials. Violators of this law were subjected to grand jury indictment, and the locally elected D.A. may not have conducted the prosecution very enthusiastically. Even if he had, city juries might not have been disposed to convict. However, if Superintendent Kennedy was right, liquor law indictments were not likely to be brought to trial at all. A precise reason for the decline of convictions compared to indictments remains elusive.

Did improper arrests or judicial leniency or mistrust of the police account for the divergence between arrests and convictions? This raises the paradox of apparent judicial and public toleration of unregulated arrest practices along with police complaints of leniency toward offenders. Perhaps refusal to convict was an effort to regulate the police, although the establishment of clearly set forth standards, as in London, would certainly have been a more effective method. In London both the police magistrates and the commissioners were agents of the law, and both were subordinate to the home secretary. In New York, especially after state take-over of the police in 1857, the police and the elected judiciary were serving different "constituencies." They seemed inclined to throw their institutional weight against each other.

The conflict with the justices was similar to the difficulties with the district attorney. Institutional conflict became a struggle for power in the political arena. As we shall see, most "respectable" citizens sided with the police, but many others supported the judiciary. The paradox of police-judicial relations, unregulated arrest practices combined with resentment of judicial leniency, did not inspire respect for the rule of law. On the one hand the police were encouraged to act outside of the law, but on the other their actions often were not validated by convictions. Contradictory signals were bound to produce frustration, and, much more than their London brethren, New York patrolmen seemed ready to take it out through "street-corner justice," violence or arbitrary arrest as punishment.

RULE OF LAW AND THE POLICE IMAGE

A New York patrolman wrote in his instruction book in 1848, "A policeman would not live one year if he acted up to these regulations."[41] In contrast, a London bobby most likely would not live — remain a policeman — very long if he did *not* act up to the regulations. Official direction, or lack of it, was the foundation of the two forces' police images because discipline could make the image into reality. We have seen that London's impersonal authority depended on tight discipline within the force and the watchfulness of outside agencies. Subordination to the rule of law as well as efficiency was discipline's goal. New York's personal authority was marked by looser internal discipline and less external concern for conformity to the rule of law. Of course the two police forces did not exist in isolation. Equally if not more important than official standards were public expectations of the police and the responses of different groups and classes to the official personality of the man on the beat. These reactions were not only responses to the police image; they helped form it.

5   SERVANT OR MASTER? POLICE AND PUBLIC IN LONDON

When a modern sociologist argued that "The efficiency of the police may . . . be less important than their responsiveness to the community they are required to serve," he echoed Richard Mayne's claim that "the real efficiency of the police depends upon the estimation in which it is held by the public." In heterogeneous cities there are many publics, many communities, with different attitudes toward and expectations of police authority. In addition, the complexity of police work, with general order maintenance and law enforcement duties covering almost all aspects of urban life, makes it difficult for a patrolman to be all things to all men. A person may view the officer as a benevolent protector or as an authoritarian oppressor, depending upon his circumstances and his attitude toward the policy or law the policeman is upholding. Nevertheless, despite the sometimes schizoid nature of public opinion, the police forces of representative governments like England and the United States could not afford for very long to flout the expectations of the citizens they policed. They could never completely become closed worlds unto themselves; they had to respond at least to influential sectors of the community, and influence was not always measured by social and economic power. As T. A. Critchley pointed out, "The point to be hammered home, whether the subject is kite flying or vagrancy or larceny or crowd control, is always the same: what matters is not so much what a policeman does as what people think of him."[1]

This chapter will explore what various sorts of people thought about the London police, how citizens of different groups and classes responded to the images the police projected for themselves. Keeping in mind the complexity of public attitudes and the stratification within social classes, it is possible to trace broad group responses to the police which reflect views of the whole social and political order as well as of specific police activities.

"RESPECTABLE" CITIZENS' ACCEPTANCE OF THE POLICE: LAW AND ORDER, 1830-60

When London bobbies first took to the streets on a rainy November day in 1829, it seemed as if everybody from the king to the humblest day laborer objected to the new force. Many people invoked traditional fears of spies and standing armies to express their more specific objections. Tories opposed to Peel resented the force as his brainchild; Whigs worried about the future of civil liberties at the hands of a Tory police; Radicals feared aristocratic oppression of the working and middle classes. Many aristocrats themselves protested police surveillance, which sometimes uncovered their irregular habits; magistrates and parish officials regretted their lost power; local ratepayers objected to the expense of the new force; soldiers, sailors, and firemen resented policemen and often assaulted them; poor street-sellers saw the police, with their orders to "move on," as greedy shopkeepers' way of stifling competition. People of all classes who drove vehicles in the streets, accustomed to going where and as fast as they pleased, resented police traffic control. Much of the public opposition was verbal, but physical attacks on policemen punctuated the early years of the force.[2]

Evoking their fear of French tyranny, people called the new police "Jenny Darbies" (gendarmes) and other uncomplimentary names. An early print pictured a husky peeler with two large pistols in his belt, brandishing a cutlass in one hand and his other arm thrust forward with fist clenched in what looks like a pugilistic pose. "History," an early critic wrote of the police, "will record them as amongst the most odious petty tyrants that have ever disgraced her pages."[3]

Perhaps more significant for police authority than fears of tyranny, however, was public contempt of the force and interference with officers making arrests. Recalling the early days to a reporter in 1864, an old officer remarked: "I do not remember ever having received any assistance from bystanders, when I've had to take into custody a troublesome customer ...; I have had frequently to fight against odds to take my man, and have generally found the mob against me." The difficulty came not only from the presumably working-class "mob." Another old bobby said, "What I most disliked ... was the interference of your clever 'gentleman,' who knew nothing about the merits of the case, had not seen the commencement, and only come up, perhaps, just at the moment when, after a hard tussle and some serious injuries, an officer had succeeded in overcoming resistance." The persistence of such interference would have undermined police efficiency as well as legitimacy.[4]

The period of almost universal opposition to the new police was brief; by 1834 Rowan and Mayne noticed a distinct decline in complaints of police tyranny. The turning point was probably settlement of the reform crisis of 1832, which united the middle and upper classes in support of the social order. British historians have made it clear that the middle classes did not rule England, but, ranging from men of great wealth to small shopkeepers, they were the largest group of voters after the 1832 reform. If they too complacently saw themselves as the "public," they nevertheless formed mid-Victorian England's "public opinion." Although hardly unified in interest and outlook, the groups making up the middle classes would have shared suspicion of a police too closely tied to the landed aristocracy. On the other hand, they condemned ineffective as well as arbitrary policemen. The post-reform Whig governments, concerned—though not always consistently—with "the liberty of the subject," had lingering doubts about the new police but at the same time found them useful in holding the line against radical protests. Similarly, the middle classes worried about arbitrary power, but by the mid-thirties they were asking the police to do more to maintain order instead of worrying about curtailment of liberty. Partly this reflects the commissioners' increasing ability to check the excesses of inexperienced men, but it is also an indication of the middle classes' identification with the social order.[5]

The middle classes came to depend for protection and order upon an institution which fostered social stability by restrained power and in many small ways helped discipline an unruly population being transformed by industrialization. Believing in orderly progress and rational social change, they were not in a mood for either violent protest or harsh repression. A police force which contained disorder with minimal violence increased people's sense of security and contributed to economic stability. Praise for the bobbies usually emphasized their restraint as much as their efficiency. Ralph Waldo Emerson tied industrial discipline to social control in his description of English orderliness: "Mines, forges, mills, breweries, railroads, steampump, steamplough, drill of regiments, drill of police, rule of court, and shop-rule, have operated to give a mechanical regularity to all the habit and action of men." Although this was "a terrible machine" to the transcendentalist, many more worldly Englishmen saw such order as their era's greatest achievement. The middle classes, who saw themselves as the custodians of such virtues, could take pride in a police force with a reputation for respectability and "habitual discretion and moderation of conduct." Although created by aristocrats who continued to dominate society, to a great extent the police were a middle-class institution.[6]

The middle classes probably benefited most directly from the new force. The upper classes certainly benefited as well, but they could if necessary mobilize human and financial resources for their own protection, while the comfortable but not rich sectors of the middle classes depended on the police as protectors against "nuisances" or criminal intrusions from below. In 1830 Edwin Chadwick pointed out that the police were usually seen in action as apprehenders of criminals: "They are viewed either as a sort of thief catchers, or as retainers of the rich to act against the labouring classes, and in either aspect their calling has strong unpopular associations which no exertions should be spared to remove." He argued that the police should seek public support by appearing more frequently in a service role — helping to prevent and assist at accidents, protecting public health, and other beneficial functions which maintained order without the application of force. Indeed, in 1868, Chadwick reported that this service role had become the mainstay of police legitimacy.[7] The middle classes seem to have been the first to appreciate the service role, and soon came to demand its expansion. Bobbies enforced regulatory legislation which improved order in "respectable" neighborhoods, including the original Metropolitan Police Act of 1829; the Police Act of 1839, which greatly expanded police powers over nuisance or petty disorder misdemeanors; and the Metropolitan Streets Act of 1867, which regulated lower-class street trading, systematized traffic control, and required muzzling of all dogs. Except for the control of dogs, which was shortly repealed, people seem to have welcomed these expansions of power as improving the quality of urban life. Even more significant was police assumption of the role of public prosecutors. Previously, private citizens bore the burden of prosecution and few except the rich could afford the time and expense of court cases. The middle classes quickly appreciated such benefits and soon lost any widespread fear of arbitrary police power.

During the thirties complaints against the police began to focus on the force's *not doing enough* to maintain order rather than doing *too much,* to the detriment of civil liberty. In place of early complaints of police harassment or arbitrariness, the commissioners began to receive "complaints from the public against the police for not doing anything (altho' they were doing their best) and the Commissioners have great difficulty in getting the public to see that the police have no powers." As early as 1830–31 the most common complaints which reached Scotland Yard concerned unregulated nuisances, insufficient policemen in the neighborhood, or neglect of duty. Charges of improper arrest or violence were the least common grievances among the middle-class letter-writers. People wanted policemen to remove annoying individuals such as streetwalkers, peddlers, sellers of indecent ballads, and nude bathers, and to do something about annoying objects such as dilapidated buildings, dirty streets, and exposed cesspools. The 1839 police act, which extended the force's power over many of these aspects of city life, was more representative of public opinion than the original measure of 1829. People had discovered many uses for the police which they had not anticipated ten years earlier. Mayne asserted in the early 1850s that the most common complaint against the police had become that there were not enough of them: "The public now expect to see a constable at all places at every moment that he may be required."[8]

Middle-class acceptance of and dependence on the police reflected growing trust in the government and a new definition of liberty which, while it limited freedom on the one hand, increased security on the other. Peel in 1829 wanted to "teach people that liberty does not consist in having their houses robbed by organized gangs of Thieves," recalling the eighteenth-century reformer Patrick Colquhoun's belief that "all true liberty depends on those fences which are established in every Country, for the protection of the Persons and Property of the People, against every attack whatsoever." In both of these statements the people referred to were those with property to protect. A mid-Victorian commentator revealed how experience with the new police taught Peel's and Colquhoun's lessons:

> Few will now deny that the power of the police has been rightly exercised, and that, instead of restraining the liberty of the good part of the community, it has extended it, by freeing them in a measure from the molestation of the bad; and no one now thinks of pointing to the police as the infringers of the liberty of the

peaceful and honest, for the more the liberty of the turbulent
and dishonest is restricted the better; the freedom of the male-
factor being the bondage of the just.[9]

The police protected the liberty and security of respectable citizens
by exercising broad but controlled powers within legal boundaries.
As has been seen, the commissioners were very much concerned that
"respectable" people not feel the police as an oppressive burden.

Upper- and middle-class Londoners felt that their persons and
property were increasingly secure from 1830 up to the early 1860s.
Although W. L. Burn reminds us that there was "a vast amount of
casual rowdyism" in the mid-nineteenth century, people dwelled
more often on the contrast between their era and the turbulent
eighteenth century: "It may not be more virtuous, but it is certainly
more safe." The bygone metropolis was "a city whose customs are as
alien to us as those in which the squabbling retainers of the Capulets
and Montagues could only be kept from fighting by all the clubs of
all the citizens." In 1821 George Mainwaring anticipated that an
improved police force would change people's behavior: "I entertain
a sanguine hope, that the very operation of a better system will so
change the manners and habits of the people, upon whom it is to act,
as to drive them to the pursuits of industry." By the late thirties the
new police seemed to fulfill his "sanguine hope." The commissioners
reported a marked improvement in the conduct of the people in
public places since establishment of the force. Contemporaries found
that "Considering the enormous, and in many parts, demoralized
population of London, it is quite marvelous that there should be so
little personal insecurity," and they gave the police credit for
improving public order. Rowan believed that people had confidence
in the police, which removed "the feeling which formerly existed,
that each man must depend on himself for the redress of his own
grievance."[10]

Hard times and political upheaval dampened Londoners' self-
congratulation during the "hungry forties," although they happily
pointed out that the climactic Chartist demonstration of April 1848
passed off without violence. By the next decade, many commentators
declared that orderliness had become a permanent part of the
English character. Dickens described Englishmen's "unobtrusive
politeness, their good humour, and their cheerful recognition of all
restraints that really originate in consideration for the general good."
Drawing an implicit contrast with eighteenth- and early-nineteenth-
century manners, he pictured "the people in general" as not

"gluttons, nor drunkards, nor gamblers, nor addicted to cruel sports, nor to the pushing of any amusement to furious and wild extremes." Many Londoners feared that reduction of the Crystal Palace admission fee from five shillings to one shilling and subsequent free admission days would create a scene of "legions of policemen combating indignant multitudes" crowded out of the exhibition. Instead, the people's orderliness "betokened the instinctive feeling of propriety by which the visitors were guided." Contemporaries felt that a general decrease of crime, especially violence, accompanied improved manners. A writer of 1852 asserted that "No member of Parliament would now venture to say that it was dangerous to walk in the streets of London by day or night." To "their betters," proletarian Londoners seemed less violent than their provincial urban counterparts, more inclined to verbal abuse than fisticuffs. Despite the Hyde Park anti-Sunday law disturbance of 1855 (which was largely the police's fault), serious mob violence seemed to be thing of the past:

> There seems to be no fear that a London mob will ever prove a
> serious thing in the face of our present corps of policemen . . . .
> Those who shudder at the idea of an outbreak in the metropolis,
> containing two millions and a half of people and at least fifty
> thousand of the "dangerous classes" forget that the capital is so
> wide that its different sections are totally unknown to each other.
> A mob in London is wholly without cohesion, and the indi-
> viduals composing it have but few feelings, thoughts, or pursuits
> in common. They would immediately break up before the deter-
> mined attack of a band of well-trained men who know and have
> confidence in each other.[11]

This writer found some good in urban anonymity: combined with a good police it could neutralize the forces of disorder. During the fifties the class tensions of previous decades seemed to be muted, expressed more often in good-natured "chaff" or teasing of well-dressed "respectables" than in violence. However, police reports of people throwing vitriol on ladies' dresses remind us of Geoffrey Best's hint that hostility may have been bottled up instead of dissipated.[12]

Charles Reith and Geoffrey Gorer have given the police exclusive credit for improved order during the mid-nineteenth century. However, the force was clearly aided by a variety of social, intellectual, and economic factors. Historians have assessed the fifties as a decade of stability, pointing to the "safety valve" of emigration; the inculcation of ideals of work and austerity through factory discipline;

the lower price of bread after repeal of the Corn Laws in 1842; the opening of parks and museums to the working classes, and cheap transportation for excursions out of the city; the spread of evangelical religion, and the growth of workers' self-help organizations; general economic expansion, albeit unequally distributed; and political, social, and legal reforms. The police operated in a context which made their duty of upholding order easier than in times of economic and political crisis.[13]

CRITICISM OF THE POLICE: THE CRIME WAVE
OF THE SIXTIES

Self-confidence and security were rudely shaken amid economic difficulties and political crisis during the sixties, and newly aroused fears centered on the metropolis.[14] Crime and political violence, including the Hyde Park protests in 1866 and Fenian terrorism in 1868, shocked Londoners who had relaxed during the peaceful fifties.

In 1862 a wave of "garottings" or muggings—violent street robberies by two or three criminals ganging up on the lone stroller—aroused Londoners' anxiety. The streets were no longer safe even for members of Parliament; one of them was among the victims. Concern extended beyond the propertied classes: the proletarian *Lloyd's* and *Reynolds's* newspapers, which Geoffrey Best has described as "definitely below" the line of respectability, shared their conservative and respectable contemporaries' worries.[15]

The crime wave caused Londoners of all classes to doubt prison reformers' emphasis on rehabilitation as a substitute for harsh punishments, arousing suspicion that leniency had removed deterrence altogether from the penal system. *Lloyd's Newspaper* reflected the general tendency to blame the increase of violence on excessive leniency: "It behooves us to reform the criminal if we can; but the first duty of the governing powers is to protect the honest against him. We must have safe streets and throats." The editor of a middle-class neighborhood newspaper said of garotting, "The effect of this new felonious profession has been to cause a reaction against the pro-criminal humanitarians." He added, "We cannot go back to hanging, which, perhaps is a pity—a thrice-convicted robber with violence would be best hung." Parliament responded by passing the first measure to increase punishment for a crime since the early part of the century. The death penalty for robbery with violence had been abolished in 1861; the Garotters' Act of 1863 added flogging to the prison sentence.[16]

The harsh reaction focused on a relatively small, but seemingly dangerous, group. This comprised paroled convicts or "ticket-of-leave men," who appeared in increasing numbers after transportation to Australia was abolished in the fifties and prisoners had to be dealt with at home. Dickens believed that the professional thief or ruffian had become "one of the estabished orders of the body politic," immune from his just deserts because the police and magistrates did not have sufficient powers to put him permanently in prison. Nobody had much sympathy for the ticket-of-leave man. The aristocratic *Saturday Review* and the working-class *Weekly Dispatch* agreed at the end of the sixties that control over incorrigible convicts was too lenient. Even navvies, themselves the objects of many respectable citizens' suspicions, regarded parolees as untouchables and refused to work alongside them. The judge in a music-hall tune summed up popular views:

> For liberty behold your thanks
> It does but clearly show
> To your former prigging pranks
> You determined are to go —
>
> Like a hardened ticket man of leave,
> One of the present time.
>
> Regretted it is much to be they ever introduced
> This ticket system, 'tis but leniency abused.

With everyone against him, the ex-convict had little choice but to relapse into crime whatever his original intentions had been.[17]

After dealing with garotters, whom most people thought were ticket-of-leave men, Parliament turned its attention to the parole and prison systems. The Penal Servitude Act of 1864 required parolees to report monthly to the police and authorized any constable to arrest and bring before a magistrate a ticket-of-leave man whom he suspected of committing a crime or breaking the conditions of his parole. Edwin Chadwick, noting the police's inability to do anything about ex-convicts unless they caught them in the act of committing a crime, had advocated a similar policy back in 1831. He assumed, as did the 1864 measure, that proof of a prison record was sufficient justification of preventive arrest. Such extension of police power would have been impossible amid the public hostility of 1831, but thirty years later people had come to accept and expect more of the force.[18]

The Prisons Act of 1865 made the convict's life more difficult inside prison as well as after release. The measure marked an official end of penal servitude as a means of rehabilitation, substituting "retribution" and "administrative convenience." Nineteenth-century prison reformers' methods seem harsh to us today, but the treadmill and silent system had been rationalized as rehabilitative. W. L. Burn thinks that the prisons act could have been called "An Act to ensure that Prisoners sentenced to Hard Labour shall duly undergo the same."[19] Treatment of lawbreakers had never been exactly benign, but increased crime in the sixties made people anxious to put the offenders away and keep them under control when they got out.

The new measures do not seem to have accomplished their main object, for crime (as measured by indictable offenses reported to the police) increased in the second half of the decade, following slight decreases after the garotting wave of 1862. Even more frightening was that police apprehensions did not keep pace with reported offenses. Between 1856/57 and 1869/70 the "Judicial Statistics" reveal a sharp rise in reported "indictable offenses," the more serious crimes requiring jury trial. The reported serious crimes more than doubled, rising from 7,632 in 1856/57 to 15,609 in 1869/70. Arrests for these crimes, however, remained between about 4,000 and 5,600 annually throughout the period. The gap between reported crimes and arrests was most striking in 1867/68 and 1868/69: 5,448 and 5,546 arrests, respectively, compared to 16,600 and 17,918 reported indictable offenses (the peaks between 1856/57 and 1869/70). Indeed, the police seemed to be falling disastrously behind.

However, these figures may have reflected an increased reporting of crime, which is part of the spurious aspects of crime waves generally. For example, when we break the total reported indictable offenses into their component crimes, we find that the *least serious* crimes make up most of the reported offenses. Taking the bad year 1868/69 as an example, of the 17,918 reported indictable offenses, 12,537 are in three minor categories—simple (petty) larceny, 9,611; larceny from the person (pocket-picking), 1,678; and larceny by servants, 1,248. The crimes which worried people the most, burglary and robbery, were respectively 531 and 119. There were 987 reported larcenies from houses to the value of five pounds, mainly stealing of clothing from entryways. Comparing reported crimes with arrests, the greatest gaps between offense and apprehension, as shown in table 10, were in the lesser thefts. Now we do not know from these figures the results of individual cases of, say, robbery, but they are all we have to go on. The figures show that arrests were made in over

TABLE 10
Reported Indictable Offenses, Arrests, 1868–69, London

Offenses	Number Reported	Number of Arrests
Simple larceny	9,271	1,409
Larceny from the person	1,597	540
Larceny by servants	1,263	285
Burglary and housebreaking	479	274
Robbery	118	160
Larceny to the value of £5, houses	956	101

SOURCE: *PP,* 1871, vol. 37, Metro. Police Annual Report 1870, table 11, p. 22.

NOTE: The "Judicial Statistics," whose figures are cited in the text, did not show arrests for *each* indictable offense; thus the above figures are from another source. The figures from the two sources vary somewhat because the Metropolitan Police report covers the entire year 1869, while the "Judicial Statistics" are from September 1868 to September 1869.

half the number of reported burglary and housebreaking cases, and there were more arrests for robbery than reported cases (perhaps because apprehension of two or three individuals might account for one robbery). In short, the police do not look too bad in the two serious crimes which aroused the most fear. In lesser crimes against property — petty larceny, pocket-picking, larceny by servants, and thefts from houses to the value of five pounds — the police did not do as well. These crimes were difficult to detect unless the thief were caught in the act, and the arrest of one person might "clear" several cases. Moreover, increased willingness to report petty thefts might account for their high numbers compared to earlier years. As early as 1836 the superintendents noticed that "trifling things" were "now reported," and the "crime wave" of the sixties may have fed itself by encouraging increased reporting. The statistics show, then, that a problem certainly existed in London at the end of the sixties, but perhaps it was not as serious as the public believed.[20]

However, contemporaries were scared, and complaints from all classes at the end of the sixties had a shrillness unheard in the previous decade. "Crimes of violence are rife, and have been for the last few years," said the working-class *Lloyd's Newspaper,* blaming the outbreak on "foreign refuse" who introduced the knife and revolver to the criminal arsenal. "The revolver's appearance . . . we owe to the importation of reckless characters from America. . . . The Fenian desperadoes have sown weapons of violence in our poorer districts. Vagabond boys have learned to carry revolvers as toys." The Rev. Henry Solly considered the London mob worse than their rural or provincial counterparts, and asked, "What would a force of 8,000 or 9,000 police be against the 150,000 roughs and ruffians whom, on some sufficiently exciting occasion, the metropolis might see arrayed against law and order?" Underlying Solly's apprehensions and those of many of his upper- and middle-class contemporaries was a foreboding about England's political future if workers obtained the vote. Disorder had ominous political implications. Another commentator spoke of the "utter recklessness and violence of the hordes of ruffians who are drawn from their customary haunts on every public occasion, and to whom the unfortunate occurrences of the summer of 1866 [the Hyde Park reform disturbances] have disclosed the secret of their strength."[21] What were the police doing?

Public attention once again focused on the ticket-of-leave men and the continued ineffectiveness of controls over them, but also the police came under a critical scrutiny by all classes which they had not endured since the thirties. The sixties were a crisis period in police-public relations; criticism was almost universal. The complaints — emphasizing organizational inefficiency and individual incompetence but also including, especially in the working-class press, charges of arbitrariness and illegality — touched the very heart of the police image of efficient but carefully controlled impersonal authority.

Critics laid many of the force's deficiencies at Sir Richard Mayne's door, charging that he had grown old and hidebound after over thirty years of service and was unable to adjust to new conditions and demands. Some asserted that he had invested all the police's energies in the service function at the expense of crime prevention and detection. The force could cope with petty nuisances but little else. *Punch*'s "A Plaint by a P'liceman" captured this grievance:

> I am a p'liceman, bold and true,
> Stand in my highlows six foot two:
> Yet what d'ye think I has to do?
>   Hoop de dooden doo.
>
> They bids me chivy little boys,
> And grab their hoops, them harmless toys,
> Which gouty gents they much annoys;
>   Hoop de dooden doo.

I muzzle dogs, both great and small,
Stop little boys from playing ball,
Or move away an apple-stall:
   Hoop de dooden doo.

Meanwhile garotters plays their game,
And roughs they also do the same;
The public cries, O what a shame!
   Hoop de dooden doo.

The streets are quite unsafe, they say,
You're robbed and mobbed in broad noon day,
But little boys they mustn't play
   With their hoop, de dooden doo.

Well, if from growls you can't refrain,
It ain't of us you should complain,
You've got to thank SIR RICHARD MAYNE.
   Hoop de dooden doo.

Such complaints reflected increasing public expectations of the police; having come to rely on them for many little services, people were quick to criticize them when they did not live up to expectations.[22]

Working-class spokesmen found more sinister sources of police inefficiency. Having charged Mayne with a "pet project" of "assimilating as much as possible the policeman with the soldier" in 1862, *Reynolds's Newspaper* asserted at the end of the decade: "The constables are thinking of drill and the 'goose step' when they ought to be watching for thieves and garotters; for their promotion is made to depend upon the excellence of their military evolutions." This militarization carried implications more ominous than its damage to police efficiency. Reviving the rhetoric of the thirties, *Reynolds's* charged:

> The Government proposes converting the English Peeler into a species of continental policeman. The revolver and cutlass will supersede the comparatively harmless truncheon. A detective force, framed upon the French model, will be organized; the police are to be drilled into becoming regular soldiers; the police-stations will be strongly armed and fortified. . . . When all this has been accomplished . . . , the mouchard, or spy, will become an established institution among us.[23]

Ancient fears of the standing army and Continental spy system were hard for many Englishmen to forget.

116

Throughout the sixties, critics charged that the police were arbitrary and brutal. These complaints may reflect the decline in the quality of recruits because of low pay, but if brutality and illegality did increase they may also have been the result of public demands for action against crime. Responding to pressures for apprehension of criminals, the police often become harsher and more casual about procedural safeguards. Moreover, during a crime wave, patrolmen may become sensitive about their inability to meet public demands and compensate by violent handling of arrestees. Asserting that "The oppressive violence of the Metropolitan Police increases as their efficiency diminishes," *Reynolds's* in 1862 compared Mayne and his force to "a cowardly and clumsy giant, who either cannot or will not cope with powerful transgressors, and who, therefore, wreaks all the meanness and malignity of his nature on every feeble and helpless creature that comes in his way." As we have seen, Mayne did indeed have to warn his men against arbitrary arrests in 1863.[24]

To many people the Metropolitan Police's tight centralization prevented accountability to the public. Critics charged that the force was increasingly cut off from local residents, that citizens with complaints against policemen were becoming exasperated by the long delays and red tape of Scotland Yard action on their letters, and "instances of this kind constantly recurring, have given birth to a growing feeling of dissatisfaction, which seeks to find expression on every possible occasion." A few years earlier another writer had noticed the same antagonism: "I have heard people in a decent station in life, who ought to have known better, condemn in unmeasured language the whole body of the constabulary, the general behaviour of constables, and the system that was assumed to screen their arbitrary and illegal proceedings." *Reynolds's* called Mayne the "Scotland Yard Bashaw" who, "it appears, is an entirely irresponsible person, and is not accountable for his deeds to any public tribunal."[25]

The "Bashaw" had a lot to answer for—his force's image and efficiency seemed to be breaking down. At one point the Disraeli government suggested that Mayne resign. He refused, but died in office shortly thereafter, on the last day of 1868. Although Mayne may have become stubborn and conservative in his old age, many of the problems he faced were beyond his control. The police could not effectively prevent crime with insufficient men on the streets and it was increasingly impossible to get men with all the desirable physical strength, mental alertness, and moral rectitude, "cut and dried, for three and twenty shillings a week." Manpower and pay were ultimately determined by the Home Office. In 1868 the home secretary did authorize a thousand more recruits to bring the police/population ratio back to 1829 levels after many years of growing disparity, but pay increases were not granted.[26]

Mayne's successor, Col. E. Y. W. Henderson, a prison official selected for his ability to discipline convicts, instituted administrative reforms which met many of the criticisms. He strengthened the Central Detective Division and established divisional detective forces, created fixed posts where a policeman could be found at all times, and decentralized the police by appointing district superintendents. These officers handled many internal matters, and, most important, all public complaints in their divisions. This change helped eliminate the bureaucratic delays and public distrust of complaint-handling procedures. Henderson did not reverse the trend toward militarization; in fact, as we have seen, apparently military discipline was increasing. His decentralization came nowhere near the local control which some people advocated, and his changes did not alter the police image as impersonal agents of the legal system. Parliament seems to have been satisfied with these changes, for it never investigated the Metropolitan Police or proposed fundamental structural or administrative changes.[27]

Parliament's satisfaction seems to have reflected an underlying public acceptance of the police, at least among the propertied classes. After listing its criticisms of Mayne, *Punch* said, "We English have been taunted with instinctive reverence for a policeman. We acknowledge it — we profess it." The solution for the crime wave was not a radical alteration of police authority, but the granting of more legal power to the force. To the *Times,* "the only question is, about the rights of civil society as against these known enemies, and that question will someday press very imperatively for an answer." The *Saturday Review* had an answer: "Before the police can half satisfy the expectations of the public, at any rate in London, it should be armed with preventive powers similar to those exercised by the Continental police." Even the proletarian *Weekly Dispatch* argued that "The police have certainly a good deal of arbitrary power, but we have no alternative, if we are really in earnest about putting down crime, but to very much increase that power." The editorial also urged that "We must be less sportsmanlike in the conduct of criminal trials" to insure conviction.[28]

This demand for less sportsmanship — legality — raises the question whether Londoners would countenance extralegal discretionary practices in the war against crime. The demand for action, as in the past, focused on new police powers specified by act of Parliament. As the *Times* pointed out, most Londoners believed that police inefficiency reflected defects in the law and they sought still stricter controls over the ticket-of-leave men, whom they blamed for their insecurity. The Habitual Criminals Act of 1869 declared that any person twice convicted of a felony and not sentenced to penal servitude should be subject to police supervision for seven years, during which time he had to satisfy the police that he was earning an honest living. The Prevention of Crimes Act of 1871 further increased police power: if a constable believed that any ticket-of-leave man was earning his livelihood dishonestly, he could take him before a magistrate, who could revoke his parole and return him to prison. The measure also provided for national photographic records of criminals.[29]

Increased police powers, accompanying stricter controls over parolees, aroused some criticisms and fears. Writing in 1847, before the abolition of transportation, a commentator warned that having to watch released convicts might make the English police into a French spy system. The parolee had to prove his innocence, that he was gaining an honest living, but many casual or seasonal lower-class occupations did not meet the criteria of a steady job. Moreover, the increase of police power was dangerous because a young and inexperienced constable seeking a reputation for "shrewdness and intelligence," acting according to his "home-bred, unofficially cultivated ideas of right and wrong," could ruin a man on mere suspicion. The legal historian Alan Harding has labeled some features of the Habitual Criminals Act and the Prevention of Crimes Act "positively mediaeval."[30]

While primitive by modern standards, the measures were significantly mid-nineteenth century rather than medieval. They granted broad discretionary powers to the police, but only over a clearly defined group feared by all classes. The journalist quoted earlier had wanted to hang thrice-convicted garotters, but the acts represented a choice of bureaucratic controls over dramatic and harsh punishments.[31] They also reaffirmed the legal basis of police power. Specific laws, rather than unchecked personal discretion or arming of the bobbies, were chosen as the main weapons in the war against crime. The crisis of the sixties prompted many criticisms of police efficiency, behavior, and administration, but did not force an abandonment of the principle of controlled impersonal authority.

WORKING-CLASS ATTITUDES TOWARD THE POLICE

So far we have discussed an area of agreement between the propertied and working classes—the fear of crime and the desire to do something about it in the sixties. However, workers often experienced aspects of police authority which "their betters" rarely noticed or discussed. Impersonal authority looked different when seen from the bottom, and many workers did not share middle-class praise of the police's "habitual discretion and moderation of conduct."[32]

In the following discussion of attitudes and perceptions, drawn largely from the press and some popular music, the old-fashioned term "working classes" will be used, as a reminder that "In no other section of society are there so many and such widely differing castes.... There is no typical working man."[33] Working-class reaction to the police was as complex as the makeup of that stratum of society, and thus it is impossible in most cases to be precise as to the views of this or that group within it.

The broadest gulf was between "respectable" and "rough" elements. Geoffrey Best speaks of the respectable worker's "unmistakable anxiety to dissociate himself from rowdies and 'roughs'"; Brian Harrison, of "a continuous guerrilla warfare between rough and respectable working men." Roughs were not necessarily criminals, although amateur thieves were among their number; they were men who worked at hard, unskilled, or casual occupations—honest, usually illiterate or semiliterate navvies, bricklayers' laborers, dockers, or costermongers. According to a clergyman they were "always in danger, under provocation, of combining with the actually criminal and violent classes for the illegal assertion of ... power, or for purposes of plunder." This is essentially a definition of the "mob" of the eighteenth and early-nineteenth century, but now lifted from the bulk of the working classes and applied to only a certain element.*

---

*See Mainwaring, *Observations* (1821), pp. 4-5: "A large mass of unproductive population ..., without occupation or ostensible means of subsistence ...; hundreds of thousands go forth from day to day trusting alone to charity or rapine; and differing little from the barbarous hordes which traverse an uncivilized land." Though Solly's language is similar, he is speaking of a rather more precisely defined "residuum" of casual laborers subject to seasonal unemployment. This more precise focus of public fears is partly the result of the researches of Henry Mayhew and his

To a modern writer the roughs formed "the borders of the underworld." Certainly members of the unskilled occupations most often ran afoul of the police. Records show that of a total of 34,629 people arrested in the second half of 1837, 22,900 were reported as having no occupation. Since there is no listing for unskilled laborers, presumably this "none" category is mostly made up of them rather than the unemployed. In 1876, of the leading categories of arrestees, laborers far outstripped the others with 14,480, laundresses taking a distant second with 2,043. In both years the crimes for which they were most frequently arrested were assault, disorderly conduct, drunkenness, and petty larceny. Skilled artisans, who probably manifested the most anxiety to avoid the taint of roughness, were rarely arrested according to the clergyman who analyzed the roughs. The police records, however, show many more of them arrested in 1837 than in 1876—perhaps a handy index of the artisan's road to respectability.[34]

While we might assume that there would be little love between roughs and the police, placing a workingman in the respectable category does not necessarily mean that he shared the propertied classes' general satisfaction with the force. In fact, the more he shared middle-class aspirations and life-style, the more political he might be. A self-educated, skilled artisan might be a Chartist or republican who had felt the truncheon at a demonstration or feared the government's political use of the police. *Reynolds's Newspaper,* perhaps the most consistent journalistic critic of the police, described itself in 1852 as "read by a large portion of the Middle Class and by all the intelligent members of the Working Class."[35] On the other hand, along with *Reynolds's* and other working-class papers in the sixties, the workingman might criticize the police for inefficiency and inability to provide the personal security he valued as much as the West Ender. Just as there was no typical workingman, it would be

---

colleagues, who sought to determine "which are in reality the dangerous classes, the idle, the profligate, and the criminal," giving precise figures of the numbers of people following various criminal occupations (see publisher's advertisement, Henry Mayhew and John Binny, *The Criminal Prisons of London and Scenes of Prison Life* [London, 1862], n.p.). The police first published official figures of the "criminal classes," listing known thieves and "depredators," receivers of stolen goods, prostitutes, "suspected persons," and vagrants, in 1858 (see "Judicial Statistics," *PP*, 1858 and later). Solly's 150,000 "roughs and ruffians" (see note 20) included the potential as well as the professional criminal, but was a more carefully defined group than Mainwaring's "hundreds of thousands" in the much smaller London of 1821.

difficult to describe a typical working-class view of the police. However, certain broad attitudes do appear in working-class literature and music which are not usually found in their middle-class counterparts.

The most sustained working-class theme during the 1830–70 period was "one law for the rich, another law for the poor"—the complaint that the legal system and its judicial and police agents enshrined and enforced class privilege. Not only did individual laws—such as the law of master and servant governing workers' relations with the boss as well as domestics' ties with their employers, and the notorious game laws—seem to be designed to keep the poor under the thumb of "their betters," but justice was slow and prohibitively expensive for the workingman. As *Reynolds's* said, "The extravagance of the law has always been a mighty weapon in the hands of the rich and powerful to crush the weak and poor. How many a poor man has suffered the grossest injustice at the hands of a rich one, because the former has not the means of paying for law, or, in other words, purchasing justice?" Important reforms of the civil and criminal statutes during the mid-nineteenth century, including mitigation of harsh punishments for petty crimes, removal of time-consuming archaisms and technicalities, and changes in procedure and jurisdiction, helped alleviate this grievance. Although the steady modernizing and humanizing of the law may, according to a lawyer, have strengthened "the attachment of the people to the laws by which they are governed," most of the reforms made prosecution easier, cheaper, and more certain of conviction instead of easing the lot of defendants. In addition to the reduction of punishments, the change probably most beneficial to the working classes was the extension in the fifties of magistrates' summary jurisdiction over juvenile offenses, minor thefts, and most embezzlements, which ended the expense of higher-court trial and the long imprisonment while awaiting trial. Even this, however, was a mixed blessing. Working-class spokesmen condemned the harshness of "justices' justice"—most often in the case of the "great unpaid" rural magistracy, but also among London's stipendiary magistrates. Things had improved since the 1830s, but the law still seemed to favor the rich. After pointing out the great accomplishments of reformers like Lord Brougham, a journalist in 1863 reminded his readers that "There are grievous hindrances in the way of cheap justice yet. The poor man remains at a disadvantage to this hour." At the end of our period Thomas Wright, "the journeyman engineer," pointed out that the inequities of the law still "sting and rankle, . . . perpetuate and intensify class jealousy and hatred." He added, "Furthermore, the poor are firmly of the opinion that there being one law for the rich and another for the poor is intentional—is the result of the rich having the 'upper hand' and being practically the lawmakers. This is the crowning sting of the grievance—the point that maddens." The resentment was fundamentally political, the grievance of the powerless against the powerful.[36]

As agents of a legal order which many workers viewed as unjust, the police naturally came under attack. A print of the thirties by George Cruikshank pictured policemen as automatons mechanically carrying out the injustice of the magistrates or "beaks," with their appropriately long noses. The bobbies are saluting the magistrates by holding their detached heads or arms in their hands while a poor woman and her child lie collapsed on the floor. The "real offenders" are the drunken and brutal rich, standing in the dock and carousing and thumbing their noses at justice. Although bobbies were expected to be polite to "all people of every rank and class," a magistrate in 1834 asserted that "there is no security to the poor, because I think they are very much ill-treated by the police." Thirty years later a journalist sympathetic to the force could still write, "Although well-dressed people always meet with civility . . . it is possible that the ragged and the outcaste may occasionally meet with the hasty word or unnecessary force from the constable, who is for them the despot of the streets." This corroborates *Reynolds's* expected view that "The victims of . . . police tyranny are invariably the poor, the needy, and the would-be honest strugglers for a living." Friedrich Engels reflected a large segment of public opinion when he argued that "A policeman will always treat a member of the middle classes with every courtesy whatever he may do. . . . But a worker who falls into the hands of the police is immediately treated in a nasty and brutal fashion. The fact that a worker is poor is sufficient for him to be suspected of every crime in the calendar."[37] Were policemen harder on the poor or working classes than on the propertied and powerful? One man's firmness may be another's brutality, but what is important here is that people believed that the force treated the poor roughly despite official ideals of civility to all classes.

Rowan's and Mayne's often-expressed concern for the rights of "respectable" citizens may not have helped Londoners who did not meet the criteria of respectability as perceived by the commissioners or by a station-house desk officer. Pointing out that their "utmost attention is at all times given to prevent any undue exercise of authority, or of any harshness, or incivility, on the part of the Police," Rowan and Mayne felt "indebted to all respectable persons who call their attention to any such instances of misconduct." To whom did they listen? Many workers must have felt that the "strong arm of the law" was "exceedingly powerful against the weak but exceedingly weak against the powerful."[38]

If they sometimes complained that the police were harsh and authoritarian, workers also felt that the force protected wealthy neighborhoods while neglecting their own. The commissioners followed a policy of "watching St. James's and other places while we are watching St. Giles's and other bad places in general"—that is, patrolling of slum areas to prevent depredators from invading wealthy districts. While there may have been a greater concentration of policemen in poor districts, it seems to have been to protect bordering "respectable" areas instead of to protect the poor from each other. In fact, the police seem to have tolerated much disorder they would have suppressed in other neighborhoods. They seem to have overlooked brawls or other disturbances, partly because interference was dangerous and stirred up a hornet's nest of angry resentment. In addition, the commissioners did not expect much of poor cockneys' behavior. Regarding rowdyism in Calmel Buildings, a rookery, Rowan wrote privately to a magistrate, "I think we can shew that the Police have not been idle as regards this sweet spot, and in fact that it is considerably improved, but far beyond the reach of the Police to make it a fitting neighbourhood for anything respectable." Five years later, disturbances there were characterized as "a sudden ebullition of temper which frequently takes place in that quarter." Concern for their own physical welfare, as well as a belief that a certain amount of disorder was endemic to the slums, made policemen scarce in some areas. Respectable workers complained at the end of the sixties that the East End was insufficiently policed while the wealthy West End was carefully protected.[39]

Where were those policemen watching St. Giles to protect St. James? Was the charge true? Official figures suggest that there was some substance to it in 1848: the working-class divisions had fewer bobbies in proportion to the population than the aristocratic and middle-class divisions. An important exception to this generalization is the E or Holborn Division, which contained both the notorious rookery of St. Giles's and a bustling middle-class shopping area. The division's one bobby for each 544 residents may be explained by the proximity of classes. This ratio resembled that of aristocratic St. James's (also disturbingly close to the rookery), with one policeman for each 540 citizens. The more isolated H or Whitechapel Division, perhaps the poorest in the metropolis, had one constable for each 698 residents; the largely working-class L or Lambeth Division on the south bank of the Thames had one bobby for each 655 citizens. Where the working class was relatively isolated, not as many men were deployed; where the propertyless and propertied rubbed elbows the bobbies were most visible. This is in line with the commissioners' general policy.[40]

Twenty years later the pattern seems to have remained. Unfortunately divisional population figures are not available, so we have to use the less meaningful measure of policemen per square mile of the division in 1869. This can be useful, however, when we recall that in poorer areas there were many more people packed into that square mile than in wealthy neighborhoods. Looking at Holborn again, we get a ratio of 330 patrolmen per square mile. This is only slightly less than St. James's, which if it made up a square mile (its area was only 0.79 m²) would have had 342 bobbies (there were 171 per half a square mile). Whitechapel, Lambeth, and by now working-class Southwark had substantially fewer policemen. Whitechapel had 228 per square mile; Lambeth, 201; Southwark, 162. Two non-working-class areas had fewer patrolmen. Westminster (B Division) had 175, perhaps because of the numerous public buildings and wealthy areas which were relatively far from poor neighborhoods (an exception being its own rookery, "the Devil's Acre"). Suburban Marylebone, increasingly being built up, had 185 policemen per square mile. Marylebone residents, in fact, led the complaints of insufficient police protection in 1868. Translating the dry statistics into human terms, fewer policemen per square mile meant that the individual bobby had to patrol a longer beat and his blue coat would be less frequently seen. Comparing themselves to St. James's and Holborn, East Enders did have grounds for complaint; they were joined by upper- and middle-class residents of Marylebone.[41]

How could the working classes see the police as both overbearing or authoritarian and inadequate to protect their neighborhoods? If it is correct to say that the police concentrated their force along the borders between rich and poor neighborhoods, the two perspectives do not seem so contradictory. Along the "front lines" bobbies would be especially suspicious of workers going into wealthy areas, looking, as the police always do, for individuals who seemed to be out of place. Ragged clothes or sometimes work dress where they were not normally seen invited patrolmen's attention. Moreover, although the police did serve the working classes in many ways in the normal course of their duties, many of the laws designed to make "respectable" neighborhoods more orderly and healthy devolved into a bobby's order to "move on" to costermongers or other street-sellers who eked out marginal livings on the pavements. To them, the police seemed to be the enforcers of shopkeepers' greed at the poor man's expense. Costermongers were always ready to assault a policeman, to "serve up a crusher," who disrupted their precarious livelihood. The other side of the picture is that the police often left the poor to their own devices on the back streets, undoubtedly to the dismay of people who valued peace and quiet despite their humble circumstances. Depending upon who they were, what they did for a living, and who their next-door neighbors were, working-class Londoners could sometimes see the police as tyrannical and other times as inefficient.[42]

If there was a conventional image of the policeman, it was of bobby — somewhat slow and plodding physically and mentally, but honest and loyal, whose worst vice was flirting with servant girls. Upper- and middle-class people, appreciative of his services, were inclined to wink at that transgression. An 1857 song concluded:

> May he long our dwellings and coffers to guard
>   from all that would rush thereunto.
> 'Gainst promise or threat, his face ever set,
> Determined his duty to do, determined his duty to do.
> Delight to use argument rather than force, both
>   sides of the question to look.
> To his sov'reign and land ever firm and true stand,
> And we'll pardon his freaks with the cook.[43]

This was the policeman's informal, or John Bull, aspect, in contrast to his official, or Britannia, side — the impersonal "institution rather than a man."

During the sixties the music hall became a popular working-class entertainment, and audiences enjoyed songs which depicted policemen with fewer virtues and more vices than "freaks with the cook." In the song and patter routine by C. P. Cove, "The Model Peeler," the policeman is rough, lazy, corrupt, and lecherous:

> Oh, I'm the chap to make a hit,
>   No matter where I goes it.
> I'm quite a credit to the force,

> And jolly well they knows it.
> I take folks up, knock others down,
> None do the thing genteeler,
> I'm number 14, double X,
> And called the Model Peeler.

Brandishing his truncheon, the Model Peeler declares that it would be bad for the health of any citizen who took his number. "Lor' bless you, when I first became a policeman I was as green as grass. . . . I actually used to walk about looking after other people's welfare and forgetting my own; but I didn't do it long, I can tell you." He is careful not to catch every burglar — "gentleman of the bar (crowbar I mean)" — for that would put the police out of business. He rifles the pockets of a drunk before sending him home in a cab, "and by so doing, I consider I remove temptation from the path of some poor wretch who might be induced through poverty to plunder the person of a fellow creature." He accepts a bribe from rowdy medical students and allows them to go their way, but when he runs up against some drunken laborers, he acts on the maxim "suit your manners according to your company" and clubs them all mercilessly. "Next morning I told his Worship of the brutal and cowardly attack the wretches had made on me, and wound up by saying that I feared I was internally injured from the kicks I had received; of course the prisoners had the impudence to say I was a liar, but his Worship (as usual), paid no attention to their statement, and fined 'em £ 5 each, or three months on the stepper [treadmill]." (The fine, which was the maximum provided by the Metropolitan Police Act for assaults on the police, was impossible for most workers to pay, so they undoubtedly went to prison. The whole principle of fines was one of the most bitterly resented aspects of "one law for the rich, another law for the poor.") The Model Peeler's "freaks with the cook" were decidedly off-color, revolving around such themes as "Yes, all the little cook maids have a welcome for me, and no wonder, for . . . I always do my duty, and by help of my trusty staff, I do it like a man," and "I tell her I have been so long engaged in keeping the peace for other people that I shall find no difficulty in keeping a piece of my own." The Model Peeler takes his leave "fully convinced that no other occupation can beat the beat of a policeman."

> For I'm the chap to wake 'em up,
> None do the thing genteeler,
> And right throughout the blessed force,
> I'm called the Model Peeler.[44]

Music-hall numbers like this clearly did not accept the official version of the police image, but they did not sympathize with criminals. As we descend the social scale from music halls to the cheapest, "penny gaff," theaters we encounter performances in which "the stage policemen were getting very much the worst of a free fight, to the unbounded delight of pit and gallery." Describing the "penny dreadful" pulp literature read by young roughs, a newspaper editor said, "In nearly all these novels the hero is the criminal. To befool the police, to escape from justice, or to foil the law are the most favourite adventures of these jaunty and charming villains. . . . The law is always put at a disadvantage. Its officers are persecutors and its punishments cruel exactions, from which every fascinated reader wishes his hero may escape." In working-class entertainment, from the respectable to the rough, the policeman emerges as an unpleasant or antagonistic figure, not as the devoted servant of an impartial legal order.[45]

Was the police image, then, simply an image for the propertied classes? To a great extent it was, for the force was part of a class society and reflected its inequalities. Moreover, the notion of a bobby as an impartial legal agent was congenial with the upper- and middle-class view of the legal system: "There is but one code of laws written in our statute-book, and . . . it stands applicable to all, without respect to persons or caste." Engels was not being particularly radical when he pointed out that legal officials saw the interests of their own class as the "true cornerstone of law and order."[46]

Yet, despite this reality and the fervid journalistic rhetoric, it would be wrong to assume that the police systematically oppressed the working classes. The commissioners had hoped to "conciliate the populace," and within the framework of a class society they took this commitment seriously. The policeman's service role, which Chadwick stressed as the ultimate basis of public acceptance, benefited workers and their families in many ways. Bobbies helped them in fires and accidents; took the destitute to workhouses for relief (though a dubious charity, it was better than freezing or starving in the street); enforced laws to keep tradesmen honest in dealing with working-class customers; attempted to enforce sanitary measures to prevent disease; and after 1851 enforced the Common Lodging Houses Act which, though designed to give the police greater surveillance over criminal elements, improved the living conditions of the poorest Londoners.[47] Moreover, as the following section will illustrate, the police were not insensitive to proletarian values which diverged from the middle-class norm.

SABBATARIANS AND THE POLICE: MEDIATION BETWEEN
MIDDLE-CLASS DEMANDS AND WORKING-CLASS RESISTANCE

The "Sunday question" was a constantly recurring and often bitterly fought political and social issue in mid-nineteenth-century London. The conflict brought the values of upper- and middle-class moral reformers into collision with the life-style of most of London's teeming working-class population. Reformers, though they often tried persuasion, also insisted on passage of laws restricting or outlawing secular business, amusements, or drinking of alcoholic beverages on the sabbath. As agents of the law, the police found themselves in the middle of the conflict.

In the 1830s the only comprehensive Sunday law on the English statute book was an act passed in 1667 under King Charles II which prohibited all Sunday labor and trading except "works of charity or necessity." Despite some additions to the law during the eighteenth century, popular customs steadily drifted away from the Puritan sabbath to the secular Sunday. Particularly among the working classes, Sunday by the mid-nineteenth century was a day of thriving street markets (the larger ones resembling fairs in which all manner of goods were sold), public-house conviviality, and excursions into the countryside. Small shopkeepers and street vendors in London and other cities busily provided food for Sunday dinners, bakers warmed up these meals for working-class families without adequate cooking facilities, and publicans provided the essential beer. In many areas of London the law of Charles II was a dead letter.[48]

The Sunday question was generally dormant until the later 1820s, when growth of the evangelical movement drew attention to sabbath observance. Among both Anglicans and Nonconformists the evangelicals were known for their missionary and philanthropic zeal, but also for inflexibility of doctrine and strict interpretation of the Fourth Commandment, "Remember the Sabbath Day to keep it Holy." Evangelicalism was particularly strong among the middle and lower-middle classes, although for many working people it was a spiritual road to the secular "respectability" they sought.[49] Not all evangelicals were sabbatarians, but most sabbatarians were evangelicals.

Although evangelicalism was a powerful force in Victorian England, giving the period much of its tone and providing the impetus for many reform movements, sabbatarians had to wage an uphill battle. Ironically, the impact of evangelicalism upon manners during the mid-nineteenth century encouraged voluntary sabbath observance among the upper and middle classes and weakened the case for

Sunday laws. Moreover, at the end of the 1830s many Nonconformist clergymen split from their Anglican brethren by adopting "voluntaryism," or opposition to legislation of religious observance. A tactic acceptable to the established church became unacceptable to those who challenged the link between church and state. Sabbatarians were also checked by important countervailing forces rooted in English social structure and institutions. Although sabbatarianism had aristocratic spokesmen in Parliament like Lord Shaftesbury and Lord Robert Grosvenor, its political force was blunted by an alliance between the top and bottom of society—sporting aristocrats and workingmen. Partly this alliance rested on upper-class toleration of amusements or customs which kept the "lower orders" contented, satiated, and out of political mischief. Another aspect was that some aristocrats shared the working-class taste for "manly" amusements and public-house camaraderie. As C. F. G. Masterman put it, the workingman was "allied in temperament and disposition to some of the occupants of the Conservative back benches, whose life, in its bodily exercises, enjoyment of eating and drinking, and excitement of 'sport,' he would undoubtedly pursue with extreme relish if similar opportunities were offered him." One of the few times available to him for such activities was Sunday afternoon. Although many working-class antisabbatarians charged that Sunday laws represented class tyranny and an effort to destroy religious liberty, resentment of puritanism sometimes bridged the gulf between "the two nations."[50]

Politically radical though many antisabbatarians were, including Karl Marx, others could appeal to the roast-beef-and-ale tradition of merry England against evangelical efforts to overturn established customs. They aroused popular resentment against foreign—Scottish and New England Yankee—puritanism. J. A. Roebuck, who spoke for aristocrats when he supported the Confederacy during the American Civil War and for workingmen when he opposed Sunday laws, depicted sabbatarianism as the convergence of "two muddy streams . . . the fanaticism of the anti-liquor gentlemen and the fanaticism of the sabbath-preservation Yankee." Politically minded workers admired American democracy but not her puritanism.[51]

Sabbatarians were most successful in communities where they could mobilize local opinion, and in some London neighborhoods achieved the orderliness they sought through encouraging prosecutions by parish authorities or private citizens.[52] However, in seeking national legislation, or measures for London only, as the basis for later extension through England and Wales, they were at a disadvantage because Parliament was situated in the cosmopolitan, heterogeneous metropolis, where antisabbatarianism was strong. Opponents formed the National Sunday League to campaign against existing restrictions, publicans lobbied in Parliament, and in the streets ("out of doors") was the threat or reality of antisabbatarian demonstrations. While many M.P.'s supported Sunday bills to satisfy religious constituents back home, they also faced the immediate threat of reaction in London. These cross-pressures came to a head in 1855, when Parliament passed Lord Robert Grosvenor's Sunday-trading bill and then hastily repealed it after demonstrations in Hyde Park. The protests dampened Parliament's sabbatarian zeal for many years.[52] The nature of London as the political capital and a center of working-class radicalism had much to do with the fate of Sunday bills.

Because of the various countervailing factors, sabbatarians obtained only a series of limited Sunday measures, following the pattern of liquor-control legislation, which rejected prohibition in favor of stricter licensing laws. They kept museums and galleries closed on Sunday, prevented Sunday military band concerts in the parks, and obtained limited Sunday closing of public houses. These relatively modest Sunday measures represented a compromise between sabbatarians and their opponents.

Sabbatarians of the 1830s primarily sought to improve religious observance. They were led by the Society for the Promotion of the Due Observance of the Lord's Day, founded in London in 1831 by a group of evangelical clergy and laymen. The society's views set the tone for debate on the Sunday question throughout the decade. In 1832 it began a protracted campaign for a comprehensive Sunday law, selecting Sir Andrew Agnew, a Scottish baronet, as its parliamentary spokesman. The following year he introduced a bill to outlaw all Sunday labor and travel except for religious, charitable, or necessary reasons, and to close the pubs all day. The law would be enforced by progressively higher fines for each offense and rewards for reporting of violators. Agnew's bill provoked a storm of opposition inside and outside of Parliament. He was pictured as a tyrant who would destroy liberty in the name of religion, a gloomy Scot importing foreign customs to merry England. He never got his bill through, although he came close in 1837, when evangelical influence was at its height among members of Parliament as well as their constituents.[53]

Although the Lord's Day Society continued its emphasis on religious observance, public rejection of making men "religious by Act of Parliament" prompted a shift of sabbatarian tactics. New organizations and parliamentary champions of the cause emphasized moderate measures which were intended to give workers and shopkeepers a day of rest and to reduce the disorderly Sunday drunkenness, which disturbed churchgoers, by closing the pubs.[54]

Growth of the temperance movement during the mid-nineteenth century aided sabbatarian efforts to restrict Sunday drinking, but all-day public-house closing was never enacted. Except for increased control of pubs, the moderate Sunday measures of the 1840s and later were unsuccessful. Bad memories of Sir Andrew Agnew's religious zeal tainted less ambitious efforts. Laissez faire liberalism opposed regulation of harmless customs and amusements. Working-class radicalism denounced efforts to regulate manners and morals, even in the interest of people who had to labor seven days a week, as one of the worst forms of hypocritical class tyranny. Some defenders of the poor argued that Sunday laws imposed real physical deprivation on people who had to buy their food on Sunday morning or do without because of inadequate storage facilities.[55] Resisted from all sides, sabbatarianism won only modest victories on some fronts.

Against this background of sabbatarian efforts and widespread resistance to them in London, one must place the attitude of the Metropolitan Police toward Sunday laws. Rowan and Mayne, heads of an independent and powerful institution which nevertheless depended upon and sought broad-based public support, clearly expressed their views and exerted official influence in Parliament to make sure they were taken into account.

The commissioners objected to comprehensive Sunday legislation. So strong was working-class sentiment against interference with familiar customs that enforcement of even the limited provisions of Charles II's act threatened to provoke popular hostility against the police. In 1833 the *Times* warned that attempts to enforce Sunday laws would arouse dangerous anger against any authorities seen as attempting to compel religious observance. Charles Dickens thought that enforcement "may well rouse a feeling abroad, which a king would gladly yield his crown to quell, and a peer would resign his coronet to allay." Amid political conflict and hostility toward the police the commissioners naturally would not welcome the burden of Sunday law enforcement. Even thirty years later, when most working-class hostility toward the police had simmered down, a member of Parliament pointed out that although "now the police were regarded as the guardians of peace and order by the population," the "humbler classes" would hate them if they enforced Sunday laws.[56]

Rowan and Mayne agreed that enforcement would bring "odium to the police which injures their general usefulness to the public and . . . is very desirable therefore to avoid." The commissioners were well aware of the awkwardness of arresting a poor orange-seller, which might result in a small riot and "more confusion and scandal than could arise from selling any quantity of oranges" on Sunday.[57]

In addition to arousing hostility on the streets, the police lacked judicial support and effective legal power to suppress Sunday trading. In the early thirties, when one of the superintendents acted upon a petition of local residents and began arresting Sunday traders, he heard a magistrate criticize his men as common informers. The commissioners, "unwilling to subject their officers to such observations," ordered cessation of arrests. Over a decade later the commissioners directed the superintendents to prevent street cries which disturbed church services but to ignore quiet selling. Rowan wrote to a friend that a "Billiard Room keeper *politely* refuses to shut his rooms on the Sabbath, and I believe I am quite correct in saying that the *Police* have no power to compel him." A tobacconist cheerfully paid his fine under the act of Charles II every Monday morning but never closed on Sunday. Years later Sunday sellers were offering to pay six months' fines in advance. Rowan and Mayne found in 1834 that it was "necessary to be cautious and not to do more than public opinion would support." In 1850 Mayne believed it "necessary to restrict the use of the police to instances in which I thought it desirable that they should interfere," and these do not seem to have been frequent. Mayne's successor, Henderson, continued the earlier policy of preventing street cries which disturbed the peace but not quiet Sunday trading.[58]

Although reluctant to enforce measures which would provoke hostility, the commissioners favored limited Sunday laws whose contribution to public order outweighed disgruntlement over their enforcement. One of these, which was prompted by a defect in existing law, specified that public houses had to close during Sunday morning Anglican services. Just as "respectable" people were on their way to church, the pubs were turning out drunk and frequently disorderly customers. A parish official described these Hogarthian scenes:

> Just as church-time approached, the gin-shops sent forth their multitudes swearing and fighting and bawling obscenely; some were stretched on the pavement insensibly drunk, while every few steps the footway was taken up by drunken wretches being dragged to the station-house by the police. I saw some of that description, and a vast number of persons following them, who occupied the whole of the pavement, and every decent person was compelled to walk in the road, so that it was physically as well as morally dangerous.

The commissioners found that this disorder was the greatest source of Sunday complaints, and clearing the streets was one of the police's most trying duties, intervention often causing a small riot. They had complained to the Home Office in 1832 that existing laws could not cope with Sunday morning disorder, and two years later Rowan recommended closing hours of 12:00 P.M. (midnight) Saturday to 1:00 P.M. Sunday. A bill to that effect was introduced in 1835, but the hours were not instituted until on Mayne's advice the provision was inserted into the government's comprehensive 1839 police act.[59]

The police found that the new law improved public order and eased their task. After the law went into operation Mayne wrote that "The effect of the clause for closing the Public Houses was very remarkable," arrests for drunkenness dropping dramatically and other good results appearing in the "improved state of the streets, and prevention of the numerous evils to the families of the individuals who had been in the habits of drinking all Saturday night and the following morning." Indirectly, the new law hastened the demise of Saturday night wage payment in public houses. Publicans, once workers could not drink all Sunday morning, lost their vested interest in Saturday wage payments, which, like the beer they sold, were often consumed "on the premises." Employers began to pay their men on Friday night, and even if still paid in pubs, workers kept most of their wages in their pockets because they did not want to risk missing the next day's work because of drunkenness. While the law benefited churchgoers most directly, it also benefited many workers.[60]

Despite improved order, the 1839 law aroused a good deal of criticism and introduced difficult problems of enforcement. Since judges required precise evidence of illegal liquor sales, publicans devised various strategies of evasion, including the use of sentinels to warn of approaching policemen, secret side doors, and hiding of the

134

evidence when bobbies came knocking. Most evasion was in slum areas, where local residents encouraged secret Sunday tippling and police interference could provoke disorder. Pub habitués resented invasion of their domain, a castle often more congenial than their tenement homes. Many public houses were important centers of radical politics and trade-union organizing where policemen would be especially unwelcome. The periodic use of plainclothesmen to detect illegal selling aroused fears of the "Continental spy system." "It behooves every man who values his civil rights and liberty to protest against a system which encourages the wily machinations of hired spies to entrap the unwary into the commission of crime," thundered a journalist. "It is now no uncommon occurrence for the police to assume disguises so ingeniously devised that the most lynx-eyed persons are deceived, and under such circumstances to become parties to a breach of the law, in order that the less guilty may be pounced upon and punished." He described the police as "a gang of interested prosecutors, who are actuated by the most sordid and unworthy motives." However, if uniformed policemen went into public houses, citizens suspected them of drinking on duty. Finally, since the police admitted extensive evasion of the law, many people suspected them of accepting bribes to ignore violations. The unpopular control and inspection of pubs was a sensitive and controversial police duty.[61]

Pleased though the commissioners were with Sunday morning closing, they were aware of the difficulty and delicacy of enforcement. They accepted increased power over publicans and their customers but exercised it cautiously. Until 1834 the police had no power to enter pubs, even at the landlord's request, unless a disturbance were in progress. Rowan and Mayne wanted increased power, but a section of the Beer Act of 1834, which gave bobbies the power of entry when they "shall think proper," was more than they thought proper. For "the protection of the Police themselves and also ensuring a due restraint on the exercise of their authority," the commissioners directed that constables and sergeants could enter pubs only on the express orders of the superintendent or inspector on duty and present at the time.[62]

They wanted control of pubs to be exercised only by men they had personally selected for integrity, admitting that they could not indiscriminately trust such power to the rank and file. Recognizing that drinking on duty was a major problem in the force's early years, and that corruption, which seems to have existed but was not systematic, was a temptation difficult to resist, the commissioners made sure they knew whom they allowed into pubs. Mayne generally discouraged use of plainclothesmen, although he resigned himself to necessity in some cases as the only way to obtain the sort of evidence magistrates required. He realized that the practice placed the police in "a very objectionable light before the public." Toward the end of his career he ordered that no disguises could be used to detect illegal sales. To reduce the opportunity of corruption the commissioners required policemen to report Sunday violations to them for decision on whether a summons should be issued. Once Rowan and Mayne authorized a summons, possible "compromise between the constable or police officer and the publican" was prevented.[63]

The force generally seems to have shared the commissioners' cautious attitude. A magistrate believed that policemen themselves would regard unlimited inspection of pubs as "a very obnoxious exercise of their power," and a tradesman found that they were "rather shy of entering public-houses" unless disorder were taking place. In fact, on some occasions, the police avoided "obnoxious exercise of their power" by ignoring Sunday law violations. The commissioners, though, seem to have preferred a "low profile" method of police work to overzealous enforcement.[64]

Despite evasion and difficulties of enforcement, after several years of experience the commissioners continued to favor limited Sunday closing as a contribution to good order. Richard Mayne, who became single head of the police after Rowan's retirement in 1850, stressed that the value of Sunday closing lay precisely in its limited nature. Too much restriction would nullify good results because of the evasion and hostility it would generate. His view was dramatically confirmed after Parliament passed the Wilson Patten Act of 1854, which closed pubs on Sundays from 2:30 P.M. to 6:00 P.M. and after 10:00 P.M. Most people seem to have been unaware of the act, so quickly was it passed. Since Sunday afternoon excursion trains usually returned to London at 10:00 P.M., many thirsty travelers were particularly incensed when they found pub doors closed on their return. The result, in the words of an M.P., was "great discontent, almost amounting to riot, and the police were called on to do their most unpleasant, and . . . un-English duty, which they did with that quietude and firmness which mark the character of the corps."[65]

Discontent boiled over into organized protest the next year when Parliament almost passed Lord Robert Grosvenor's bill to outlaw all Sunday trading in London. Mayne, who had "some doubts as to whether the public feeling would go along with" increased restrictions of Sunday trading, became a leading opponent of the 1855 measure. After some preliminary meetings, a demonstration in Hyde Park turned into a confused melee when the police tried to ban the crowds from the park and prevent their harassment of aristocratic equestrians on the park's carriageways. Many people, including innocent spectators, were injured and some of the policemen were justly charged with excessive violence. The *Times* asserted that "The sympathies of nine-tenths of the educated population are on the side of the rioters. . . . The people of London don't want a Sunday bill, and there's an end of it." The proletarian *Reynolds's Newspaper* had earlier agreed: "The 'saints' are public nuisances, and by persevering in their present vexatious crusade against the liberties of the working class, they will make the name of religion hated and detested by the people." For Mayne the worst result of the incident was that his fears had been realized: public anger over sabbatarianism had placed the police in an embarrassing position and tarnished their reputation.[66]

Many people, including Mayne, believed that the crowd's anger could be traced back to the Wilson Patten Act. Along with Grosvenor's bill, the act was dropped by Parliament as quickly as it had earlier been passed. Afternoon closing was retained as a concession to sabbatarians, who remained influential, but the new hours were 3:00 P.M. to 5:00 P.M. and, most important, the 10:00 P.M. closing was changed to 11:00 P.M., enabling excursionists to obtain their "refreshment." Pubs now remained open eight hours on Sunday, compared with five and a half hours under the Wilson Patten Act. Popular anger simmered down, and during the next decade magistrates interpreted Sunday closing hours very liberally, allowing people who walked from one part of London to another to qualify as travelers who could be served throughout Sunday afternoon.[67]

Sabbatarians persisted in their efforts to outlaw Sunday trading and drinking, but memories of the 1855 riot made Parliament shy away from further restrictions and Mayne continued his opposition. In 1867, however, sabbatarians obtained a Select Committee investigation of the desirability of closing pubs all day Sunday. The committee concluded by an eight-to-four majority that "the safe limit of restrictive legislation [had] been reached, and that further measures . . . would be unwise and injudicious." The investigation gave Richard Mayne, a few months before his death, the opportunity to state his most forceful view of police policy toward Sunday closing. He believed that existing restrictions reduced drunkenness and improved public order, but that further measures would cause so much discontent and evasion as to negate their contribution to orderliness. The best policy to follow was limited restrictions which struck "a balance between good and evil." Too many restrictions threatened the rule of law itself: "If you increase the restrictions you increase the danger of evasion," he said, "and all evasions are bad, and accustom people to disregard the law and give them a general disrespect for observance of the law." Mayne left an enduring legacy for the London police. Officials of a later era echoed his views when they dreaded "passage of laws making a crime of actions which a great many people regard as innocent." Since the police presented themselves as agents of the law who sought to win public support as impartial upholders of order, having to enforce widely resisted laws would have undermined the foundations of their impersonal image.[68]

THE POLICE AND THE POLICED

In attempting to assess the degree of police legitimacy among the working classes, it is probably safest to say that the force won a certain grumbling acquiescence to its authority — a fragile toleration which sometimes broke down in periods of political crisis when workers saw the police as an instrument of oppression, but an improvement over the violent opposition of the thirties. A good deal of this acquiescence may have been achieved by a simple yielding to superior force: "People feel that resistance is useless," said Mayne in the fifties. The police's technique for dealing with recalcitrant Irish slum residents illustrates this basis of the force's power. If a single bobby attempting to serve a warrant was driven away, more men were sent in to reinforce him until the offenders were taught that "it was not the single policeman alone who was to be considered, but the large indefinite force that was behind to back him." After this lesson, "the single policeman walked into these places with the prestige of strength, and resistance, known to be fruitless, was not attempted."[69]

Chadwick, who wrote this, was exaggerating somewhat, for there remained a reservoir of violent resistance. Bobbies still avoided certain courtyards in 1870 unless they were armed or had the support of large numbers; there were 2,858 arrests for assaults on policemen (all but 203 offenders convicted by magistrates or higher courts) in 1869, despite the Habitual Criminals Act's raising the fine to twenty

138

pounds or a maximum of six months' imprisonment. At least some members of the working classes, who had led opposition to the police in the thirties, still carried on guerrilla warfare in 1870.[70]

Ultimately the working-class view of the police was a political response to the force which upheld political, economic, and social institutions on which workers had no direct influence. Michael Banton points out that "To do his job properly the policeman ... has to be to some extent a 'classless' figure. He has to deal with subjects of different class and his relationships with them must be determined by his office, not by his class position. But despite the powers conferred and the restrictions imposed upon him, the policeman is never completely separated from the class structure."[71] As long as people believed that there was one law for the rich and another law for the poor, the bobby would be seen as an upholder of inequality. Legal and political reforms helped secure middle-class attachment to the government and the police force which upheld it. The reform of 1867 opened the way for growth of similar working-class attachment, but that remained only a potential in 1870. Since the police generally subordinated themselves to the law, they were attacked when the laws were attacked, but they could also benefit when the laws improved and more people had faith in the administration of justice.

The public respect which the London police have gained in the twentieth century (at least until the last decade) was built on foundations laid in the nineteenth century, but it is also important to remember that a large sector of the public feared and despised the force they called "crushers." Chapter 1 discussed the force's policy of restrained power; it is best to view this as a sort of continuum. The bobbies seem to have emphasized restraint when dealing with "respectable" Londoners, power when confronting the "lower orders." In neither case was one element totally missing; it was a matter of emphasis.

6 THE FINEST?
POLICE AND PUBLIC
IN NEW YORK

Like their London peers, upper- and middle-class New Yorkers expected efficient police protection. However, they often felt unprotected and, especially in the late fifties and the sixties, sometimes formed vigilance committees and armed themselves when disorder became intolerable.[1] Reformers' efforts to professionalize the police resulted in some improvements, but ultimately only substituted one political party's control for the other's. Respectable citizens continued to criticize partisan domination of the force, especially when political conflict reflected the native-immigrant, Protestant-Catholic disputes which divided the city. While the London force was also the subject of political controversy, election victories did not turn out one group of officials and substitute another. Moreover, the working classes, who were most prone to view the police as political instruments, did not have direct access to, or influence upon, police administration. In New York, on the other hand, Whig and, later, Republican citizens feared Democratic control of the force because that party depended on the "turbulent" or "dangerous" unskilled, largely Irish workers for votes. Perhaps out of fear that a partisan police would abuse broad legal powers, whatever party was in the saddle, New Yorkers did not legislate such comprehensive increases of police power as were provided in London's 1839 police act or its Habitual Criminals Act of 1869. The question of police efficiency was always a matter of political controversy: the outs uniformly charged the ins with destroying the morale and discipline of the force.

"NEW YORK'S FINEST": THE USE OF DISCRETIONARY POWER
TO CHECK THE "DANGEROUS CLASSES"
The effectiveness of the New York police did not depend on professionalism or growing legal powers. Instead, the citizens who

criticized many aspects of the force tolerated informal or extralegal discretionary power in the street and station house as their only bastion against the underworld. Leaving the police to their own devices was convenient, for they could be attacked if they stepped outside the limits of toleration — if respectable people became victims of brutality or illegality — but praised for harsh treatment of the "dangerous classes." Police discretion was part of New York's "netherside," something everybody knew existed but did not talk about very much unless it threatened to escape its informal boundaries. Such attitudes gave patrolmen a free hand but did not communicate clear public expectations of behavior. The end, control or apprehension of members of the "dangerous classes," allowed policemen to choose their own means. Now, to some extent this was also true of London, but there the policy of restrained force, even though it grew more forceful toward those on the lower rungs of the social ladder, was backed by legal and judicial constraints on police discretion which were generally lacking in New York.

Propertied New Yorkers remained ambivalent about the police, objecting to partisan control and inefficiency but also demanding quick action against criminal elements, not through new laws but by accepting policemen's own discretion. The phrase "New York's Finest," coined in the mid-seventies, was ambiguous in the mouths of citizens who condemned inefficiency and corruption but entrusted policemen with much broader uncontrolled power than in London.[2]

Mid-nineteenth-century New Yorkers were never certain that they had obtained the ordered liberty which the English middle classes enjoyed in the 1850s. They could point to some visible improvement in public order by 1870, such as the disappearance of volunteer fire company rowdies after the creation of a paid fire department in 1865 and improvement of the city's notorious slum area, the Five Points. More often, however, they dwelled on the city's disorder and violence, which seemed to increase dramatically after the Civil War, and feared that the "dangerous classes" would explode into social revolution. The traumatic draft riots of 1863 and the Orange riot of 1871 confirmed the existing insecurity. A writer of 1860 warned, "We are sleeping over a volcano, from which already there are irruptions, spreading ruin in their track, while investigation will insure the conviction, that these are the comparatively mild premonitions of the more terrible irruptions that are certain by-and-by to belch forth with an all-consuming power." The draft riots made him a prophet, and the image of a volcano under the city became a cliché. Charles Loring Brace argued that past experience indicated

141

that the Paris Commune of 1871 was possible in America: "Let the law lift its hand from them for a season, or let the civilizing influences of American life fail to reach them, and, if the opportunity offered, we should see an explosion from this class which might leave this city in ashes and blood."[3]

New Yorkers' rhetoric recalls Londoners' fears of social explosion during the sixties. However, Americans believed that the "metropolis of the New World" was considerably more violent than the British metropolis. From the early 1850s on, contemporaries pointed to statistics revealing that crimes against the person consistently outnumbered crimes against the property of New Yorkers, while the reverse was true in London. Brace argued that although London had greater numbers of the poor than New York, the American metropolis could claim "elements of the population even more dangerous" than the worst of London. As Americans, "their crimes have the unrestrained and sanguinary character of a race accustomed to overcome all obstacles. They rifle a bank where English thieves pick a pocket; they murder, where European prolétaires cudgel or fight with fists; in a riot they begin what seems about to be the sacking of a city, where English rioters would merely batter policemen, or smash lamps."[4]

Like their London counterparts, respectable New Yorkers knew who the "dangerous classes" were. They were foreign-born, largely Irish, unskilled workers who possessed ominous political influence because of universal male suffrage. The English reformers who opened the door for working-class political participation in 1867 hoped to strengthen society by broadening the franchise. Americans could not devise such a conservative solution, for the very means which gave immigrants access to American institutions—loose naturalization laws which allowed them to become voting citizens—made them all the more threatening to many people. Democracy seemed to be the means of its own destruction.

New Yorkers counted up professional criminals during the sixties, although the police did not provide the precise figures Londoners relied upon and there was no Mayhew to chronicle criminal lifestyles. Most commentators, however, argued that the really dangerous elements were the immigrant poor who occasionally turned to crime. "No class is more costly or in a certain way more offensive to the metropolis than that which drops into crime . . . as an occasional interlude to more reputable employment . . . , constantly hovering on the outermost edge of the law, where only the slightest influence is required to push them beyond it." They were "part of that vast and ignorant multitude, who, in prosperous times, just keep their heads above water, who are pressed down by poverty and misfortune, and who look with envy and greed at the signs of wealth and luxury all around them, while they themselves have nothing but hardship, penury, and unceasing drudgery." New Yorkers were convinced that among the immigrants only "the dregs" settled in the city, while the better elements sought homes in the West. As David Montgomery observes, only in the big cities like New York or Boston did it seem as if the whole unskilled working class was made up of immigrants. Swelling statistics of the urban immigrant poor and their children arrested by the police, convicted by the courts, and confined in the prisons, hospitals, asylums, and almshouses reinforced many people's ancient attitudes toward poverty: the poor were indigent through their own failings, and crime was the natural result of their vices. James W. Gerard, the police reformer, asked why immigrants committed violent crimes in New York when they had been peaceful at home. He did not look to overcrowded living conditions and uncertain employment among unskilled workers, but argued that immigrants' "passions and criminal instincts" had been checked by strict laws and efficient police in Europe, whereas the law and police of democratic America did not compel their respect.[5]

American democracy added a political fear of immigrants to general concern about their vices and crimes. The Irish especially seemed not to be a group seeking an equal political role with natives but a socially dangerous element which took advantage of democratic institutions to weaken democracy itself. "That's the reason I dislike the Irish so much," a New Yorker told Francis Grund in the 1830s:

> They are scarcely a year in the country before they pretend to be equal to our *born* citizens. I should have no objection to their coming here, provided they would be contented to remain servants, — the only condition, by the by, they are fit for; but when they come without a cent in their pockets, pretending to enjoy the same privileges as our oldest and most respectable citizens, my blood boils with rage.

With rising immigration in the forties and fifties these sentiments crystallized into the nativist movement, and many New Yorkers argued that democracy was too lenient in granting the vote to "dangerous" elements, a leniency which would undermine democracy. Irish Catholic voters and public officials, they contended, threatened to impose European authoritarianism. Representative democracy could not survive demagogic politicians' manipulation of ignorant masses with alien beliefs and customs.[6]

One of the most disturbing manifestations of immigrant power was the "shoulder-hitter," the rough in his political role. The rough was a youth in his teens or early twenties, usually Irish or, by the sixties, the native-born son of immigrants. According to contemporaries, his rowdyism was a diversion from his occupation as cartman or laborer. Often armed with a club or pistol, the rough's drunken brawls contributed much of the city's violence. Good citizens found nothing good in him: "He is a social hyena, a rational jackal, utterly devoid of reverence or respect, whom education does not reach, and Society cannot tame." The roughs were "far more brutal than the peasantry from whom they descend.... They are our *enfants perdus,* grown up to young manhood.... They are ready for any offense or crime, however degraded or bloody." In the days of the volunteer fire laddies, they often found an outlet in the frequent brawls at fires, and were the rank and file of gangs like the Dead Rabbits and Bowery B'hoys. More disturbing to respectable citizens was the roughs' usefulness to political bosses as the kind of striking force suggested by the name "shoulder-hitter." They were always good for starting a brawl at the polls, intimidating voters, or roaming the city in gangs, repeatedly voting for their patrons and knocking down anyone who interfered. Because of their usefulness to elected officials, reformers charged that the roughs were the "protected powers" of the city, immune from the law. Riots and intimidation were certainly not unknown in English elections, and the fear of London roughs was at root political, but to New Yorkers roughs seemed to be a dangerously well-organized and pervasive alien element in democratic politics, which ideally rested on rational decisions by educated voters.[7]

Since they feared the "dangerous classes" as much, if not more, than did Londoners, upper- and middle-class New Yorkers expected firm police action against them. In the end, the British Parliament turned to new laws which expanded police power but also defined its limits. New York did not pass new laws, instead relying on the policeman's discretionary power to keep the lid on the volcano. There was a certain impatience with the forms of legality. If to put down crime, editorialized the *Herald* in 1856, "it were necessary for us to have a Turk as Chief of Police, we, for our own parts, would go for the Turk, turban, koran, and all." In an extreme expression of frustration, the New York Prison Association, founded in 1844 to reform prisons and aid discharged convicts, suggested abandonment of the principle of innocence until proven guilty when dealing with hardened criminals. The maxim "has, in our times and under our circumstances, become, so at least it appears to us, inconsistent with the security of society and with the dictates of true justice, when administered with all its ancient rigor." Nor was the *Times* patient with legal principles when it commented on a shocking case of gang-rape:

> It makes a Christian's blood curdle to read of such things, and while all sober impulses and all the rules of reason look to the strict administration of law as the only proper punishment for such crimes, there is a rising wrath that will not be calmed by forms and statutes: if every one of the ruffians engaged in this awful outrage had been then and there tied to the stake and very slowly roasted alive, there would not have been a tear shed over their fate.

Some of this language resembles that which preceded passage of the English Habitual Criminals Act of 1869. However, it was not precisely focused on released convicts, and there were no proposals for new laws resembling the English measure. New Yorkers looked to their policemen instead.[8]

Public acceptance of armed policemen as a necessary evil in the war against crime reflected the belief that legal procedures could not cope with urban violence. One of the earliest occasions of police use of firearms, the Seventeenth Ward German riot of July 1857, in which an innocent bystander was fatally shot, aroused considerable hostility to the new Metropolitan force. However, much of the criticism was soon dispelled by the shooting of Patrolman Anderson while arresting a notorious burglar. Civilian friends of the murdered officer twice tried to lynch the assailant; at one point the police had to threaten to fire into the crowd to save the prisoner's life. At Anderson's funeral a minister expressed many people's sympathy not only for him but for all policemen:

> He did not die as an individual. The customs of all time invest the officer of justice with peculiar sacredness. . . . He is the per-sonification of justice. He is the eye, soul, and arm of power. He is the sleepless guardian of private and social rights. . . . He is the defense of our property—the guardian of public peace and honor. When such a man falls the victim of lawless violence, the dearest rights of the community are struck down. It is felt as a blow at the heart of all that is dear and sacred in the blessings of life and of home.

145

A week after Anderson's death, the *Herald,* generally critical of the Metropolitan Police, advocated summary punishment of criminals: "The greatest terror that can be held out to these lawless vagabonds is the strong probability that exists of their being shot down in the act.... The law justifies and public opinion applauds the man who shoots down the burglar and the footpad."[9]

Similar attitudes prevailed over a year later when a policeman did inflict such summary punishment. While Patrolman Cairnes was taking "Sailor Jack," an Irish longshoreman considered dangerous and disorderly, to the station house the man struck him and tried to escape. Cairnes fired at the fleeing prisoner, killing him on the third shot. Witnesses' opinions were divided, some condemning the policeman as needlessly violent, others praising him for "his attempt to uphold the majesty of the law." A fellow officer arrested him, according to the law which subjected policemen to the same penalties as civilians for the improper use of firearms. He told Cairnes that he "must have been crazy to have used his pistol when he had plenty of assistance at hand," to which Cairnes replied that if he had to do it over, he would not do it again. Cairnes was generally respected as a "quiet inoffensive man" by his brother officers, who seemed "to feel keenly his position, but [were] in expectation that he will soon be liberated." A coroner's jury (usually composed of local tradesmen or artisans) found Cairnes guilty of unjustifiable homicide, and he had to remain in the Tombs without bail until his appearance before the court of general sessions, where his $10,000 bail was posted by one of New York's most prominent merchants. The grand jury (usually composed of more substantial citizens — business or professional men — than the coroner's jury) dismissed the case and freed the policeman.[10]

Except for the *Times,* the press withheld editorial comment. The *Times* pointed out that most people probably supported Cairnes because of "a general, and perfectly natural feeling in the community, that it is a positive godsend to get rid of one of the many scoundrels who infest our streets, by any means and through any agency possible." Many argued that crime was so serious that "there is absolutely no safety but in summary and even lawless measures, — that the Police are our sole reliance, and that they must have power to shoot down every ruffian who resists arrest or attempts to escape."[11] In light of the contrasting verdicts of the coroner's jury and the grand jury, these attitudes may have been more characteristic of upper- and middle-class than of working-class New Yorkers, who in some circumstances were liable to be taken for "ruffians."

Despite widespread trust in the police, the same *Times* editorial was apprehensive over a future in which "Every Policeman is to be an absolute monarch, within his beat, with complete power of life and death over all within his range, and armed with revolvers to execute his decrees on the instant, without even the forms of trial or legal inquiry of any kind." Reliance on armed policemen instead of on the rule of law was a grim reminder of "the degradation into which our local government has fallen, — nothing could show half so strongly the utter failure of an attempt to govern ourselves *by law,* and according to the fixed principles of justice." If crime were as serious as people believed, "let us meet the fearful emergency in some way less fatal to every conception of regulated republican freedom." No proposals were forthcoming, and the worst aspect of the next decade's growing number of shooting incidents was that they aroused "neither surprise nor remark in any quarter." [12] Instead of a government of law, New Yorkers accepted a government of men, the policemen whom their taxes supported to wage war on the "dangerous classes."

As in England, the 1860s were a pessimistic period. American reformers had originally placed their hopes on the rehabilitation of criminals through penal reform. Prison reformers had considered offenders individually capable of rehabilitation, and even though they blamed society for most crimes, they had not developed the notion of a permanent criminal class during the 1830s. By the fifties, however, increasing immigration and consequent social conflict focused attention on the growing proletariat and dispelled much of the early optimism. The police as an instrument of social control grew increasingly important during the fifties and sixties as prisons abandoned rehabilitation in favor of mere custody. [13]

The development of preventive police had followed the growth of prison reform in America — it was logical that if criminals were to be removed from social contamination by a poor environment, an efficient police would be the best means to remove them. In both England and America, however, the police functions of surveillance and apprehension outlived the prisons' reformatory efforts and became the dominant means of coping with crime in the nineteenth century. After the apparent failure and abandonment of prison reform in England, Parliament increased police powers over "habitual criminals"; New Yorkers (and other Americans) did not increase police legal powers but relied instead on informal or extralegal discretionary powers. Typically, the English turned to impersonal legal authority, the Americans to the policeman's personal authority on the street. The English tightened surveillance of the "dangerous classes"; the Americans tolerated informal police toughness. The difference was in the choice of means for the same end of crime control.

I have suggested earlier that "respectable" New Yorkers did not extend police legal powers because of their fears of how these might be used in the wrong hands. Consequently, perhaps, the law never seemed to be quite the bulwark of property and respectability that it was in England. American laws had never been as harsh as the old English "bloody code," and most of the cruel punishments of colonial laws were old-fashioned curiosities by the 1830s and 1840s.[14] Thus there was not the sense of steady legal improvement which Englishmen felt. Americans were proud of the humanity of their criminal codes, but, as we have seen, respect for the law seemed to be yielding to a disposition to take the law into one's own hands during the thirties. Unlike England, which witnessed steady amelioration of the legal system and a growth of respect for the law among the middle classes, America seemed to be growing increasingly impatient with legal forms and procedures.

The reason for this impatience among upper- and middle-class New Yorkers was not in the nature of the law itself, but in how it was administered by the courts. Respectable citizens shared the police view that judges, especially in the lower courts, were too lenient. They charged that judges acted corruptly from mercenary or political motives. Although some middle-class Londoners like Charles Dickens shared the working-class view of the police magistrates as unduly harsh, attacks on judicial leniency were rare and the magistrates were generally considered honest. New Yorkers, though, mistrusted the judiciary and turned to the police for justice in the battle with the "dangerous classes" because they lacked faith in "the capacity or common honesty of our legal tribunals."[15]

WORKING-CLASS RESPONSE TO THE POLICE

How did the largely immigrant working classes, lumped together by many citizens into the "dangerous" category, respond to the police? Unfortunately their views are much more difficult to trace than those of London workers. One problem is that it is hard to distinguish between the partisan arguments advanced by Democratic politicians and journalists, in their dispute with Republicans over control of the police, and the actual views of their working-class constituents. Did the Democratic spokesmen who claimed to represent the common

148

man really express his attitudes? When the Democrats controlled the police force, did they mold policy and practices according to the will of their constituents? Was there an Irish view or a working-class view of the police distinct from the opinions of politicians? These questions are difficult to answer because elected officials both reflect public opinion and manipulate or whip it up. For example, the outburst of Irish working-class hostility toward the Republican-controlled Metropolitan Police in 1857, the violence against policemen during the draft riots of 1863, and the simmering hostility toward the force throughout the sixties have elements of both spontaneity and the efforts of politicians trying to regain control of the police. While the voteless English working classes developed views of society and the political order which transcended differences among various groups and were independent of the middle-class-based political parties, American workers, apparently including the unskilled Irish, believed that through the ballot the existing political parties would reflect their interests. American democracy made it difficult to separate constituents' opinions from political partisanship.

One apparent effect of democracy seems to have been the undercutting of the "one law for the rich, another law for the poor" argument by legal reform and popular election of the judiciary. Radicals of the 1830s and 1840s argued that the complexity and expense of the legal system guaranteed that the rich would monopolize power and privilege. In 1836 the state convention of the Loco-focos, or radical wing of the Democrats, declared that "the practices of our courts of law are as aristocratic, arbitrary and oppressive as they were in the dark ages of feudalism." They argued that republican simplicity should replace inherited complexity and obscurity: "In a Republic but few laws are necessary, and those few plain, simple, and easy of comprehension." They urged that the English common law be supplanted by American statutes; if a statute did not exist, juries should act "according to principles of natural right and justice." Judges should be elected for limited terms. By 1846 these ideas were no longer so radical: Whigs and Democrats agreed to provisions of the new state constitution for codification of the criminal and civil laws and reform of judicial procedure, as well as popular election of the judiciary. Legal reformer David Dudley Field at once set to work, and after producing complete civil and criminal codes he secured passage of an act in 1857 for full codification of state law. The legislature actually moved very slowly and did not adopt many of Field's ideas, but there was a sense that democracy had breached the last citadel of aristocracy.[16]

Popular election of the judiciary became the bugbear of the "aristocrats." There is some evidence that the much-maligned police justices were sympathetic to poor defendants. The "Big Judge," Michael Connolly, won popular support in his feud with police Superintendent Kennedy over the liquor laws, and was known as "the very embodiment of good nature, and his kind heart and liberality to the poor, combined with his well-known social qualities, made him one of the most popular men in New York." Justice Joseph Dowling, a former police captain, "has sympathy with the poor creatures who are on trial, leans to the side of mercy, stands between the prisoner and the oppressor, becomes an advocate when the complainant is disposed to be crushing, and with the advice he gives, his warnings and admonitions, and even in his judgments, he sits more as a father than as a stern judge." Dowling uniformly discharged nondisorderly drunks and petty offenders who had been arrested for the first time. The quality of judicial mercy was sometimes strained by political considerations. A journalist familiar with the police courts found that in cases of assaults committed by young roughs — useful as "shoulder-hitters" at election time — the justices frequently dismissed the charges with a paternal warning to "go and sin no more." Even if mercy was tempered by politics, support of the judge at the next election was for a poor man a much smaller price than several nights in jail. What the police and many citizens condemned as leniency and corruption, many working-class New Yorkers may have seen as sympathy and humanity. At least one does not find their spokesmen attacking the popularly elected judiciary in the manner of London working-class journalists' criticism of the appointed magistracy.[17]

Although the laws were simpler and more democratically administered than in London, New Yorkers could still point to injustices. We have already heard criticisms of arbitrary police and judicial practices. Perhaps worst of all, because it was not directed at criminals or suspects, was the requirement that witnesses to a crime (including the victim if he were the only witness) had to post bail for their appearance at the trial. This often amounted to imprisonment simply because an individual was poor, for judges had no choice but to incarcerate witnesses who could not post bail. The bail requirement was originally instituted in New York in 1830 to preserve the prisoner's right to confront all witnesses against him. However, an imprisoned witness often suffered more punishment than the person charged with a crime. Flagrant abuses sometimes came to light.[18]

Witnesses were treated like criminals while imprisoned, and the "difference in favor of the felon is, that upon the trial he cannot be baited and questioned, racked and maddened by an insolent petti- fogger; while the witness, less happy, most assuredly must and will." The harshness of witness detention was relieved by the segregation of witnesses from other prisoners in the 1850s and by construction of the comfortable and well-run House of Detention for Witnesses in 1862, but detained witnesses were still not compensated for lost wages.[19]

In London witnesses unable to post bail had been incarcerated until the early 1840s, when public outcry forced magistrates to release them on their own recognizance. The New York Prison Association and the Metropolitan Police both suggested this simple solution for New York, and the state legislature's commission for revising the criminal code advised it; but nothing was done. Witnessing a crime, whether as complainant or observer, carried a grave risk of impoverishment after weeks of imprisonment while trial was pending. People learned that the safest thing was not to complain or testify at all, and justice was frustrated because witnesses hid until the offender was released on the basis of insufficient evidence. Tight-lipped silence must have greeted many police in- quiries about crime in working-class neighborhoods.[20]

Despite such injustice, the law was closer to the citizen than in England, and was administered by popularly elected officials. Similarly, the policeman who enforced the law was closer to the local community than his counterpart in London. Did this proximity foster amicable police-community relations? Many factors suggest that there was less tension between working-class New Yorkers and the locally controlled Municipal Police than was the case after 1857, under the state-controlled Metropolitan force. However, complaints of inefficiency and corruption keynote journalistic criticism of the Municipal Police. The force's most vociferous early critic was Mike Walsh, the anti-Tammany editor and politician who claimed to speak for the city's working classes. Walsh's expectations of the new police, expressed in his newspaper *The Subterranean,* were dim indeed. Three-fourths of the new officers "will be 'deadheads,' 'asses,' 'bootjacks,' and 'blaitherskites.'" The rest will be the corrupt members of the old police forces, with only a few "from among the boys, and perhaps a scattering decent, clever fellow, who may have luck or brass enough to secure a place." Even most of these men, however, will soon learn the old police officers' "base and unlawful mode of transacting business, as has been practiced for years in this city." Walsh called portly Chief Matsell a "walking mass of moral and physical putrefaction" and a "degraded and pitiful lump of blubber and meanness." The police regulations? "The regulations, as they stand, would disgrace a school boy, and any attempt to enforce two-thirds of them would result in the maiming of all the menial hirelings in the department." Generally he regarded the police as "very properly despised and detested by the community."[21] It is difficult to know just how much of the community Walsh represented, but certainly his readers must have shared his feelings. His language makes British working-class criticism of the police seem quite restrained.

Attacks on inefficiency and corruption continued under the Metropolitan force, but charges of secrecy, arbitrariness, and brutality dominate papers like the *Herald* and *World,* which claimed to speak for broader segments of the working classes than Walsh reached. These papers generally endorsed the views of the "regular" Democratic local politicians. While the Republican *Times* criticized the uncontrolled use of firearms, it did not share the Democratic *Herald*'s sympathy with the German Seventeenth Ward rioters of 1857 or its denunciation of "Mr. Fouché Kennedy's" force, "fast assuming an aspect so odious, and insufferable that the people will be compelled at last to revolt against it and overthrow it altogether." Some indication of the level of hostility to the new force is the jump in arrests for assaulting policemen after 1857, although it is difficult to know whether the figures measure police policy or actual assaults. The assault arrests dropped in 1862, suggesting some reconciliation with the new force, but the draft rioters' brutality toward the police in 1863 belies such an interpretation. The violence suggests a settlement of old scores against a force created and imposed by Republicans and against active enforcers of the draft law and the hated Sunday blue laws. Moreover, the Metropolitan force patrolled the streets of the Five Points more actively than the old Municipal Police had.[22] Table 11 gives some idea of how the force was concentrated.

After the Civil War the police were the object of political and judicial campaigns against Sunday law enforcement, as well as a target of the home rule campaign which culminated in return of the force to municipal control under the Tweed Charter of 1870. Signs indicate a deterioration of police relations with the largely Irish unskilled working class, fostered by partisan conflict over control of the force.

To what extent did the Metropolitan Police's abandonment of the

TABLE 11
Police-Population Ratios in Selected Wards,
New York City*

Ward	1855	1860	1864
1	1 : 228	1 : 204	1 : 156
6	1 : 464	1 : 460	1 : 282
15	1 : 601	1 : 520	1 : 370
17	1 : 1,240	1 : 1,158	1 : 1,420

SOURCES: My computations are from numbers of police (patrolmen only) given in D. T. Valentine, comp., *Manual of the Corporation of the City of New York,* for the year following the one given. Population is from the table on p. 216 of Joseph Shannon, comp., *Manual of the Corporation of the City of New York 1868.* The figure for the 1864 computation is the 1865 population for the ward.

local residency requirement worsen public relations? Was the policeman's personal authority more acceptable when he was a local figure known to his neighbors? The old residency requirement produced a large number of Irish policemen in Irish neighborhoods. Did common ethnicity lead to better community relations? Did Irish patrolmen soften the law's impact upon their compatriots? These questions are extremely difficult to answer on the basis of available evidence; also, police-community relations depend on complex personal interaction, which does not show up in tangible ways. Nevertheless, figures can provide some leads.

James Richardson cites nativist accusations that Irish law enforcement officials were lenient toward their countrymen during the 1850s, but available arrest records suggest that Irish-surname officers made at least as many arrests as their WASP colleagues for the largely Irish misdemeanors of drunkenness, disorderly conduct, and petty larceny. Blotters for the Tenth Ward (13 percent Irish-born residents in 1855) for the summer months of 1855 and 1856 are the only surviving documents which provide both the arresting officer's name and his prisoner's name and nativity. Irish offenders accounted

*In every ward here except the Seventeenth, there was a substantial increase of policemen between 1860 and 1864, probably as a result of the draft riots. The Seventeenth Ward was not near the rioting and did not provide rioters in large numbers. The Sixth Ward contained the Five Points and was called "The Bloody Old Sixth." The First Ward contained a substantial Irish population (46 percent in 1855, compared to the Sixth Ward's 42 percent) *and* Wall Street. That may well explain the concentration of police there. The Fifteenth Ward was a wealthy residential area, containing Washington Square and part of fashionable Fifth Avenue. It was near the riot areas, but did not border directly on the city's toughest wards.

153

for about 40 percent of the arrests recorded, mostly for drunkenness and disorderly conduct. Irish-surname officers arrested between 20 and 40 percent of these Irish-born offenders. This proportion was close to the approximately 25 percent Irish-surname officers on the Tenth Ward force. Finally, under the locally controlled Municipal Police, complaints of violence and/or improper arrest, averaging some 29 a year, were not much fewer when Irish patrolmen dealt with Irish citizens than when WASP officers confronted them. Of 261 complaints of violence and improper arrest heard before the mayor in 1845–54, 44 involved Irish-surname policemen and Irish-surname civilians, while 54 involved WASP-surname officers and Irish-surname complainants. Common ethnicity does not seem to have significantly affected arrest and complaint patterns.[23]

Richardson is well aware of the difficulty of deciding whether Irish policemen would be easier on their countrymen because of common ethnicity, and is forced to conclude, "Unfortunately, there seems to be no way of measuring . . . or even forming defensible impressions."[24] However, there does seem to be some evidence for forming a defensible — if not definitive — impression that more factors separated local policemen from their countrymen than united them. As indicated by frequent use of the word "may," the following discussion is impressionistic and speculative.

High turnover among policemen before good-behavior tenure was established in 1853 may have interfered with the development of close police-community ties. Moreover, the great amount of geographical mobility which historians have discovered among mid-nineteenth-century unskilled workers does not suggest lasting acquaintance between policemen and the class with which they most often came into official contact. Class, in fact, may have separated Irish policemen from local residents in areas dominated by unskilled Irish laborers and their families. New York policemen were better paid than their London brethren, earning $800 per year in the later fifties (raised to $1,200 in 1860) compared to the equivalent of $239–$378 for the various classes of London patrolmen. London's low pay resulted in a high proportion of recruits from the ranks of unskilled labor, but New York policemen made about as much as the most skilled workers — in the early 1850s they earned $500 per year compared to the $520 or so per year that highly skilled workers received in 1851. Fragmentary surviving data reveal that out of forty-three successful applicants to the force in 1855, there were twenty-two skilled artisans of various sorts, one "mechanic" or skilled industrial worker, five shopkeepers, five clerks and other white-collar workers, seven drivers or other transportation workers, and only three unskilled laborers. Skilled-worker policemen of the forties and fifties, who according to the 1850 and 1860 censuses usually lived among artisans or small tradesmen, may not have had much sympathy for the unskilled group at the bottom of the social ladder. Finally, family and age differences between policemen and the most common group of offenders, single men in their teens and twenties, may also have counterbalanced common ethnicity or local residence. New York patrolmen in 1850 and 1860 were mostly married men with one or two children, and they averaged about 35 years of age, being ten years older than their London brethren. Thus various social factors seem to have mitigated the possible cohesive effects of a common ethnic background between policemen and unskilled laborers, the group which most often ran afoul of the law.[25]

It is possible that the Irish background of both policemen and offenders may have encouraged rather than dampened violence. Policemen and local residents may both have been inclined to settle disputes by violence instead of by persuasion or legality, a trait which modern writers have described as inherited from centuries of oppression in the old country. Policemen and citizens alike may have expected roughness as a matter of course. Furthermore, the Irish policeman's experience may have been similar to that of the modern black patrolman in New York. A sociologist has documented the cross-pressures from the police department and different sectors of the community which beset black policemen. Some officers respond by ignoring petty offenses to avoid hostile confrontations and accusations of serving "the man"; others become tough in order to win personal respect based on fear, and meet the demands of many people in the community for order. We cannot recapture the mentality of the mid-nineteenth-century Irish patrolman, but when we read of an Irish ex-Municipal policeman being beaten up by rioters who recognized him, the suggestion is strong that there was little love between policemen and at least some elements of their neighbors whom they kept in line.[26]

Since Irishmen remained a strong element of the Metropolitan Police, it seems clear that the policies of the men in charge of the force and the political controversy surrounding it were the main factors in the worsening of public relations after 1857. With growing class antagonism after the draft riots, the propertied classes and many skilled workers placed greater faith in the police than before,

155

and the unskilled Irish workers grew more hostile. The draft riots were a recognized turning point, a crucible from which the loyalty of Irish policemen to the force emerged, tested by battle with their countrymen. Even when more unskilled workers came into the force after the Civil War because of lagging salaries, it was clear that policemen's first loyalty was to the force. Their personal authority embodied the expectations of probably most New Yorkers that the "dangerous classes" should be dealt with firmly. Citizens were divided, often bitterly, over who should control the police and what laws they should enforce, but there were few articulate challenges to the patrolman's broad discretionary power. That did not change when the city regained control of the force in 1870.

SABBATARIANS AND THE POLICE: LAWS, RESISTANCE, AND DILEMMAS

The New York force's experience with the "Sunday question" highlighted all the ambivalent public responses to the police and revealed its inability to maintain an independent position amid social and political conflict. As in the similar case of the policy to be followed in drunkenness arrests, middle-class reformers overrode their usual tolerance of broad discretion and demanded that the police strictly enforce the letter of the law. In this controversy, it was the working classes that favored broad discretion, which would allow them to evade the Sunday laws as long as they were orderly. This seems to have been the view of many policemen as well, but after 1857 political pressure prevented them from acting as they thought best. As a result, the police lost authority among the working classes instead of improving their position as occurred in London.

Like England, mid-nineteenth-century America witnessed a surge of evangelicalism which was channeled into social reform as well as religious revival. English evangelicals were more successful as a moral influence than as a political pressure group; American evangelicals managed to obtain the laws they wanted but had less effect upon the habits of the groups they sought to reform. This difference cannot be traced to differences in doctrine, for English and American sabbatarians communicated with each other and exchanged ideas. Nor, although there is some evidence to suggest it, were American evangelicals politically successful because America was more religious than England. The explanation of New York sabbatarians' legislative success lies in differences between the social structure and institutions of England and America.[27]

156

Sabbatarianism in New York was principally the product of the settlement of both the city and the state by New Englanders in the early nineteenth century. In 1813 the state legislature passed a Sunday law as strict as the measure Sir Andrew Agnew sought for London in 1833. Sabbatarians looked back on the early years as a time when New York City enjoyed the benefits of the traditional New England Puritan sabbath, although violations were inevitable in a heterogeneous port city. Beginning in the later 1820s, the growth of immigration made the city seem more disorderly and less respectful of traditional ways. Sabbatarians increasingly rallied in defense of the quiet Sunday, especially with the influx and concentration of Irish and Germans in certain neighborhoods during the 1840s and 1850s. They argued that the "Continental Sunday" as a day of recreation and potation would contaminate the native population and destroy the old-fashioned Yankee sabbath, the foundation of American free government.[28]

Unlike the situation in London, New York sabbatarians had tradition on their side; it was the antisabbatarians who were foreign. Sabbatarianism reflected not only the evangelical impulse but also WASP resentment of immigrants, which took the political form of nativist parties. Sunday laws were strictly enforced when the Native American party captured the municipal government in 1844.[29] The appeal of sabbatarians as defenders of tradition against an alien onslaught was an important part of their legislative success.

Moreover, in defending their tradition, sabbatarians did not confront a traditional aristocracy which supported working-class sabbath-profaners for political and social reasons. America's elite seems to have been more "Victorian" than much of England's aristocracy. New York City sabbatarians came from the urban elite: the nativist mayor of 1844, James Harper, belonged to the prestigious publishing family, while wealthy merchants, doctors, and lawyers joined clergymen as the backbone of the New York Sabbath Committee, the city's most influential sabbatarian organization.[30] Although similar types supported English sabbatarianism, upper-class supporters had to face many of their own rank on the other side of the issue. Also, in New York it was puritanism rather than antipuritanism which transcended class lines: native American workers often resented the alien customs as well as the economic threat of immigrant workers.

New York City, the "metropolis of the New World," was not even the political metropolis of its own state. The state legislature, which

157

sat in Albany amid predominantly sabbatarian citizens, enacted the city's Sunday laws for it. The battle over the Sunday question was not really a conflict of rural and urban values; initiative for legislation came from urban dwellers who, though they lost influence in city politics, commanded respect upstate and could afford to travel for extensive lobbying activities. The legislature was an essential ally in one urban group's efforts to reform the manners of a larger urban group which could outvote sabbatarians in local elections. As long as Republicans, the party of puritanism, controlled the state legislature, sabbatarians had a good reception.[31] Urban antisabbatarians, like their London counterparts, organized and protested, but their complaints were ignored until the Democrats gained control of the state legislature in the late 1860s. New York City residents, who were predominantly antisabbatarian, like Londoners, had less direct influence on legislative action. Only a minority, the sabbatarians, reached the ears of the upstate legislators.

As in London, the attitude of the police toward Sunday laws was important, but since the New York force was a creature of politics it was not as independent and consequently reflected which party controlled it rather than its own views. As we shall see, however, there was some tension between the men who actually had to enforce the laws and the high officials who set general policy. If working policemen had had their way, New York's experience would have resembled London's.

The Sunday question aroused most controversy from 1858 to 1870, because the antisabbatarian Irish and Germans had become powerful political blocs and the sabbatarians had formed their first large-scale organization, the New York Sabbath Committee, in 1857. Before 1858 the police responded to intermittent sabbatarian pressures by sporadic enforcement campaigns which lasted only as long as public pressure was on them. They preferred to ignore the matter, as in London, avoiding trouble instead of creating it, for antisabbatarianism was strong and generally supported by local politicians. On one occasion in 1854, when the city council demanded that the police chief report "without delay" why "groceries and rum-holes" remained open on Sunday, he replied that enforcement was not up to the police but to the justices of the peace and aldermen of each ward. If these elected officials were willing to risk their popularity by closing saloons and groceries, the chief, perhaps a bit wryly, promised police cooperation. Few officials took up Matsell's invitation. In addition there were many legal restrictions on police surveillance of places selling liquor. Officers could not enter any saloon unless an actual disturbance were in progress, proof of illegal sales was difficult to obtain, and liquor sellers could not be arrested without a warrant. Attitudes and institutions seemed to weigh against sabbatarianism.[32]

In 1855 Mayor Fernando Wood, who won election as a reformer, mobilized the police for an all-out Sunday closing drive. Newspapers were astounded at his immediate success: *"On Sunday the liquor shops were shut up!"*; "The age of miracles is evidently not yet past." Policemen even watched secret back doors, and a reserve corps in plain clothes was placed on duty to detect violators. "Fast young gentlemen . . . might be seen in groups of three and four passing from one grog shop to another to see if they couldn't 'wet up' as they termed it," but their search was in vain. Many Democrats who voted for Wood complained of betrayal. The mayor pointed with satisfaction to improved public order: in the first two months of 1855 the police made less than half the number of drunkenness arrests as in the same period the previous year. He prided himself on securing Sunday closing without arrests or revocation of liquor licenses. His secret of success may have been the saloons' tie to Wood's own party, the Democrats. He may also have told liquor sellers what he reportedly said to an alderman: he favored Sunday closing as a way to "head off" the state legislature's contemplated total prohibition law.[33]

The legislature did indeed pass a prohibition law, the Act for the Prevention of Intemperance, Pauperism, and Crime. This was New York's version of the Maine law, which outlawed all liquor sales except for "mechanical, chemical or medicinal purposes" and sacramental wine. Temperance advocates thought that Wood would enforce the new law against "all offenders, high and low, rich and poor" because of his "high moral attitude" as revealed in the Sunday closing and other reform campaigns. However, with the cooperation of other city officials Wood launched a program of nullification and interposition which John C. Calhoun would have admired. Not only did the loosely worded law arouse public hostility, but it was full of holes which imaginative officials and liquor sellers took full advantage of. Prohibition quickly became a dead letter. People arrested for intoxication swore that they got drunk in New Jersey, or that somebody gave the liquor to them, or that they did not know where they got it. Some corner groceries closed their bars but welcomed well-known patrons "behind the scenes." The *Times* lamented that

"This spectacle of law, enacted for so benevolent a purpose, so completely nullified and contemned, does not excite in the public mind any such feeling of indignation as it would naturally be expected to create." Wood's sabotage of prohibition, assisted by the same police force which had previously enforced Sunday closing, marked his falling-out with moral reformers.[34]

Prohibition's informal, and later official, demise forced reformers to return to sabbatarianism. Sunday at least should be free from the week's vices, and the principal target was drinking, for Sunday food sales do not seem to have been as extensive in New York as in London. Sabbatarians obtained stricter liquor controls from the legislature and succeeded in abolishing German Sunday theaters which featured music or melodrama and foaming steins of beer. The years 1857–58 were propitious for sabbatarians for two reasons. First was the state legislature's passage in 1857 of the Metropolitan Police Act, which wrested control of the force from Fernando Wood and placed it in the hands of state-appointed commissioners. In practice this meant Republican control of the force and a greater sympathy among police officials for moralistic reform. The act contained a Sunday closing provision with a fifty-dollar fine for each violation. Second, 1857–58 witnessed a religious revival, greatly accelerated by the financial panic of late 1857 but having its beginnings before the crisis. By the spring of 1858 daily noon prayer meetings were held throughout the city. Now attitudes and institutions seemed favorable to sabbatarian efforts.[35]

Coinciding with passage of the new police law and the beginnings of the revival, in the spring of 1857 thirty-eight influential "Christian laymen of the various evangelical churches," alarmed at flagrant violations of the Sunday laws, called a meeting to discuss ways of improving sabbath observance. The meeting led to formation of the New York Sabbath Committee, which stressed the need for a "civil sabbath" as a day of rest to allow people to worship as they saw fit. The well-heeled committee promptly began lobbying with city and state officials and instituted missionary work among the Germans, a religiously and politically divided, largely middle- and skilled working-class group whom the Republicans were wooing in the late fifties. The working-class Irish Catholics were apparently beyond redemption.[36] Not only was the committee able to influence legislators in Albany, but the heads of the police supported their crusade. Unlike the London commissioners, the predominantly Republican Metropolitan Police commissioners favored strict Sunday laws, including all-day saloon closing.

Before the sabbath committee's campaign got under way, New York witnessed a premonition of the opposition that Sunday closing would arouse. Police Captain Jedediah W. Hartt of the Seventeenth Ward, a self-proclaimed "cold-water man," determined to close beer halls on Sunday in the city's German district. His efforts aroused the anger of normally peaceful Germans and led to a two-day riot in which shots were exchanged between the police and the crowd, killing an innocent bystander. A protest meeting attended by over three thousand people accused "the Commissioners of the Metropolitan Police and their tools to be the rioters, and that the Commissioners, in order to parade their authority, jeopardized the peace and lives of the citizens; and by so doing justify the contempt which they have deserved so richly." The German press condemned German policemen for being involved in the affair.[37] Unlike London's Hyde Park demonstration, however, this incident did not daunt sabbatarians, and police officials continued to support Sunday closing.

Having spent 1858 in a campaign against the minor nuisance of newsboys crying Sunday papers for sale, the sabbath committee attacked the Sunday liquor traffic in 1859. The police had not closed saloons and beer halls because the district attorney rarely prosecuted and juries rarely convicted violators. After the committee presented the commissioners with a petition signed by some thousand respectable citizens, the police moved toward vigorous enforcement. German and WASP antisabbatarians counter-petitioned, but the commissioners replied that "The laws of the land, in conformity with the opinion of the masses of the people . . . are not to be disregarded or repealed, because of peculiar notions of morals entertained by small portions of the community."[38] Unfortunately, the portions were quite large, which policemen on the beat appreciated more than did their commanders.

Despite official determination, Amos Pilsbury, the general superintendent or chief executive officer of the police force, moved cautiously. Although antisabbatarians called him "pious Pilsbury," he seems to have been more sensitive than his superiors to the difficulties of Sunday closing enforcement. While many people had expected dramatic police "descents" and seizures of illegal liquor, and Pilsbury declared he would enforce the law, it was actually enforced as in the past: merely taking violators' names for subsequent prosecution by the district attorney. Since the law specified *closing* of saloons, the police were not exercising their full powers. Pilsbury continued this policy for about a month, despite the urgings of many, including four "teetotal" police captains, for strict enforcement and the commissioners' resolution that violations should be prevented by "the whole power of the police force."[39]

Under this pressure Pilsbury ordered the complete closing of places selling liquor on Sunday. This order, strict as it seemed on the surface, was considerably qualified in the superintendent's directions for carrying it out:

> In the enforcement of these Sunday statutes, while you are required to be firm, impartial, and discreet, you will neverthe- less be expected to pay careful regard to the rights of our citi- zens, who, without injury to public order or private immunity, are entitled to observe their respective and accustomed methods of rest, devotion, or relaxation.

This directive left much up to individual captains, and even patrol- men, in deciding what "rights" or "accustomed methods" of rest and relaxation were. Moreover, Pilsbury "did not deem it his duty or that of the police to interfere with side [secret] entrances, or with hotel proprietors in furnishing liquor to their guests." As to closing lager beer halls, he would leave it to the captains' judgment whether beer was an intoxicating beverage, a matter of controversy in New York courts at the time. Since policemen were not allowed into a public house unless a disturbance were in progress, they could do little if anything about secret drinking even if determined to stamp it out.[40]

The antisabbatarian *Herald* asserted that Pilsbury's campaign was motivated by hypocritical political considerations, but sabbatarians were glad to see quieter Sundays even though they noticed that the police were not using their full powers. If Pilsbury was not political, he was at least politic: while orderly Sundays were obtained, the law did not bear too hard on anybody who wanted to tipple in secret, or for that matter to indulge in lager beer in a precinct where the captain had decided that beer was not intoxicating. Secret drinking seems to have been more orderly than open indulgence, perhaps because no one was willing to stagger into the street and reveal the source of his liquor. Pilsbury managed to close down Irish "low groggeries," places selling cheap whiskey which were generally disorderly, but he seems to have declared an armistice with beer halls and other German recreations. Irish whiskey seems to have had more violent effects than German lager, and the superintendent acted accordingly. Like the London commissioners, he was more con- cerned with improved public order than moral reform.[41]

In 1860 Amos Pilsbury resigned and was replaced by John A.

Kennedy, an active Republican who exercised his authority with determination. Kennedy, backed by the commissioners, undertook stricter enforcement of Sunday laws. Enforcement was irregular until he ordered the arrest of open violators and confinement in the station houses. This move intimidated many saloon-keepers, who did not want to stay locked up all night even though they knew that on Monday morning the police justices, who owed their office to immigrant votes, would probably discharge them. Open sales were rare, though sabbatarians still complained of side-door business. The commissioners were satisfied that "the practice hitherto so general, has in great degree ceased, and, though there are many public desecrations of the Sabbath, offensive to the moral portion of the community, yet enforcement . . . has removed the most prominent and objectionable."[42]

Since the police were enforcing Sunday closing of politically influential saloons, the city officials who had nullified the 1855 prohibition law interposed themselves between the state-controlled police force and their constituents' drinking habits. Their campaign seriously crippled Sunday law enforcement by 1865. Typical of elected officials' attitudes was Justice Brennan's remark after discharging a group of violators: "When I go into such places to get some oysters, I generally call for something to drink after eating, and I would like to see anyone bother me." City Judge McCunn delivered an interesting opinion on Sunday laws, defining "beverage" as "the act of *publicly,* with open doors, selling and drinking spiritous liquors." Therefore Sunday drinking behind closed doors was legal; saloons could not be prevented from operating in this discreet manner.[43]

Because of the municipal judiciary's attitudes the police could do nothing about Sunday violations by 1865. Places were wide open, and disorder increased. Sunday drunk and disorderly arrests now exceeded weekday arrests by 25 percent, whereas from August 1859 to February 1861, despite secret drinking, Sunday arrests had been 50 percent less than weekday arrests. Fighting back, the police commissioners and the sabbath committee both called for a stricter liquor law.[44]

In 1866 the state legislature granted this wish, passing the toughest liquor control measure yet enacted. The sabbath committee claimed credit for preparing and securing passage of the new law. The Excise Act of 1866 gave the police commissioners full control over liquor licensing and for the first time allowed policemen to arrest Sunday violators without a warrant. The measure did not enact new principles of liquor regulation, seeking rather to secure more effective licensing and Sunday closing.[45]

The new law aroused further opposition and nullification efforts. Democrats charged that it was simply a means of securing Republican control of the liquor trade. WASPs who believed that beer was a harmless substitute for hard liquor joined Germans in opposing the measure's specification of beer in its Sunday closing provisions. Three judges issued 854 injunctions against police interference with beer halls. They were seeking to establish a compromise: most people recognized whiskey's contribution to disorder and consented to closing of whiskey saloons. Moreover, beer was no longer an exclusively German beverage; by the later sixties WASPs and Irishmen were also enjoying lager. Public order improved after the injunctions. No longer did "thirsty infuriated swarms" flock to New Jersey or the suburbs. Beer halls thrived under judicial blessing, and the police reported decreased drunkenness despite their operation. Later the law was suspended entirely pending the outcome of test cases in higher courts. Liquor sales were unrestricted until the Court of Appeals upheld the excise law's constitutionality on the last day of 1866. The police noticed that during the law's suspension drunkenness arrests increased, presumably due to the free flow of hard liquor.[46]

Following the court action Superintendent Kennedy ordered both whiskey and beer sellers to be "completely and effectually closed" on Sunday. Special hourly "liquor watches" were able to enforce the law during the winter; however, during the summer the police could only eliminate visible disorder, not secret drinking. Disorder migrated to New Jersey, which had no Sunday closing. Many of those who stayed home on Sunday had laid in an extra amount of liquor on Saturday night and spent the sabbath in "a state of beastly intoxication." According to the *Times,* the police were not to be blamed for enforcement difficulties, for "probably three-fourths of the adult community believe in free traffic in liquor."[47]

Nullification having failed, opponents of liquor control sought repeal of the excise act. They were unsuccessful until 1870, when the new Democratic-controlled state legislature enacted a new city charter which not only abolished the excise law but also did away with the Metropolitan Police, returning the force to local control. A German paper chided the sabbatarians: "However gladly they would continue their Sunday tricks, they have absolutely not the power to do so; they must see with silent anger in their heart how the Puritan prejudice is mocked and violated."[48]

Horace Greeley had pointed out in 1867 that Sunday closing was enforced only because the policemen were responsible to state, not city, officials. Without state enforcement of the law, he warned that the city would be in the hands of the antisabbatarian forces, whom he saw as men who "gratify their own sensual desires in defiance of morality" or who "make money out of such gratification by others." Enforcement did break down in 1870–71: Sunday sales were open, with a consequent increase of disorderly drunkenness. Even after reformers had vanquished the Tweed ring, the *Times* complained that

> Sunday, in this city, still maintains its bad pre-eminence as a day of drunkenness, and of the crimes and offenses that come from drunkenness. The list for yesterday is terribly long, and includes every variety of stand-up and knock-down fight, shooting, stabbing, wife beating and street rowdyism. Most of these crimes are attributable to the looseness of the Excise law, and the negligent way in which it is enforced.[49]

Liquor traffic was technically regulated by the state Excise Act of 1867, which the Tweed ring and other politicians found useful "to exert discipline and to exact a fee from saloons on the wrong side of the political tracks" who remained open on Sunday. The combination of a weak law which could be selectively enforced for political reasons and popular resistance to all Sunday measures became the basis of systematic corruption of the police force. The payoff at the saloon's side door, while it undoubtedly occurred under the Municipal and Metropolitan Police, was the foundation of a pyramid of graft which became quite complex by the end of the nineteenth century. The story of Sunday laws in New York closes differently than its counterpart in London, where a police official warned of the consequences of unenforceable laws. Here such laws remained on the books as a useful tool of political discipline rather than an agency of moral reform.[50]

Repudiating any accommodation between public order and popular habits of the kind that Amos Pilsbury and some members of the judiciary had tried to work out, sabbatarians brooked no compromise. Dedicated to what Thurman Arnold has called the "Creed of Law Enforcement," they demanded adherence to the letter of unenforceable laws. As Charles Loring Brace, himself a reformer, said, "Our reformers ... as a class, are exceedingly adverse to concessions; they look at questions of habits as absolute questions of right and wrong, and they will permit no halfway or medium ground."[51] Such rigidity proved in the end to be the source of their defeat. It also weakened public and police respect for the rule of law. The policeman, caught between conflicting notions of order, found discretion to be the better part of valor by ignoring the law. If so minded, he was also in a position to exploit it for his own profit. However he acted, he was not likely to see himself or to be seen as an impartial agent of the law.

POLICEMEN AND THEIR PUBLICS

In both London and New York the policed reacted to the police according to their social position and political beliefs. London's propertied classes accepted the impersonal authority of the bobby as a means of maintaining order with a minimum of violence, turning to tougher laws when the police had difficulty coping with crime. The working classes continued to resent the force's role in upholding "one law for the rich, another law for the poor," but most of their violent hostility was diverted to grumbling acquiescence by a policy of restrained force. If the police seemed to be more forceful than restrained, they nevertheless did not ride roughshod over the working classes. In New York the propertied classes and many of the skilled workers who valued American democracy accepted the policeman's personal authority as the best means of coping with the "dangerous classes" of immigrant unskilled workers who threatened social revolution. Such acceptance persisted even though the police were the center of partisan conflict and continued to be criticized for inefficiency and corruption. The largely Irish immigrants reacted to the police mostly according to who controlled the force and what policies it pursued; politicians championed their cause against the successful efforts of reformers to divorce the police from local control, eventually regaining it for city officials. Public response to both police forces was as mixed as the public itself, reflecting the social structure with its stratification and conflicts.

EPILOGUE
THE LEGACY OF
POLICE TRADITION

One can recognize modern London and New York policemen in the portraits I have drawn of their great-grandfathers. Nevertheless, in spite of the family resemblance, both forces have undergone numerous changes since 1870, and many of their problems of public relations have been experienced in cities with similar social conflicts. Generally in recent years the New York police have consciously sought a more professional, impersonal image, tying themselves more closely to the rule of law than in the past through both external pressures and internal efforts. The old emphasis on broad personal discretion has hardly disappeared, but it is being somewhat modified. Many citizens believe that the hands of the police have been tied by too many legal and administrative regulations, but an equally significant group argues that the police need still more control. The London force, apparently not so consciously, seems to be moving away from its strict legalism toward a more personal, discretionary authority which reflects public expectations more than legal restraints. As in New York, many Londoners applaud this departure from police tradition while others decry it as oppressive and dangerous. The changes in both forces reveal that the two police traditions are growing fuzzy around the edges rather than undergoing any major qualitative transformation. As was the case in the contrast of styles in the nineteenth century, the changes are more of degree than of kind, and they also reflect two changing societies.

Mid-twentieth-century America no longer shares the broad faith in democratic political and social institutions which existed a hundred years ago. Class conflict has a racial dimension which, while it recalls earlier ethnic conflicts, is more ominous because the traditional channels of mobility for foreign white immigrants are

167

scarcely available to today's urban blacks. Conflict reached its peak in the 1960s, arousing public fears but also prompting politicians to coopt blacks into the lower levels of the "establishment," just as England's reforming elite did with first the middle classes and later the workers. This combination of fear and efforts to soothe black anger recalls the position of "respectable" people toward the nineteenth-century English working class. Both reactions influenced the New York and other urban police forces. On the one hand, a large segment of the public demanded instant suppression of crime and violent protests; on the other, blacks and civil libertarians demanded increased minority recruitment and regulation of police practices.

At first in these racial conflicts the police acted as they had always done, applying the usual informal and unregulated methods of crime control and maintenance of public order. However, these seemed to provoke still more disorder and mounting criticism of the force. Police officials, often prodded from outside, realized the dangers of traditional practices and responded to court rulings and the unwillingness of many influential citizens to tolerate the practices they had taken for granted in the past. As in London during the mid-nineteenth century, many New York police officials seem to have realized that restoration of a tarnished image required measures designed to moderate instead of exacerbate social tension. The resulting changes, which may or may not have achieved their goal, influenced many areas of police work.

An important emphasis of recent police reform has been professionalization, including testing and training programs, establishment of uniform procedures and internal accountability, and other measures which reduce policemen's personal discretion and promote general efficiency. While professionalization did improve the force, many critics charge that it has produced excessive centralization and bureaucratization which alienates the police from black and Puerto Rican communities. They advocate a return to decentralized local control, much in the spirit of the Jacksonian public officials who first established New York's police.[1] Community control is unlikely, but the department has made some moves toward decentralization and restoration of police-community contact.

Many reformers believe that extensive recruitment of minority group members will reduce tensions, although it has become clear that common ethnicity is not a panacea for police-public relations. New York began stepping up black recruitment in the sixties, and recently the police abolished the height requirement which in-advertently excluded shorter Puerto Rican recruits. Increasing attention to minority recruitment has brought one reform into conflict with another. Almost immediately after police officials accepted the professionalizers' emphasis on strict admission standards and full educational testing of recruits, advocates of increased minority recruitment began urging a relaxation of standards to admit capable but often poorly prepared applicants. The conflict remains to be worked out.

Sophisticated technological advances have reduced the necessity of force in police work, but New York policemen, despite stricter regulations and greater caution in the use of firearms than in the past, have not been able to escape the cycle of violence which has haunted America. Policemen have inflicted death deliberately and accidentally, and have often themselves been victims. An interesting recent development, however, was the department's dismissal of an officer whom the jury had acquitted of the charge of murdering a black youth. The department criticized his lack of judgment in firing the shots at all.[2] Clearly the jury and the patrolman's superiors had different expectations of his conduct. The episode reveals the sort of cross-pressures of public and official opinion to which the cop on the beat is subject.

The New York policeman's subordination to the rule of law has increased greatly since the nineteenth century, largely due to Supreme Court decisions under Chief Justice Warren. The more conservative Burger Court has weakened some of the protections for suspects in favor of greater police discretion in arrest and interrogation practices. However, what is different from the past is the explicit judicial sanction of broadened police powers, which results in greater integration of the police and court systems. While different judgments may be made about this integration, at least it reduces the past conflict and frustration which fostered extralegality.

One venerable and persistent aspect of New York's police tradition is corruption. Despite professionalization and the elimination of old-time political favoritism in most large urban forces, the Knapp Commission revealed widespread corruption in many branches of the New York force. Many of the tried and true methods of the past continue today; much of this modern corruption is the legacy of unenforceable vice laws.

In London, crimes of violence and political protests also increased markedly during the 1960s. Although the level of violence was still far below that of American cities, it was disturbing to Englishmen who prided themselves on their orderly society. As in New York, many Londoners pressured the police to suppress disorder regardless of the means, demanding that bobbies be released from some of their traditional restraints. This is the important difference between the demand for order in the two cities: in New York the public urged the police to act as they had in the past; in London the pressure was against a well-established tradition of subordination to the rule of law. The important question is whether tradition can survive such pressure. Evidence that it may not be surviving can be found in the growing protests against police arbitrariness in dealing with newly arrived West Indian blacks and violence in handling political protests. The London police seem to be facing a crisis similar to the crisis of the 1860s. As they did a century ago, different segments of the public complain of too much or too little police power.

English blacks, though able to obtain low-level civil service positions, are not as powerful a political force as their American brethren. They are a large enough group to arouse fears of disorder (largely misdirected, for the blacks are not England's most violent group) but not yet large enough to prompt police officials to exercise restraint and large-scale minority recruitment efforts.[3] They are not in the position of the organized mid-nineteenth-century working classes, but, although their social and economic position is much better, they are akin to the almost universally despised "residuum" of marginal laborers. American blacks, underrepresented though they are, carry more political weight.

Until the last few years there were no blacks on the London police force. Officials argued that the policeman was an important national symbol and that people would not respect a black bobby. Their view seems analogous to Mayne's reluctance to recruit Irish policemen.[4] London's tradition of impartial aloofness from local communities is increasingly coming under attack. In a society that is much more democratic now than in the mid-nineteenth century, there is concern for democratizing the police.[5]

Another segment of public opinion, less concerned with democracy than with efficiency in an increasingly violent society, has urged firearms for the London police. Yet many people condemn an apparent increase of police violence. Nevertheless, relative to American cities, of which New York is by no means the worst, London and its police force seem quite orderly. English society is still, although decreasingly so, one in which "The criminal has to obey the rule of robbing cleverly and without violence; let him bring out a cosh or gun and he's beyond the social pale."[6] Of course, if more people are considered beyond the pale, traditional restraints may be abandoned in dealing with them. Still, T. A. Critchley could publish *The Conquest of Violence* in 1970, which argued that England had moved far in the extirpation of collective violence by relatively peaceful means. This may be overly complacent, for England today seems to be in an ambivalent position. Traditional restraint, exemplified in police handling of the Grosvenor Square anti-Vietnam War protests of 1968, is contradicted by the violent suppression of a left-wing demonstration, in 1974, in which one protestor was killed by the police.[7] The police never perfectly achieved the ability to peacefully control demonstrations, and now there seems to be less expectation that they should do so.

It seems, though, that the official response to pressures for increased police powers leans toward passage of laws which weaken the rights of suspects and broaden discretionary practices. As in the 1860s, officially defined power seems to be preferred over extra-legality.[8]

One recent development not entirely consistent with most of London police tradition involves charges of corruption. The problem is principally in the detective rather than in the uniformed forces. The detectives seem particularly susceptible because of their contact with criminals, as they were in 1877 when the three highest officials of the Criminal Investigation Division were discovered to be accomplices of an international ring of confidence-men.

Many conflicts and problems are endemic to police work, and my nineteenth-century sources often sound quite modern. I have traced the London police's impersonal authority and the New York force's personal authority to the political and social circumstances of two different societies. The style of police authority reflected decisions made in light of ideological expectations and class relationships in an aristocratic and a democratic nineteenth-century city. Since both forces were formed by their social milieux, changing political and social conditions have altered the nature of police authority and public responses to the police image. Nevertheless, though the police face new pressures and expectations, their traditions remain influential shapers of their image. The London and New York police are products of both the past and the present.

ABBREVIATIONS
OF DOCUMENTS

AD   New York State Assembly Documents
BAD   New York City Board of Aldermen Documents
CCP   City Clerk Papers, New York Municipal Archives
CP   Edwin Chadwick Papers, University College Library, London
HO   Home Office Records, Public Record Office, London
Mepol   Metropolitan Police Records, Public Record Office, London
NYPA   New York Prison Association
NYSC   New York Sabbath Committee
PD   Hansard's Parliamentary Debates
PO   Police Orders, Metropolitan Police Records, Public Record Office,
        London
PP   Parliamentary Papers
SD   New York State Senate Documents

NOTES

Notes to Chapter 1

1. Quotations from Walter Bagehot, *The English Constitution* (New York, n.d,; first pub. 1867), p. 64 (original emphasis); and Edwin Chadwick, "On the Consolidation of the Police Force and the Prevention of Crime," *Fraser's Magazine* 67 (January 1868): 16. Full discussion of the consensual basis of police power is in Allan Silver, "The Demand for Order in Civil Society: A Review of Some Themes in the History of Urban Crime, Police, and Riot," in *The Police: Six Sociological Essays,* ed. David J. Bordua (New York, 1967), pp. 6-15; see also W. L. Melville Lee, *A History of the Police in England* (London, 1901), p. 329; Parker, quoted in Michael Banton, *The Policeman in the Community* (New York, 1964), p. 1 (original emphasis).

2. The Metropolitan Police Act is in *PP,* 1829, vol. 2, Bills, n.p. Detailed accounts of the origin and development of the preventive concept are in Leon Radzinowicz, *A History of English Criminal Law and Its Administration from 1750,* 4 vols. (London, 1948-68), vol. 3; and Charles Reith, *The Police Idea: Its History and Evolution in England and in the Eighteenth Century and After* (London, 1938), throughout. For Rowan and Mayne, see Charles Reith, *A New Study of Police History* (Edinburgh, 1956), and Belton Cobb, *The First Detectives and the Early Career of Richard Mayne, Commissioner of Police* (London, 1957), both throughout; see also J. F. Moylan, *Scotland Yard and the Metropolitan Police* (London, 1929), pp. 35-36; and R. H. Vetch, "Henderson, Sir Edmund Yeamans Walcott," *Dictionary of National Biography,* 22 vols. (London, 1922), 20: 834-36.

3. See James F. Richardson, *The New York Police: Colonial Times to 1901* (New York, 1970), chaps. 2-7.

4. For the old system, see T. A. Critchley, *A History of Police in England and Wales, 900-1966* (London, 1967), throughout; Reith, *Police Idea;* and Richardson, *N.Y. Police,* chap. 1; quotation from James F. Richardson, "The History of Police Protection in New York City, 1800-1870" (Ph.D. diss., New York University, 1961), p. 100.

5. Silver, "Demand for Order," pp. 12-14; Lee, *History of Police,* pp. 246-49; E. P. Thompson, *The Making of the English Working Class* (New York, 1963), pp. 662-63; and Richardson, *N.Y. Police,* pp. 21-22.

6. J. J. Tobias, *Crime and Industrial Society in the Nineteenth Century* (London, 1967), pp. 24-27, 35-37; N.Y. population figures in Joseph Shannon, comp., *Manual of the Corporation of the City of New York, 1868* (New York, 1869), p. 216; see also Kellow Chesney, *The Victorian Underworld* (London, 1970), pp. 95-96; Herbert Asbury, *The Gangs of New York: An Informal History of the Underworld* (New York, 1928), chap. 1; quotations from Edwin Chadwick, "Preventive Police," *London Review* 1 (February 1829): 254-55; *BAD,* 1837, III, no. 88, Police Report, p. 564; and [J. Wade], *A Treatise on the Police and Crimes of the Metropolis....* (London, 1829), pp. 6-7.

7. For the heterogeneity and class isolation of mid-nineteenth-century London, see Asa Briggs, *Victorian Cities* (New York, 1963), pp. 60-63, 326; Gareth Stedman Jones, *Outcast London: A Study in the Relationship between Classes in Victorian Society* (London, 1971), pp. 13-14; and *The Great Metropolis,* 2d ed., 2 vols. (London, 1837), 1: 10; on New York, see Frederika Bremer, *The Homes of the New World: Impressions of America,* 2 vols. (New York, 1853), 1: 15; Edward Crapsey, *The Netherside of New York: or, The Vice, Crime, and Poverty of the Great Metropolis* (New York, 1872), pp. 7-8; and Edward Pessen, *Riches, Class, and Power before the Civil War* (New York, 1973), chap. 9; quotation from Patrick Colquhoun, *A Treatise on the Police of the Metropolis,* 7th ed. (London, 1806), p. 562.

8. See David J. Rothman, *The Discovery of the Asylum: Social Order and Disorder in the New Republic* (Boston, 1971), chaps. 3-4; and W. L. Burn, *The Age of Equipoise: A Study of the Mid-Victorian Generation* (New York, 1964), pp. 176-79.

9. [George Mainwaring], *Observations on the Present State of the Police of the Metropolis* (London, 1821), pp. 16-21; Chadwick, "Preventive Police," pp. 260-62; and Richardson, *N.Y. Police,* pp. 25-26; on London, see also *PP,* 1828, vol. 4, Metropolitan Police Report, throughout; and Charles Reith, *British Police and the Democratic Ideal* (London, 1943), pp. 48-49. Richardson does not deal with the question of perception versus reality in New York, but Roger Lane, *Policing the City: Boston 1822-1885* (Cambridge, Mass., 1967), p. 29, addresses the problem for Boston. There is no reason to expect New York to be different.

10. Silver, "Demand for Order," pp. 15-24; Reith, *Police Idea,* pp. 82-83; and T. A. Critchley, *The Conquest of Violence: Order and Liberty in Britain* (New York, 1970), pp. 87-88, quoting the solicitor general on the Gordon riot; the Doctor's riot was described by Joel Tyler Headley, *The Great Riots of New York, 1712-1873* (New York, 1873), pp. 56-65.

11. Quotation on stock market from Karl Polanyi, *The Great Transformation* (New York, 1944), pp. 186-87 (phrase order changed); Wellington quoted in Radzinowicz, *English Criminal Law,* 4: 156-57; see also A

Police Magistrate, *Remarks on the Present Unconnected State of the Police Authorities of the Metropolis.* . . . (London, 1821), p. 14, which states that a new police force could do away with military riot control; and Richardson, *N. Y. Police,* chap. 2; quotation from "The Great Want of New-York City—a Government," *New-York Quarterly* 3 (April 1854): 82.

12. Banton, *Policeman,* esp. chap. 8, pp. 240-41; see also sources cited in note 7 above.

13. Bagehot, *English Constitution,* p. 14; Disraeli quoted in Asa Briggs, *The Making of Modern England, 1784-1867: The Age of Improvement* (New York, 1965), p. 514—for a general description of English political developments, see chaps. 5-10, and also Halévy, *History,* throughout.

14. For the significance of America's federal system in violence and its control, see David J. Bordua, "Police," in *International Encyclopedia of the Social Sciences,* ed. David L. Sills, 17 vols. (New York, 1968), 11: 175-76; and Richard Hofstadter, "Reflections on Violence in the United States," in *American Violence: A Documentary History,* ed. Richard Hofstadter and Michael Wallace (New York, 1970), p. 10.

15. George Templeton Strong, *Diary,* quoted in Richardson, *N. Y. Police,* pp. 141-42; *Fincher's Trades Review,* July 25, 1863, quoted in David Montgomery, *Beyond Equality: Labor and the Radical Republicans, 1862-1872* (New York, 1967), pp. 106-7. The general interpretation of working-class views is from Montgomery; see also, although it deals with Philadelphia, Bruce Laurie, " 'Nothing on Impulse': Life Styles of Philadelphia Artisans, 1820-1850," *Labor History* 15 (Summer 1974): 327-66; for nativism in general, see Ray A. Billington, *The Protestant Crusade, 1800-1860* (New York, 1938); and Clifford S. Griffin, *Their Brothers' Keepers: Moral Stewardship in the United States, 1800-1865* (New Brunswick, N.J., 1960).

16. Reith, *British Police,* p. 11; quotation from *Poor Man's Guardian,* October 11, 1830, p. 3; on the reforming elite's crisis management, see Allan Silver, "Social and Ideological Bases of British Elite Reactions to Domestic Crisis in 1829-1832," *Politics and Society* 2 (February 1971): 179-201.

17. Commissioners to J. Scanlon, March 2, 1842, Mepol 1/41, letter 88301; *PP,* vol. 19, 1839, First Report, Constabulary Force Commissioners, p. 324.

18. Peel to Commissioners, December 10, 1829, HO 65/11, p. 36; for Rowan's and Mayne's adherence to the standards, see, for example, their replies to future Whig Home Secretary Lord Melbourne, December 19, 1829, Mepol 1/1, p. 321; to Charles Hebbert, the manufacturer who supplied police clothing, December 10, 1829, Mepol 1/1, pp. 303-4; and to various nobles and politicians; for bobbies and the vote, see Lee, *History of Police,* pp. 399-401; see also Mayne to L. W. Freemantle, May 22, 1867, Mepol 1/47, n.p.; and PO, September 21, 1832, Mepol 7/2, fol. 95.

Bobbies were enfranchised in 1887, after agricultural laborers received the vote. Cf. the civil service reforms described in William Holdsworth, *A History of English Law,* 16 vols. (London, 1909-65), 14: 133-37; quotation from "The Metropolitan Police and What Is Paid Them," *Chambers's Magazine* 41 (July 2, 1864): 426.

19. Critchley, *Conquest,* p. 125; *London Morning Chronicle,* July 3, 1855, p. 4; for instances of the breakdown of control, see *PP,* 1833, vol. 13, Cold Bath Fields Meeting, Report, pp. 3-4; F. C. Mather, *Public Order in the Age of the Chartists* (Manchester, 1959), p. 101; *PP,* 1856, vol. 23, Hyde Park Meeting, Report, p. xxx; and Joseph H. Park, *The English Reform Bill of 1867* (New York, 1920), pp. 102-5.

20. They never entirely did away with troops in reserve for really big demonstrations. Troops were ready in the Cold Bath Fields demonstrations and the 1855 Hyde Park meeting, and were brought up in the 1866 reform demonstrations. See sources cited above; also *PP,* 1833, vol. 13, Cold Bath Fields Meeting, testimony of Rowan, p. 21, q. 196. PO, August 20, 1842, Mepol 7/8, fol. 246 (quotation); Mather, *Public Order,* pp. 98-101; Peel, in Commons, *PD,* 1830, 3d ser., vol. 1, col. 577; Baring, *PD,* 1830, n.s., vol. 25, cols. 362-63; Peel, *PD,* 1834, 3d ser., vol. 20, col. 129; Hardinge, ibid., col. 130; and Graham Wallas, *Life of Francis Place* (London, 1918), pp. 248-49. Place is supposed to have invented the baton charge, in which the police charged into violent crowds to seize the leaders and disperse the demonstrators, retiring in good order instead of standing their ground and fighting it out.

21. Quotations from Rowan to Patrick Colquhoun, March 31, 1835, Mepol 1/18, letter 29350; and S. Maccoby, *English Radicalism, 1832-1852* (London, 1935), pp. 382-83; see also PO, October 25, 1830, Mepol 7/1, fol. 253; and November 1, 1830, Mepol 7/1, fol. 128.

22. Quotations from "Principles of Police, and Their Application to the Metropolis," *Fraser's Magazine* 16 (August 1837): 170; and "The Police of London," *London Quarterly Review* (July 1870), p. 48, quoted in Silver, "Demand for Order," p. 14. Police and the rule of law is discussed fully in chaps. 3 and 4 below.

23. The notion of impersonal police authority, as well as the later discussion of personal authority, represents my distillation of various similar concepts, principally those of Michael Banton, in *Policeman,* chaps. 4-8. I am also indebted to James Q. Wilson, *Varieties of Police Behavior: The Management of Law and Order in Eight Communities* (Cambridge, Mass., 1968), chaps. 4-6; and Jerome H. Skolnick, *Justice without Trial: Law Enforcement in Democratic Society* (New York, 1966), pp. 42-70. For Weber's definition of bureaucratic professionalism, see *The Theory of Social and Economic Organization,* ed. and trans. A. M. Henderson and Talcott Parsons (New York, 1964), pp. 333-34; quotation from A. Wynter, "The Police and the Thieves," *Quarterly Review* 99 (June 1856): 171, also quoted in Silver, "Demand for Order," pp. 13-14.

24. PO, October 15, 1831, Mepol 7/2, fol. 41.

25. See note 23 above.

26. Quotations from *BAD,* 1839, vol. 6, no. 1, Mayor's Annual Message, p. 19; and First Annual Message, in James D. Richardson, comp., *A Compilation of the Messages and Papers of the Presidents,* 22 vols. (New York, 1897, ed. of 1915), 3: 1012; for antiprofessionalism, see Daniel Calhoun, *Professional Lives in America: Structure and Aspiration, 1750-1850* (Cambridge, Mass., 1965), pp. 4-15, 193-94; on the military, see ibid., pp. 16-17; Alexis de Tocqueville, *Democracy in America,* ed. Francis Bowen, 2d ed., 2 vols. (Cambridge, Mass., 1863), 2: 334-35; and Thomas H. Benton, *Thirty Years' View: or, A History of the Working of the American Government for Thirty Years, 1820-1850,* 2 vols. (New York, 1854-56), 1: 184. Studies that reveal the impact of antiprofessionalism in other American cities are George A. Ketcham, "Municipal Police Reform: A Comparative Study of Law Enforcement in Cincinnati, Chicago, New Orleans, New York, and St. Louis, 1844-1877" (Ph.D. diss., University of Missouri, 1967); David R. Johnson, "The Search for an Urban Discipline: Police Reform as a Response to Crime in American Cities, 1800-1875" (Ph.D. diss., University of Chicago, 1972); and Lane, *Policing the City.*

27. For a full treatment of political changes and developments, see Richardson, *N.Y. Police,* chaps. 3-7.

28. Bagehot, *English Constitution,* p. 63.

29. *New York Times,* December 9, 1857, p. 4; *BAD,* 1856, vol. 23, no. 10, Mayor's Annual Message, pp. 33-34.

30. *Journal of Commerce,* August 26, 1836, p. 2; and Augustine E. Costello, *Our Police Protectors: History of the New York Police from the Earliest Period to the Present Time* (New York, 1885), p. 466.

31. Contemporary quotation from George W. Searle, "Report on the Penal System of Massachusetts, " *AD,* 1865, vol. 3, no. 62, app. H, Annual Report, NYPA, pp. 96-97. Silver's comment from his remarks on my paper, "Police and the Rule of Law: London and New York City, 1830-1870," presented at the 85th American Historical Association meeting, Boston, December 1971.

32. Tocqueville, *Democracy,* 1: 265-68.

33. Quotations from ibid., 1: 267n.; and Max Weber, *On Law in Economy and Society,* ed. Max Rheinstein (Cambridge, Mass., 1954), p. 355.

34. "Municipal Government," *United States Magazine and Democratic Review* 25 (June 1849): 484; for the riot, see Headley, *Great Riots,* chap. 8; and Richard Moody, *The Astor Place Riot* (New York, 1958).

35. In 1857, for example, the police were backed by troops and used revolvers in the Bowery B'hoys-Dead Rabbits gang fights; used revolvers in the Seventeenth Ward German riots; and were armed with repeating rifles, with a six-pounder in reserve, during the Quarantine riots. See Richardson, "History of Police Protection," pp. 290-93, 309-11. The best contemporary account of the draft riots from the police viewpoint is David M. Barnes, *The*

Draft Riots in New York, July 1863: The Metropolitan Police, Their Honorable Record (New York, 1863); the best brief modern account is Richardson, *N.Y. Police,* chap. 6; and the latest and most comprehensive is Adrian Cook, *The Armies of the Streets* (Lexington, Ky., 1974). The phrase "exemplary punishment" is reiterated in Barnes's account. For the riot squad, see *AD,* 1864, vol. 2, no. 28, Metro. Police Annual Report, 1863, p. 10; *AD,* 1865, vol. 2, no. 36, p. 10; and Headley, *Great Riots,* pp. 20–23.

36. Accounts of the Orange riot are in Headley, *Great Riots,* chap. 21; and Richardson, *N.Y. Police,* pp. 166–67. I am grateful to Jonathan Katz for the Whitman quotation, which is from a letter to Peter Doyle, July 14, 1871, in E. H. Miller, ed., *The Collected Writings of Walt Whitman: The Correspondence,* 2 vols. (New York, 1961), 2:126. Costello, *Protectors,* p. 254, mentions the flag presentation.

37. Harriet Martineau, *Morals and Manners* (Philadelphia, 1838), p. 192. The New York police she describes are the old constabulary and night watch, but the principles of the new force remained the same.

NOTES TO CHAPTER 2

1. Geoffrey Gorer, in *Exploring English Character* (New York, 1955), p. 308, suggests that the height requirement reflected the commissioners' awareness of a big man's ability to command respect and the belief that tall men are of "Constitutionally equable temperament." There may be something to this, as an American policeman's comment suggests: "I am kind of big, I don't have to rough them up much.... But take my partner. Now he is small. He has to rough people up" (quoted by William A. Westley, *Violence and the Police: A Sociological Study of Law, Custom, and Morality* [Cambridge, Mass., 1970], p. 128). See also Michael Banton, *The Policeman in the Community* (New York, 1964), p. 175, n. 1; for examination of applicants see *PP,* 1834, vol. 16, Metro. Police, testimony of Rowan, p. 2, q. 33; and Belton Cobb, *The First Detectives and the Early Career of Richard Mayne, Commissioner of Police* (London, 1957), p. 43; quotation from Harriet Martineau, "The Policeman: His Health," *Once A Week* 2 (June 2, 1860): 523.

2. On "improper connections," see *PP,* 1834, vol. 16, Metro. Police, test. Rowan, p. 10, q. 154; for historians' views, see J. F. Moylan, *Scotland Yard and the Metropolitan Police* (London, 1929), p. 98; Gorer, *English Character,* 306–7; James F. Richardson, *The New York Police: Colonial Times to 1901* (New York, 1970), p. 49; and Raymond B. Fosdick, *European Police Systems* (New York, 1915), pp. 200–201. The distribution of the force was 11 percent former soldiers and sailors; 5 percent shopkeepers; 7 percent servants; 26 percent skilled workers and artisans of various sorts; and 40 percent laborers. (Eleven percent came from a scattering of other occupations.) I computed these rounded percentages from figures in J. L. Thomas, "Recruits for the Police Service," *Police Journal* 19 (October–December 1946): 293, which was Gorer's source. For

the commissioners' policies, see Commissioners to Charles Steward, June 27, 1831, Mepol 1/6, letter 7128; to Parish Overseers, Woolwich, May 4, 1833, Mepol 1/12, letter 17600; to (?), April 23, 1834, Mepol 1/15, letter 23500; quotation from Rowan to Wm. Blackwood, February 20, 1837, Mepol 1/45, n.p.

3. Quotations from Rowan to Earl of Malmsbury, February 26, 1840, Mepol 1/35, letter 73467 (original emphasis); and A. Wynter, "The Police and the Thieves," *Quarterly Review* 99 (June 1856): 170; on the testimony of the policemen, see *PP*, 1856, vol. 23, Hyde Park Meeting, pp. 298-502.

4. Quotation on constables from provincial towns from Wynter, "Police and Thieves," p. 170. This view contrasts with that of a later commissioner that Fosdick quoted, who praised agricultural laborers for their "slow and steady" qualities (*European Police*, p. 201). Quotation on agricultural laborers from Henry Mayhew, *London Labour and the London Poor*, 2d ed., 4 vols. (London, 1861-62), 2:153; for evidence of their increased hiring, see the *Times* (London), January 30, 1868, p. 6; and cartoon, "Letting the Cat out of the Bag," *Punch* 54 (January-June 1868): 202: "Very sorry, mum, but I'm a stranger here in London, mum, — only just come up from the country, same as you, mum!! " This poked fun at both the affected lady and the policeman.

5. *PP*, 1834, vol. 16, Metro. Police, test. Rowan and Mayne, pp. 52-53, qq. 770-71; test. Rowan, p. 10, qq. 144-49; *PP*, 1864, vol. 25, Police Statistics, p. 2; Commissioners to Home Office, November 12, 1829, Mepol 1/1, pp. 201-6; PO, June 15, 1831, Mepol 7/1, fol. 220; and July 24, 1860, Mepol 7/21, p. 175.

6. Rowan to J. E. Dowdeswell, January 4, 1842, Mepol 1/41, letter 87251; and Luke O. Pike, *A History of Crime in England*, 2 vols. (London, 1876), 2:465-66.

7. *BAD*, 1839, vol. 6, no. 1, Mayor's Annual Message, p. 19.

8. Richardson, *N.Y. Police*, p. 55.

9. Quotations from *AD*, 1857, vol. 2, no. 127, Police Report, statement of District Attorney Hall, pp. 2-3; and *AD*, 1859, vol. 2, no. 63, Metro. Police Annual Report 1858, p. 4; see also Richardson, *N.Y. Police*, pp. 80, 159-64; and *SD*, 1859, vol. 2, no. 113, Police Investigation, pp. 4-6.

10. Quotation from *AD*, 1857, vol. 4, no. 127, Police Report, p. 2; see also Complaints against Policemen, May 8, 1848, CCP, box 3203; and *New York Times*, November 23, 1855, p. 3. I estimated the percentages of policemen living and working in the same ward by comparing policemen listed in the ms. Federal Census of 1850 (microfilm, U.S. National Archives and Record Center) in the First, Fourth, Sixth, Tenth, and Fifteenth wards, with policemen's names listed for these wards in David T. Valentine, comp., *Manual of the Corporation of the City of New York* (New York, 1851). I want to thank Eldridge Pendleton for suggesting use of the census.

11. See Robert Ernst, *Immigrant Life in New York City, 1825-1865* (New York, 1949), p. 165; for the Irish, see James F. Richardson, "The

History of Police Protection in New York City, 1800-1870" (Ph.D. diss., New York University, 1961), p. 194.

12. For objections to change in local residency requirements, see *AD,* 1857, vol. 4, no. 49, Minority Report on Metro. Police Bill, p. 5; and *New York Herald,* July 7, 1857, p. 1. The conclusion that most policemen ceased to live in their ward beats is based on an analysis of the 1860 ms. Federal Census for the same wards as in 1850. On the fall and subsequent rise of Irish police in Irish wards, I made a rough count of Irish surnames in the lists of policemen in each ward in Valentine, *Manual,* 1856, 1858, and 1861 (the last year in which policemen's names are listed). On commuting policeman, see *New York Times,* August 12, 1869, p. 2.

13. For night watch, see James Grant, *Sketches in London* (London, 4th ed., 1850), pp. 216, 385; and *PP,* 1828, vol. 6, Metro. Police, test. Joseph S. Thomas, Parish Constable, p. 25; for Irish bobbies, see *PP,* 1856, vol. 23, Hyde Park Meeting, test. Mayne, p. 258, qq. 6670, 6668; for restrictions on families, see PO, October 4, 1837, Mepol 7/5, fol. 280; Mayne to (?), June 7, 1838, Mepol 1/29, letter 50385; *Times* (London), January 30, 1868, p. 6; and Martineau, "Policeman," p. 525; decline of Irish bobbies computed from figures in *PP,* 1834, vol. 16, Metro. Police, test. Mayne, p. 10, q. 153; for Irish population, see John A. Jackson, *The Irish in Britain* (London, 1963), p. 10; quotation from W. H. Watts, *London Life at the Police-Courts* (London, 1864), p. 161.

14. On bobbies' uniforms, see Charles Reith, *A New Study of Police History* (Edinburgh, 1956), p. 143; Ronald Howe, *The Story of Scotland Yard* (London, 1965), p. 29; Moylan, *Scotland Yard,* pp. 38, 142; PO, August 28, 1863, Mepol 7/23, p. 223; March 7, 1864, Mepol 7/25, p. 78; and *PP,* 1828, vol. 6, Metro. Police, app. G, pp. 325-35. The uniform, in its resemblance to civilian fashions, might be compared to the blue blazers and gray trousers adopted as an experiment by some modern American forces. As dress styles changed, however, the uniform became more unlike civilian attire.

15. On acceptance of uniforms, see *PP,* 1822, vol 4, Metro. Police, test. Sir Richard Birnie, p. 17; PO, January 29, 1834, Mepol 7/3, fol. 16; Moylan, *Scotland Yard,* p. 152; Mayne to Home Office, June 26, 1850, Mepol 1/53, letter 951; and *PP,* 1833, vol. 13, Police Spies, test. Rowan and Mayne, p. 177, qq. 4012-13.

16. On uniforms as deterrents, see J. L. Thomas, "The Scarecrow Function of the Police," *The Police Journal* 18 (October-December 1945): 298-304. F. C. Mather, *Public Order in the Age of the Chartists* (Manchester, 1959), pp. 210-11, and Elie Halévy, *A History of the English People in the Nineteenth Century,* 4 vols. (New York, 1949), 4: 247-48, report use of plainclothes informers hired by the police in 1848. Apparently the men were not policemen. In 1850 the commissioners ordered all policemen attending Chartist meetings to appear in uniform (PO, December 3, 1850, Mepol 7/15, fol. 263). Quotation from *PP,* 1833, vol. 13, Police Spies, Report, p. 3.

17. Moylan, *Scotland Yard,* pp. 150–55; and memo from Mayne to Superintendents, January 23, 1854, Mepol 2/28, loose; see also PO, December 10, 1845, Mepol 7/11, fol. 28; May 25, 1863, Mepol 7/24, p. 131; June 26, 1846, Mepol 7/11, fol. 264; November 12, 1862, Mepol 7/23, p. 269; and March 7, 1866, Mepol 7/29, p. 79.

18. On expansion of detectives, see *PP,* 1870, vol. 36, Metro. Police Annual Report 1869, pp. 3–4; PO, November 15, 1869, Mepol 7/31, p. 321; on exposure of swindle, see Moylan, *Scotland Yard,* p. 157.

19. James W. Gerard, *London and New York: Their Crime and Police* (New York, 1853), p. 17 (original emphasis).

20. According to A. E. Costello, *Our Police Protectors: History of the New York Police from the Earliest Period to the Present Time* (New York, 1885), p. 127, the copper badge led to "copper" or "cop," but the *Oxford Universal Dictionary* derives these words from a slang expression, meaning "to catch," going back to the eighteenth century. However, the nouns were not used in England until the later 1850s and thus could have been American imports. Incidentally, the modern epithet "pig" dates back to at least the mid-nineteenth century in both America and England. See extracts from Chief Matsell's "Vocabulum: or, The Rogue's Lexicon" (New York, 1859), in Herbert Asbury, *The Gangs of New York: An Informal History of the Underworld* (New York, 1928), p. 378; and "Glossary of Colloquial and Cant Words," in Kellow Chesney, *The Victorian Underworld* (London, 1970), pp. 377–84, at 382.

21. Richardson, "History," pp. 129–30; and Costello, *Protectors,* pp. 103, 127.

22. For proponents' views, see Gerard, *London and N.Y.,* pp. 17–18; and *New York City Board of Assistant Aldermen Documents,* 1842, vol. 9, no. 56, Police Report, pp. 209–10; for citizens' complaints, see *New York Tribune,* June 26, 1845, p. 2; July 30, p. 2; October 22, p. 2; and Complaints against Policemen, December 2, 5, 1845; March 7, July 3, 1846 (the black woman's case was on January 31, 1846), CCP, boxes 3198–99, 3201; see also Complaints, 1847, CCP, boxes 3201–2. Chief Matsell, in contrast to Gerard, argued that increased assaults reflected judicial leniency (see *BAD,* 1852, vol. 19, pt. 1, no. 7, Chief's Semi-Annual Report, p. 107).

23. Richardson, *N.Y. Police,* p. 65; quotation from *New York Times,* June 30, 1854, p. 4; see also Alexis de Tocqueville, *Democracy in America,* ed. Francis Bowen, 2d ed., 2 vols. (Cambridge, Mass., 1863), 2: 362. Richardson rightly stresses objections to servants' livery, but anti-English and antinativist feelings may be equally important.

24. On adoption of uniform, see Costello, *Protectors,* pp. 128–29; and Richardson, "History," p. 214; for dismissals and quotation, see Complaints, June 29, 1854, CCP, box 3210; Matsell quotation from *BAD,* 1854, vol. 21, pt. 2, no. 51, Chief's Semi-Annual Report, pp. 944–45. There were 251 arrests for assaults and other interference with policemen in 1852, compared to 103 in 1853, 120 in 1854, and 35 in 1855 (figures in *BAD,* 1856, vol. 23,

no. 16, Chief's Semi-Annual Report, p. 12). Arrests jumped in 1858-61 amidst general hostility toward the new Metropolitan force—236 in 1858, declining to 106 in 1861 (see Metro. Police Annual Reports 1858-61 in *AD*, 1859-62).

25. *PP*, 1830, vol. 23, Police Instructions, p. 4 (original emphasis); *Rules and Regulations for Day and Night Police of the City of New-York* (New York, 1846), p. 21; ibid. (New York, 1851), pp. 30-31; and *Manual for the Government of the Police Force of the Metropolitan Police District of the State of New York*, in *AD*, 1860, vol. 2, no. 88, p. 103.

26. On suspicion of detectives, see *SD*, 1856, vol. 2, no. 97, Police Investigation, test. Capt. James Leonard, p. 130; *New York Herald*, September 14, 1860, p. 6; and George S. McWatters, *Knots Untied: or, Ways and By-Ways in the Hidden Life of American Detectives* (Hartford, Conn., 1872), pp. 659-65. McWatters defends detectives as a necessary evil. On shortage of policemen, see Reith, *New Study*, p. 224; *BAD*, 1856, vol. 23, no. 10, Mayor's Annual Message, p. 35; *AD*, 1859, vol. 2, no. 63, Metro. Police Annual Report 1858, pp. 6-7; and Edward Crapsey, *The Netherside of New York: or, The Vice, Crime, and Poverty of the Great Metropolis* (New York, 1872), p. 12.

27. For reward system, see *SD*, 1856, vol. 2, no. 97, Police Investigation, test. ex-Police Justice Daniel Clark, p. 45; quotation from Crapsey, *Netherside*, pp. 12, 51; and for the continuity between old and new practices, see David R. Johnson, "The Origins of Police Corruption, 1800-1860." (Paper delivered at 65th Meeting of the Organization of American Historians, New Orleans, April 1972).

28. *Poor Man's Guardian*, October 11, 1830, p. 3.

29. These orders, also appearing in the Mepol mss., are printed in *PP*, 1830, vol. 23, Metro. Police, pp. 15-17, and *PP*, 1830-31, vol. 8, Metro. Police, pp. 18-21; for later repetitions, see PO, September 21, 1846, Mepol 7/11, fol. 269; January 17, 1849, Mepol 7/14, fol. 278; February 8, 1850, ibid., fol. 246; March 3, 1851, Mepol 7/15, fol. 274; and January 25, 1861, Mepol 7/22, p. 176.

30. Quotations from Mrs. J. C. Byrne, *Undercurrents Overlooked*, 2 vols. (London, 1860), 1: 54; James Greenwood, *The Seven Curses of London* (London, 1869), pp. 94-95; and *PP*, 1834, vol. 16, Metro. Police, test. anonymous journalist, p. 258, q. 3654.

31. For length of service and mobility, see Martineau, "Policeman," pp. 523, 526; for misconduct, see *PP*, 1834, vol. 16, Metro. Police, test. Rowan and Mayne, pp. 7-8, qq. 104-7; PO, December 29, 1838, Mepol 7/5, fol. 365; *PP*, 1856, vol. 23, Hyde Park Meeting, test. Mayne, p. 297, qq. 6663, 6666; for various wage levels, see Arthur Bowley, *Wages in the United Kingdom in the Nineteenth Century* (Cambridge, 1900), p. 70; for force as temporary refuge, see *PP*, 1834, vol. 16, Metro. Police, test. Rowan, pp. 394-95, q. 6273; Mayne to Sir Wm. Somerville, April 21, 1847, Mepol 1/45,

n.p.; quotations from G. C. Smith, *Weeding the New Police....* (London, 1830), p. 2; and *Times* (London), January 30, 1868, p. 6; for pay problems, see Moylan, *Scotland Yard,* pp. 40–43; Mayne to H. Fitzroy, September 29, 1853, Mepol 1/46, n.p.; and Mayne to Home Office, August 30, 1839, Mepol 1/33, between letters 55806 and 55807.

32. Quotations from Cobb, *First Detectives,* pp. 44, 53, 86; "Our Police System," *The Dark Blue* 2 (February 1872): 693; and *PP,* 1834, vol. 16, Metro. Police, test. G. H. Kent, p. 174, q. 2514.

33. For police structure, see Cobb, *First Detectives,* pp. 12, 28–39; for higher ranks, see Moylan, *Scotland Yard,* p. 32; *PP,* 1860, Metro. Police Statistics, p. 1; PO, March 10, 1837, Mepol 7/4, fol. 344; June 28, 1831, Mepol 7/1, fol. 228; December 5, 1857, Mepol 7/19, p. 82; and February 20, 1835, Mepol 7/3, fol. 79.

34. Quotations from *PP,* 1830, vol. 23, Instructions to Metro. Police, p. 10; see also PO, February 28, 1830, Mepol 7/1, fols. 33–34; Rowan to James Traill, February 28, 1837, Mepol 1/45, n.p.; PO, March 11, 1830, Mepol 7/1, fol. 41; July 17, 1858, Mepol 7/19, p. 273; and December 30, 1863, Mepol 7/24, p. 329.

35. Moylan, *Scotland Yard,* p. 102; *PP,* 1830–31, vol. 8, Metro. Police, p. 20; Wynter, "Police and Thieves," pp. 169–71; *PP,* 1856, vol. 23, Hyde Park Meeting, letter from Mayne, p. 549; and *PP,* 1871, vol. 28, Metro. Police Annual Report 1870, p. 38.

36. *PP,* 1834, vol. 16, Metro. Police, test. Rowan, p. 6, q. 74; for dismissal figures, see Mather, *Public Order,* p. 97; *PP,* 1856, vol. 23, Hyde Park Meeting, test. Mayne, p. 297, qq. 6663, 6666; and *PP,* 1871, vol. 28, Metro. Police Annual Report 1870, table 5, p. 18.

37. Commissioners to M. Jones, January 20, 1835, Mepol 1/16, letter 27957; Charles Reith, *British Police and the Democratic Ideal* (London, 1943), p. 63; and Reith, *New Study,* pp. 152–53. Henderson, Mayne's successor, decentralized the system, creating district superintendents who handled all complaints (*PP,* 1870, vol. 36, Metro. Police Annual Report 1869, p. 12). Quotation from *Illustrated London News* 1 (August 27, 1842): 250. Most of the letter-writers are clergymen, shopkeepers, or individuals who attach "esq." to their names. Only one man, a baker, seems to have been from the working class (Mr. Davis to Commissioners, June 15, 1831, Mepol 1/6, letter 6891).

38. For instructions on behavior, see *Rules and Regulations,* 1846, p. 6; ibid., 1851, pp. 6–7; and *Manual,* 1860, p. 90; Mickle quotation from mayor's decision, Complaints, September 1846, CCP, box 3201. The conclusion on punishments rests on a comparison of the decisions on complaints against policemen in New York, 1846–48 (CCP, boxes 3198–99, 3201-3), with published reports of brutality and improper arrest charges which the London commissioners sent for trial by magistrates, 1846–48 (recording whether the man was retained or dismissed by the commissioners,

as well as the court's punishment). See *PP,* 1849, vol. 44, Metro. Police Charged with Offenses 1844-48, pp. 5-9. Quotations from Complaints, August 11, 1851, CCP, box 3205.

39. I have compared police earnings with workers' wages as cited in George R. Taylor, *The Transportation Revolution, 1815-1860* (New York, 1951), pp. 295-97. See also applications for the force, 1855, CCP, boxes 3209-10, which reveal that out of 43 successful applicants, 10 were in various "white collar" jobs, 23 were skilled workers and only 10 were transport workers or unskilled laborers. Commissioners' quotation from *AD,* 1864, vol. 3, no. 28, Metro. Police Annual Report 1863, p. 5; journalist's quotations from Junius Henri Browne, *The Great Metropolis: A Mirror of New York* (Hartford, Conn., 1869), pp. 50, 51; on complaints, see Matthew H. Smith, *Sunshine and Shadow in New York* (Hartford, Conn., 1868), p. 305; and Richardson, *N.Y. Police,* pp. 157-58.

40. For friction, see Costello, *Protectors,* pp. 118-19; see also the fight between Patrolman Thorne and Capt. Bowyer, which the mayor decided was purely personal (Complaints, May 30, 1848, CCP, box 3203). Matsell quotation from *BAD,* 1854, vol. 21, pt. 1, no. 17, Chief's Semi-Annual Report, pp. 328-29; and quotation of critic from *AD,* 1857, vol. 4, no. 127, Police Report, Statement of District Attorney Hall, pp. 3-4.

41. Commissioners' quotation from *AD,* 1865, vol. 2, no. 36, Metro. Police Annual Report 1864, p. 5; see also *New York Times,* March 13, 1865, p. 4; contemporary quotation from James D. MacCabe, *The Secrets of the Great City: A Work Descriptive of the Virtues and the Vices, the Mysteries, Miseries, and Crimes of New York City* (Philadelphia, 1868), p. 71.

42. *SD,* 1859, vol. 2, no. 113, Metro. Police Investigation, test. Supt. Frederick Tallmadge, p. 18; and *AD,* 1861, vol. 1, no. 27, Metro. Police Annual Report 1860, statement of Supt. Amos Pilsbury, p. 8; quotation from Crapsey, *Netherside,* p. 12; for other disciplinary problems, see *New York Times,* August 12, 1869, p. 2; August 31, p. 3; December 14, pp. 2, 4; and December 16, p. 2.

Notes to Chapter 3

1. Michael Banton distinguishes between the patrolman who maintains general order, often without invoking any specific law as a "peace officer," and specialized detectives (such as the narcotics squad) who enforce specific statutes as "law officers" (*The Policeman in the Community* [New York, 1964], pp. 6-7). See also John R. Lambert, *Crime, Police, and Race Relations: A Study in Birmingham* (London, 1970), p. 166.

2. See Egon Bittner, *The Functions of the Police in Modern Society: A Review of Background Factors, Current Practices, and Possible Role Models* (Washington, D.C., 1970), chap. 15; Jerome H. Skolnick, *Justice without Trial: Law Enforcement in Democratic Society* (New York, 1966), p. 14; Wayne R. LaFave, *Arrest: The Decision to Take a Suspect into Custody* (Boston, 1965), pp. 110-11; and Lambert, *Crime, Police, Race,* pp. 138, 159-75.

3. LaFave, *Arrest,* p. 429.

4. Delmar Karlen, Geoffrey Sawer, and Edward M. Wise, *Anglo-American Criminal Justice* (New York, 1967), pp. 98, 101, 32.

5. Cf. similar questions in Skolnick, *Justice,* p. 1, and Herbert L. Packer's "due process" and "crime control" models of police work in *The Limits of the Criminal Sanction* (Stanford, Calif., 1968), pp. 149-73.

6. *PP,* 1839, vol. 19, First Report, Constabulary Force Commissioners, p. 331 (Rowan was one of the authors); and Francis Lieber, *On Civil Liberty and Self-Government,* enl. ed. in 1 vol. (Philadelphia, 1859), p. 113.

7. Lieber, *Civil Liberty,* p. 302, n. 1.

8. For general discussion of this problem in the modern American context, see William A. Westley, *Violence and the Police: A Sociological Study of Law, Custom, and Morality* (Cambridge, Mass., 1970), chaps. 3-4; on the truncheon, see Charles Reith, *British Police and the Democratic Ideal* (London, 1943), p. 36; A. Wynter, "The Police and the Thieves," *Quarterly Review* 99 (June 1856): 170; and PO, October 29, 1863, Mepol 7/24, p. 276; quotation from "The Police System of London," *Edinburgh Review* 96 (July 1852): 11 (original emphasis).

9. PO, September 6, 1832, Mepol 7/2, fol. 93; August 21, 1830, Mepol 7/1, fols. 95-96; and *PP,* 1834, vol. 16, Metro. Police, testimony of Rowan, p. 29, qq. 449-50.

10. For pistols and cutlasses, see *PP,* 1834, vol. 16, Metro. Police, test. Rowan, p. 12, q. 180; Kellow Chesney, *The Victorian Underworld* (London, 1970), pp. 111, 119; Rowan to Home Office, January 5, 1832, Mepol 1/8, letter 1075; quotations from Melbourne to Commissioners, January 9, 1832, HO 65/11, p. 387; and PO, January 12, 1832, Mepol 7/2, fol. 55 (original emphasis); on rural areas, see Wynter, "Police and Thieves," p. 167; PO, March 14, 1864, Mepol 7/25, p. 88; Chesney, *Victorian Underworld,* pp. 87-89; and T. A. Critchley, *A History of Police in England and Wales, 900-1966* (London, 1967), p. 159.

11. PO, November 24, 1842, Mepol 7/8, fol. 254; August 1, 1848, Mepol 7/14, fol. 267; August 30, 1848, ibid., fol. 270; December 20-27, 1867, Mepol 7/29, pp. 291-98; August 28, October 17, November 19, 1868, Mepol 7/30, pp. 258, 304, 343; and January 28, 1869, Mepol 7/31, p. 32.

12. Melodrama quotation from Tom Taylor, *The Ticket-of-Leave Man* (London, 1863), act 4, sc. 3, p. 82; on lack of violence, see W. H. Watts, *London Life at the Police-Courts* (London, 1864), pp. 180-83; and [Thomas Wontner], *Old Bailey Experience* (London, 1833), p. 338; for incidents of the 1840s, see Chesney, *Victorian Underworld,* pp. 111-14; on concealed weapons, see *PP,* 1830, vol. 22, Instructions to Metro. Police, p. 12.

13. *New York Herald,* July 15, 1857, p. 1. In his diary of 1851, policeman William Bell described a battle in which he drew his pistol, which miraculously never went off despite some heavy fisticuffs after Bell had "threatened to shoot the first man who touched" him (*Journal,* 1850-51, entry for January 28, 1851, in New-York Historical Society). None of the

Complaints against Policemen, 1845-54, in CCP, boxes 3198-99, 3201 ff., mention shooting incidents.

14. A *Herald* reporter, shortly after the shooting of an innocent bystander by the police in the Seventeenth Ward German riots of 1857, uncovered the fact that policemen were armed (*Herald,* July 14, 1857, p. 1); see also James D. MacCabe, *The Secrets of the Great City: A Work Descriptive of the Virtues and the Vices, the Mysteries, Miseries, and Crimes of New York City* (Philadelphia, 1868), p. 72.

15. *Herald,* July 15, 1857, p. 1.

16. Both quotations from text of Tallmadge's request printed in the *Herald,* November 6, 1857, p. 2. He was not seeking armament of the whole force, but a specialized riot squad, a proposal which foreshadows the commissioners' own scheme for a riot squad in 1864. James F. Richardson, *The New York Police: Colonial Times to 1901* (New York, 1970), p. 113, discusses this episode, but gives an impression that the superintendent sought more extensive armament than he actually seems to have requested.

17. Quotations from *New York Times,* May 18, 1855, p. 4; *AD,* 1865, vol. 2, no. 36, Metro. Police Annual Report 1864, pp. 12-13; see also *AD,* 1859, vol. 2, no. 63, Metro. Police Annual Report 1858, p. 14; and *AD,* 1866, vol. 1, no. 12, Metro. Police Annual Report 1865, p. 13.

18. On enforcing weapons law, see *Times,* January 7, 1865, p. 4; January 11, p. 4; April 30, 1866, p. 4; June 10, pp. 4, 8; June 9, 1867, p. 4; and James F. Richardson, "The History of Police Protection in New York City, 1800-1870" (Ph.D. diss., New York University, 1961), pp. 393 ff.; quotations from Edward Crapsey, *The Netherside of New York: or, The Vice, Crime, and Poverty of the Great Metropolis* (New York, 1872), p. 30 — a compilation of articles originally published in the late sixties; James D. Burn, *Three Years among the Working-Classes in the United States during the War* (London, 1865), pp. 36-37; and *AD,* 1866, vol. 1, no. 12, Metro. Police Annual Report 1865, p. 7; see also complaints of violence in the *Times,* January 6, 1868, p. 5; November 14, p. 4; January 8, 1869, p. 4; February 6, p. 4; February 12, pp. 1, 6; February 13, p. 4; and February 14, p. 4.

19. *Times,* November 7, 1857, p. 4.

20. Ibid., May 10, 1867, p. 4; see also Richardson, *N.Y. Police,* pp. 157-58.

21. For commissioners' views, see PO, January 27, 1830, Mepol 7/1, fol. 30; and January 7, 1850, Mepol 7/14, fol. 244; for magistrate's statement, see *PP,* 1834, vol. 16, Metro. Police, test. W. A. A. White, pp. 129-30, q. 1869.

22. Quotations from James Fitzjames Stephen, *A History of the Criminal Law of England,* 3 vols. (London, 1883), 2: 273-74; and *PP,* 1834, vol. 16, Metro. Police, test. W. A. A. White, p. 129, q. 1868.

23. Commissioners to W. Sheppard, June 22, 1830, Mepol 1/3, pp. 255-56; to D. Richards, June 26, 1830, ibid., p. 279; PO, March 8, 1830, Mepol 7/1, fol. 243 (quotation); April 9, 1831, ibid., fol. 193; *PP,* 1837,

vol. 31, 3d Report, Criminal Law Commissioners, app. 1, test. Mayne, p. 20 (quotation); PO, August 4, 1831, Mepol 7/2, fol. 20; and Bittner, *Functions of the Police*, p. 10 (quotation).

24. For arrest on suspicion provision, see *PP*, 1837, vol. 31, 3d Report, Criminal Law Commissioners, app. I, test. Mayne, p. 20; Commissioners to Home Office, March 22, 1831, Mepol 1/5, unnumbered letter between 5242 and 5243; Karlen et al., *Anglo-American Justice*, pp. 115-16; and PO, January 7, 1850, Mepol 7/14, fol. 244; for complaints, see *Illustrated London News* 1 (December 31, 1842): 534; PO, September 17, 1842, Mepol 7/8, fol. 250; December 31, 1845, Mepol 7/11, fol. 28; and June 13, 1850, Mepol 7/15, fol. 250.

25. PO, March 1, 1843, Mepol 7/8, fol. 259; and *PP*, 1871, vol. 28, Metro. Police Annual Report 1870, p. 8.

26. *PP*, 1845, vol. 14, 8th Report, Criminal Law Commissioners, app. A, letter of J. P. Cobbett, barrister, p. 293; letter of Chief Justice Denman, p. 220; letter of H. Woolrych, barrister, pp. 280-81 (complaining of higher court strictness); and pp. 55-56. *SD*, 1856, vol. 2, no. 97, Police Investigation, test. J. W. Edmonds, State Supreme Court Justice, p. 166.

27. On shift of jurisdiction, see J. J. Tobias, *Crime and Industrial Society in the Nineteenth Century* (London, 1967), pp. 227-28. The basis of the conclusion on what constituted "reasonable cause" is the committal and conviction figures in the *PP*, "Returns of Criminal Offenders," before 1855, and the "Judicial Statistics," 1856 on. There is a growing convergence of convictions and committals in the 1840s and 1850s, but in the 1860s they begin to diverge, perhaps due to the "crime waves" at the beginning and end of the decade, which might have prompted magistrates to be less scrupulous about evidence and the police to make more unfounded arrests. The "crime waves" are discussed in chapter 5. On restriction of provision, see Karlen et al., *Anglo-American Justice*, p. 116.

28. Quotations from *Rules and Regulations for Day and Night Police of the City of New-York* (New York, 1846, 1851), pp. 28-30; 43 (original emphasis in both).

29. Since police orders like those of London are not available for New York, it is impossible to know whether the heads of the force cautioned their men against improper arrests on suspicion. However, the weight of the evidence in the following discussion suggests that any efforts must have been unsuccessful. Quotations from George W. Walling, *Recollections of a New York Chief of Police* (New York, 1887), pp. 196, 387; see Matthew H. Smith, *Sunshine and Shadow in New York* (Hartford, Conn., 1868), p. 180-81, for a similar comparison with London.

30. Robert Livingston, *Criminal Code of Louisiana*, pp. 211-12, quoted in *AD*, 1855, vol. 7, no. 150, Report of Select Committee on Code of Criminal Procedure, pp. 85-86; see also pp. 88-89, which spells out powers of arrest without warrant in the proposed criminal code. The identical code is in *AD*, 1850, vol. 3, no. 18, the original report of the commissioners on the criminal code. I have consistently used the 1855 edition, which matches the

earlier report exactly. Neither John W. Edmonds, ed., *Statutes at Large of the State of New York,* 1st ed., 5 vols. (Albany, 1863), nor George W. Cothran, ed., *The Revised Statutes of the State of New York,* 6th ed., 3 vols. (Albany, 1875), has a section on arrest without a warrant.

31. *SD,* 1856, vol. 2, no. 97, Police Investigation, Report, p. 3; test. Abraham Beal, General Agent, N.Y. Prison Assoc., pp. 103-4; test. Police Justice Daniel Clark, p. 43; *AD,* 1849, vol. 6, no. 243, Annual Report, NYPA, 1848, p. 59; and *AD,* 1855, vol. 7, no. 150, Code of Crim. Proc., pp. 99-101.

32. *AD,* 1855, vol. 7, no. 150, Code of Crim. Proc., pp. 101, 105; Edmonds, *Statutes,* 2: 731-32; and Cothran, *Statutes,* 3: 1000.

33. *SD,* 1856, vol. 2, no. 97, Police Investigation, test. State Supreme Court Justice J. W. Edmonds, p. 166; *AD,* 1850, vol. 8, no. 198, NYPA, 1849, p. 26; and *AD,* 1855, vol. 7, no. 150, Code of Crim. Proc., pp. 93-95 (quotation, original emphasis, at 94).

34. *AD,* 1849, vol. 6, no. 243, NYPA, 1848, p. 44.

35. *AD,* 1850, vol. 8, no. 198, NYPA, 1849, pp. 25-26.

36. *AD,* 1855, vol. 7, no. 150, Code of Crim. Proc., p. 95; *SD,* 1856, vol. 2, no. 97, Police Investigation, test. J. W. Edmonds, p. 166; Edmonds, *Statutes,* 2: 731; and Cothran, *Statutes,* 3: 1000.

37. *SD,* 1856, vol. 2, no. 97, Police Investigation, test. Police Justice G. W. Pearcey, pp. 15, 23, 24; Capt. G. W. Walling, pp. 91-92; ex-Police Justice W. J. Roome, p. 34; and Capt. J. Dowling, p. 149; see also Walling, *Recollections,* pp. 38-39.

38. *SD,* 1861, vol. 2, no. 71, Police Investigation, test. Kennedy, pp. 6-9; and Police Justice Matthew Brennan, p. 31; see also *Herald,* December 22, 1860, p. 6; and MacCabe, *Secrets,* p. 70.

39. *SD,* 1861, vol. 2, no. 71, Police Investigation, Report, pp. 2-3; quotation from MacCabe, *Secrets,* pp. 70-71.

40. Quotations from James Grant, *Sketches in London,* 4th ed. (London, 1850; first pub. 1838), p. 204; and *Punch's Almanack for 1854,* p. 4, in *Punch's 20 Almanacks, 1842-1861* (London, 1862?). Paul Chevigny, *Police Power: Police Abuses in New York City* (New York, 1969), chap. 8, discusses cover charges in a modern context.

41. Quotations from PO, January 25, 1830, Mepol 7/1, fol. 29; and June 3, 1830, ibid., fols. 63-64; on overzealousness, see Commissioners to Home Office, August 9, 1830, Mepol 1/3, pp. 422-26; *PP,* 1834, vol. 16, Metro. Police, test. W. A. A. White, pp. 129-30, q. 1869; and PO, June 29, 1842, Mepol 7/8, fol. 239.

42. PO, March 31, 1830, Mepol 7/1, fol. 46; and June 24, 1867, Mepol 7/29, p. 206. Mayne's successor, Sir E. Y. W. Henderson, changed the policy, only requiring reports of special incidents (PO, March 23, 1869, Mepol 7/31, p. 85).

43. PO, July 13, 1833, Mepol 7/2, fol. 152. Again, Henderson changed the policy, requiring a record of discharges to be kept only at the station

house and expecting his new district superintendents to report any cases needing investigation (PO, March 11, 1869, Mepol 7/31, p. 4).

44. Quotations from PO, March 15, 1845, Mepol 7/11, fol. 3; and *PP*, 1834, vol. 16, Metro. Police, test. W. A. A. White, p. 126, q. 1818; see also PO, January 4, 1863, Mepol 7/24, p. 12; September 30, 1865, Mepol 7/26, p. 275; September 12, 1866, Mepol 7/27, p. 287; and January 6, 1865, Mepol 7/26, p. 12.

45. *Rules and Regulations*, 1846, p. 6; *Manual for the Government of the Police Force of the Metropolitan Police District of the State of New York*, in *AD*, 1860, vol. 3, no. 88, p. 90; cf. PO, January 25, 1830, Mepol 7/1, fol. 29.

46. Quotations from *SD*, 1861, vol. 2, no. 71, Police Investigation, test. T. C. Acton, p. 29; Police Justice J. H. Welch, p. 14; and Crapsey, *Netherside*, p. 27. The 1851 figures are from *PP*, 1852-53, vol. 81, Arrest Statistics, p. 290; and *BAD*, 1856, vol. 13, no. 16, Police Chief's Semi-Annual Report, pp. 12-13. I computed the ratios from London's estimated 1851 population in the above source, and New York's 1851 population in Joseph Shannon, comp., *Manual of the Corporation of the City of New York 1868* (New York, 1869), p. 215. 1869 figures are in *PP*, 1870, vol. 36, Metro. Police Annual Report 1869, table 5, p. 18 (this lists "disorderly characters," which I assume to be the same as "disorderly conduct"); and figures for November 1, 1868, to October 31, 1869, are in *AD*, 1870, vol. 2, no. 16, Metro. Police Annual Report 1869, p. 74. See also Crapsey, *Netherside*, p. 30; cf. Packer, *Criminal Sanction*, pp. 293-94.

47. *PP*, 1834, vol. 16, Metro. Police, test. Mr. Williams, parish official, pp. 240-41, qq. 3387-89. He said that the old constabulary and night watch would arrest for assault on the charges of local inhabitants whom the officers personally knew to be respectable, but the new police as "perfect strangers" would not arrest unless they had seen the incident (q. 3373). Quotation from Commissioners to Home Office, January 8, 1831, Mepol 1/4, letters 4014-15; see also PO, February 5, 1831, Mepol 7/1, fol. 170; circulars to magistrates, Mepol 1/4, letters 4390-98; and Reith, *British Police*, pp. 84-85.

48. Quotations from *PP*, 1834, vol. 16, Metro. Police, test. Mr. Williams, p. 240, q. 3372; and Commissioners to Home Office, June 13, 1833, Mepol 1/12, letter 18227.

49. Commissioners to Home Office, June 19, 1833, Mepol 1/12, letter 18337; Commissioners to all magistrates, June 22, 1833, ibid., letter 18449; and PO, June 25, 1833, Mepol 7/2, fol. 14.

50. *PP*, 1837-38, vol. 15, Police Offices, test. Rowan, p. 84, q. 876; *PP*, 1837, vol. 21, 3d Report, Crim. Law Comms., app. I, test. Mayne, p. 22; and *PP*, 1834, vol. 16, Metro. Police, Report, p. 12. The 1839 act is printed in a pamphlet, *The New Police Act* (London, 1839).

51. *Rules and Regulations*, 1846, p. 39; ibid., 1851, p. 55.

52. On commissioners' conflict with Melbourne, see *PP*, 1834, vol. 16,

Metro. Police, test. R. E. Broughton, magistrate, citing correspondence with Rowan and Mayne, p. 114, q. 1661. I did not find such correspondence in the Mepol letter books. See also Commissioners to Home Office, February 15, 1832, Mepol 1/8, letter 11491; and Melbourne to Commissioners, February 22, 1832, HO 65/11, p. 396. Charles Reith, *British Police,* pp. 105-6, states that the issue was left unresolved, but Melbourne's reply indicates his acquiescence (PO, January 19, 1830, Mepol 7/1, fol. 242).

53. Karlen et al., *Anglo-American Justice,* p. 114; PO, August 29, 1833, Mepol 7/2, fol. 164; August 6, 1831, ibid., fol. 20; and *PP,* 1837-38, vol. 15, Police Offices, test. Mayne, p. 84, q. 878.

54. *PP,* 1837-38, vol. 15, Police Offices, test. Mayne, p. 84, qq. 877-78; and Karlen et al., *Anglo-American Justice,* p. 114.

55. *PP,* 1832, vol. 7, Sabbath, test. Rowan, p. 56, q. 732.

56. Commissioners to Home Office, July 31, 1833, Mepol 1/13, letter 19112; PO, August 29, 1833, Mepol 7/2, fol. 164; and January 20, 1859, Mepol 7/20, p. 19.

57. For O'Connor, see *Northern Star,* April 21, 1838, p. 6, quoted by Brian Harrison, *Drink and the Victorians: The Temperance Question in England, 1815-1872* (Pittsburgh, Pa., 1971), pp. 389-90; on magistrates' views, see *PP,* 1834, vol. 7, Drunkenness, test. Rowan, pp. 25-26, qq. 240-53; and the acid comments of magistrate Allen Steward Laing, as fictionalized in Charles Dickens, *Oliver Twist,* ed. Peter Fairclough (Harmondsworth, England, 1966), n. 1 to chap. 11, p. 488; for figures on intoxication, see *PP,* 1867-68, vol. 14, Sunday Closing, app. 1, p. 413; and *PP,* 1847-48, vol. 16, Sale of Beer, test. Rowan, p. 3, q. 3.

58. *SD,* 1861, vol. 2, no. 71, Police Investigation, Report, pp. 1-2; and Richardson, "History," p. 208.

59. Richardson, "History," pp. 208-9; *New York Tribune,* March 25, 1850, p. 2; May 14, 1850, p. 2; *SD,* 1856, vol. 2, no. 97, Police Investigation, test. Police Justice G. W. Pearcey, pp. 15-16; and complaints against Asst. Capt. Webb, Fifth Ward, August 4, 1846, and Asst. Capt. Hannigan, Sixteenth Ward, July 21, 1847, CCP, boxes 3199, 3201.

60. *AD,* 1858, vol. 3, no. 80, Metro. Police Annual Report 1857, p. 5; *AD,* 1859, vol. 2, no. 63, Metro. Police Annual Report 1858, p. 14; and *SD,* 1861, vol. 2, no. 71, Police Investigation, test. Kennedy, pp. 4-5, 12.

61. *SD,* 1861, vol. 2, no. 71, Police Investigation, Report, pp. 1-2; and 1864 police act, as printed in Shannon, *Manual of N.Y. 1868,* p. 140 (italics added).

62. Quotations from *Manual, Metro. Police, AD,* 1860, vol. 3, no. 88, p. 92n.; and *SD,* 1861, vol. 2, no. 71, Police Investigation, test. Commissioner T. C. Acton, p. 25; see also test. Superintendent Kennedy, p. 6; and Commissioner J. C. Bergen, p. 19.

63. *SD,* 1861, vol. 2, no. 71, Police Investigation, Report, pp. 1-2; quotations from ibid., test. Police Justice James Connolly, p. 16; and Crapsey, *Netherside,* pp. 46-47; see also Smith, *Sunshine and Shadow,* p. 166.

64. *SD,* 1856, vol. 2, no. 97, Police Investigation, test. Pearcey, p. 14; quotations from MacCabe, *Secrets,* p. 99; *AD,* 1850, vol. 8, no. 198, NYPA, 1849, p. 28; and *SD,* 1861, vol. 2, no. 71, Police Investigation, test. Kennedy, p. 15; see also ibid., Acton, p. 27.

65. Quotations from *Rules and Regulations,* 1846, p. 37; ibid., 1851, p. 53; and *SD,* 1856, vol. 2, no. 97, Police Investigation, test. Carpenter, p. 141; arrest figures from *BAD,* 1856, vol. 23, no. 16, Chief's Semi-Annual Report, p. 12; and *PP,* 1867-68, vol. 14, Sale of Liquors on Sunday, app. 1, p. 413 (London 1855 figures not available); see Tenth Ward Blotters, May 25-August 27, 1855, July 27-August 26, 1856, N.Y. Municipal Archives, for fines and imprisonment.

66. Arrest figures from *SD,* 1861, vol. 2, no. 71, Police Investigation, test. Kennedy, p. 10; Police Justice J. H. Welsh, p. 13; *PP,* 1870, vol. 36, Metro. Police Annual Report 1869, table 5, p. 18; and *AD,* 1870, vol. 2, no. 16, N.Y. Metro. Police Annual Report 1869, p. 74; quotation from Walling, *Recollections,* p. 196.

67. The Boston police followed a policy like London's, discharging many drunks from the station houses or helping them home—until 1869, when they adopted New York's strictness. Roger Lane argues that the change was due to Boston's increasing orderliness in the sixties and seventies. The police could arrest and punish drunks because there were fewer of them. However, this does not explain New York's policy, for there is no evidence that Gotham was growing more orderly. Perhaps officials' strict policy in New York was based on their continuing fears of lower-class disorder. For Boston, see Roger Lane, *Policing the City: Boston, 1822-1885* (Cambridge, Mass., 1967), pp. 112-13.

NOTES TO CHAPTER 4

1. *PP,* 1834, vol. 16, Metro. Police, testimony of Mayne, p. 59, qq. 875-80.

2. Quotations from *PP,* 1854-55, vol. 12, Public Prosecutors, test. A. J. A. Cockburn, p. 186, q. 2396; and *PP,* 1845, vol. 14, 8th Report, Criminal Law Commissioners, app. A, letter of J. P. Cobbett, p. 293.

3. See decision in the case of *Regina* v. *Furley,* Central Criminal Court, 1844, 1 Cox 76; *PP,* 1845, vol. 14, 8th Report, Crim. Law Comms., app. A, p. 281.

4. PO, November 3, 1837, Mepol 7/5, fol. 284.

5. Quotations from PO, May 15, 1844, Mepol 7/9, fol. 245; *PP,* 1845, vol. 14, 8th Report, Crim. Law Comms., app. A, letter of Lord Denman, p. 211; and William Forsyth, "Criminal Procedure in Scotland and England" (1851), in *Essays Critical and Narrative* (London, 1874), pp. 4-42.

6. Court of Queen's Bench, 1852, 2 Dennison 430; and James Fitzjames Stephen, *A History of the Criminal Law of England,* 3 vols (London, 1883), 1:447.

7. On commissioners' caution, see unsigned memorandum, probably by Mayne, undated but found among material for 1854, Mepol 2/28, loose. For

admissibility of confessions induced by private prosecutors, see *Regina* v. *Jarvis*, Court of Criminal Appeal, 1867, 10 Cox 574. In this case a policeman was present, but not conducting the interrogation. For a similar case, without a policeman present, see *Regina* v. *Parker*, Court of Criminal Appeal, 1861, 8 Cox 465. Mayne's orders are in PO, September 22, 1865, Mepol 7/26, p. 268; January 2, 1866, Mepol 7/27, p. 13 (quotation). The latter order informs policemen of the exceptions mentioned in the text as well as cautioning them.

8. Delmar Karlen, Geoffrey Sawer, and Edward M. Wise, *Anglo-American Criminal Justice* (New York, 1967), pp. 118-19.

9. For codification commission's attitude, see *AD,* 1855, vol. 7, no. 150, Report of Select Committee on Code of Criminal Procedure, p. 225. The original report is in *AD,* 1850, vol. 3, no. 18, with an identical text. I have consistently used the 1855 edition. For court cases, see *People* v. *Thoms,* Court of Appeal, 1855, 3 Parker 256; *Duffy* v. *the People,* Supreme Court, 1862, 5 Parker 321; and *Jefferds* v. *the People,* Supreme Court, 1862, 5 Parker 523; quotation from ibid., 548 — the incident took place and the case was first tried in New York City.

10. For British interpretation, see *Rex* v. *Warickshall,* Court of King's Bench, 1783, 1 Leach (3d ed.) 198, the original case, which is cited in *Regina* v. *Jarvis,* Court of Criminal Appeal, 1867, 10 Cox 574; for American interpretation, see *People* v. *Smith,* Supreme Court, 1848, 3 Howard 230; and *Duffy* v. *the People,* Supreme Court, 1862, 5 Parker 323, giving a history of British precedents.

11. *AD,* 1865, vol. 3, no. 62, Annual Report, NYPA, 1864, app. II, pp. 96-97.

12. *AD,* 1866, vol. 3, no. 50, NYPA, 1865, letter of E. C. Wines of NYPA to Matthew D. Hill, Recorder of Birmingham, England, January 30, 1866, p. 134; and *PP,* 1854-55, vol. 12, Public Prosecutors, test. Henry E. Davis, N.Y. City corporation counsel, p. 58, qq. 575, 578.

13. Quotations from *AD,* 1866, vol. 3, no. 50, NYPA, 1865, E. C. Wines' letter, p. 134. *New York Times,* December 12, 1869, cited by Alexander Callow, Jr., *The Tweed Ring* (New York, 1965), p. 148; see also *AD,* 1866, vol. 3, no. 50, NYPA, 1865, pp. 149-50; and Edward Crapsey, *The Nether-side of New York: or, The Vice, Crime, and Poverty of the Great Metropolis* (New York, 1872), p. 47.

14. *AD,* 1865, vol. 3, no. 62, NYPA, 1864, p. 222; and *AD,* 1866, vol. 3, no. 50, NYPA, 1865, letter of M. D. Hill to E. C. Wines, June 18, 1866, p. 128. Plea bargaining now dominates American criminal justice. Defense attorneys criticize the practice as a means of oppressing innocent people or covering up police abuses under threat of conviction for a serious offense. Policemen attack bargained pleas, on the other hand, as frustrations of their efforts. For criticisms, see Leonard Downie, Jr., *Justice Denied* (New York, 1971); for a defense, see Thurman Arnold, *The Symbols of Government* (New Haven, Conn., 1962; first pub. 1935), chap. 7. Karlen et al., *Anglo-American Justice,* p. 155, balances pros and cons.

15. T. A. Critchley, *A History of Police in England and Wales, 900–1966* (London, 1967), p. 37; quotation from Robert Townshend, famous Bow Street Runner, in Stephen, *Criminal Law,* 1: 231; for salaried justices, see Frederick W. Maitland, *Justice and Police* (London, 1885), p. 100.

16. Angus B. Reach, "The Police Offices of London," *Illustrated London News* 9 (August 22, 1846): 125.

17. *Punch* 28 (January–June 1855): 132; quotations from A. Wynter, "The Police and the Thieves," *Quarterly Review* 99 (June 1856): 200; see also *PP,* 1834, vol. 16, Metro. Police, test. Charles K. Murray, magistrate, p. 189, q. 2721; and *Reynolds's Newspaper,* May 2, 1852, p. 8; April 5, 1863, p. 4; and February 9, 1868, p. 4.

18. Leon Radzinowicz, *A History of English Criminal Law and Its Administration from 1750,* 4 vols. (London, 1948–68), 4: 172; and William Holdsworth, *A History of English Law,* 16 vols. (London, 1909–65), 13: 237.

19. Rowan to Home Office, June 21, 1832, Mepol 1/44, pp. 44–47; and *PP,* 1834, vol. 16, Metro. Police, test. Rowan, p. 12, qq. 196–99.

20. *PP,* 1834, vol. 16, Metro. Police, test. Sir F. A. Roe, pp. 88–89, qq. 1426–30; p. 105, q. 1555.

21. Rowan to Home Office, June 21, 1832, Mepol 1/44, pp. 45–46; *PP,* 1834, vol. 16, Metro. Police, Report, pp. 15–17; and *PP,* 1837–38, vol. 15, Police Offices, Report, pp. 12–14. In 1842 the commissioners complained to the Home Office that a magistrate had sent a policeman outside of his division to execute a warrant, without seeking their permission. They viewed this as a threat to their authority and requested the home secretary to lay down a rule which would prevent such conflicts in the future (see Commissioners to Home Office, January 31, 1842, Mepol 1/41, letter 87737). Presumably the matter was settled, for it does not appear in later correspondence.

22. Charles Reith, *British Police and the Democratic Ideal* (London, 1943), p. 7; and Reith, *A New Study of Police History* (Edinburgh, 1956), pp. 150–51.

23. *PP,* 1837–38, vol. 15, Police Offices, test. Mayne, pp. 88–89, q. 912; test. Rowan, p. 101, qq. 1079–80; and *PP,* 1867–68, vol. 14, Sunday Closing, test. Mayne, p. 15, q. 267; inspector's comments from summary of B Division reply to constabulary commissioners' questionnaire, 1837, in CP, box 11; quotation from "Our Police and Its Difficulties," *Saturday Review* 26 (November 14, 1868): 654.

24. PO, November 5, 1830, Mepol 7/1, fol. 130. They also expected that "every Police Constable in the force, shall at all times upon going into the several Police Offices, touch their hats in a respectfull [*sic*] manner to the Sitting Magistrates and the same when ever they meet them" (PO, November 29, 1829, Mepol 7/1, fol. 241). See also *PP,* 1837–38, vol. 15, Police Offices, test. Rowan, p. 101, q. 1078.

25. Quotation from *Reynolds's,* August 15, 1869; see also the song, "A Victim from the Country," *Diprose's Music-Hall Song-Book* (London, 1862), p. 62; *PP,* 1854–55, vol. 12, Public Prosecutors, test. Henry Avory, clerk of

Central Criminal Court, p. 178, q. 2320; p. 175, qq. 2265-75; test. Alexander Cockburn, atty. general of England, p. 186, q. 2396; and test. Horatio Waddington, undersecretary of state, pp. 160-61, qq. 2072-73. Creation of the director of public prosecutions in 1879, to advise private and official prosecutors and to initiate government prosecutions, did not alter the police's role. Today the director, unlike the American district attorney, must rely entirely on police investigation of a case. He can prevent police prosecutions (now conducted by attorneys rather than by constables) but he has rarely used this power. He is not a free agent like the district attorney when it comes to dropping or compromising charges. See Karlen et al., *Anglo-American Justice,* pp. 22-23, 28.

26. Quotations from PO, July 26, 1851, Mepol 7/15, fol. 290; see also report of superintendent of A (Whitehall) Division, December 12, 1843, Mepol 4/6, fol. 2; PO, February 26, 1869, Mepol 7/31, p. 58; Mayne's 1854 memo, Mepol 2/28, loose; and PO, December 6, 1851, Mepol 7/15, fols. 242-43.

27. On previous convictions, see PO, April 28, 1834, Mepol 7/3, fol. 31; quotations from PO, July 19, 1834, ibid., fol. 45; September 27, 1837, Mepol 7/5, fol. 279; June 23, 1838, ibid., fol. 326 (manner in court); December 3, 1833, Mepol 7/3, fol. 10; August 29, 1842, Mepol 7/8, fol. 249 (stolen property); September 20, 1838, Mepol 7/5, fol. 356 (language); May 13, 1865, Mepol 7/26, p. 138 ("mate"); and Mayne's 1854 memo, Mepol 2/28, loose. The word, which "proper-thinking" people may now utter, must be "bloody." For early reports, see PO, September 14, 1833, Mepol 7/2, fols. 166-67.

28. PO, April 7, 1831, Mepol 7/1, fols. 192-93; and April 14, 1849, Mepol 7/14, fol. 255.

29. William A. Westley, *Violence and the Police: A Sociological Study of Law, Custom, and Morality* (Cambridge, Mass., 1970), pp. 81-82.

30. For arrest on attempt, see *PP,* 1837, vol. 31, 3d Report, Crim. Law Comms., app. I, test. Mayne, p. 23; see also Reith, *New Study,* p. 183, for punishment. Kellow Chesney, *The Victorian Underworld* (London, 1970), pp. 92-93, asserts that light punishments for assaults on policemen "cannot have inclined them to restraint and strict regularity in their dealings with dangerous criminals." He cites Wiliam Hoyle, *Crime in England and Wales in the Nineteenth Century* (London, 1876), but gives no page number; I searched, but could find no such statement in Hoyle's book. During the 1850s and 1860s fines were by far the most frequent punishment inflicted by police magistrates, followed by a much smaller proportion of imprisonments for less than one month and a still smaller number of imprisonments for over a month (see *PP,* 1857-71, "Judicial Statistics").

31. David T. Valentine, comp., *Manual of the Corporation of the City of New York 1859, 1860* (New York, 1860, 1861), p. 114; p. 128.

32. For criticism of police justices, see *SD,* 1870, vol. 1, no. 21, NYPA, 1869, pp. 41-42; *SD,* 1856, vol. 2, no. 97, Police Investigation, test. Capt.

G. W. Walling, pp. 92-93; test. Police Justice G. W. Pearcey, p. 13; test. F. A. Tallmadge, ex-city judge and later Metropolitan Police superintendent, p. 233; and Crapsey, *Netherside,* p. 9; quotations from James D. Burn, *Three Years among the Working-Classes in the United States during the War* (London, 1865), pp. 40-41; "The Judiciary of New York City," *North American Review* 105 (July 1867): 150, 166, 176; and Junius Henri Browne, *The Great Metropolis: A Mirror of New York* (Hartford, Conn., 1869), p. 532.

33. *SD,* 1856, vol. 2, no. 97, Police Investigation, test. Capt. J. W. Hartt, p. 101; and test. Capt. J. Dowling, p. 157. Capt. Daniel Carpenter, however, got along with the justices (p. 175). Matsell quotation from *BAD,* 1852, vol. 19, pt. 1, no. 7, Police Chief's Semi-Annual Report, p. 107.

34. Quotation from *SD,* 1856, vol. 2, no. 97, Police Investigation, test. Police Justice J. A. Welch, p. 84; see also test. Justice G. W. Pearcey, p. 26.

35. Quotations from *AD,* 1861, vol. 1, no. 27, Metro. Police Annual Report 1860, p. 5; and *AD,* 1867, vol. 8, no. 220, Metro. Police Annual Report 1866, pp. 11-12; see also *AD,* 1865, vol. 2, no. 62, NYPA, 1864, table 10, pp. 252-53, which points out that only three counties had lower average county jail sentences (for petty offenses) than New York's nineteen days.

36. *SD,* 1856, vol. 2, no. 97, Police Investigation, test. ex-Police Justice Napoleon Mountfort, p. 284.

37. Kennedy quotation from *New York World,* February 9, 1867, p. 5; Connolly quotations from ibid., February 11, p. 5; *Times,* March 20, 1867, p. 2; and April 14, p. 5; see also *World* editorial, February 11, 1867, p. 4.

38. *Times,* March 1, 1867, p. 2; and James F. Richardson, *The New York Police: Colonial Times to 1901* (New York, 1970), p. 156.

39. The median for 1851-55 is 44 percent; for 1858-67, 34 percent.

40. *AD,* 1870, vol. 2, no. 17, Metro. Police Annual Report 1869, p. 24 (arrests); ibid., vol. 6, no. 108, Annual Report of Secy. of State on Criminal Statistics 1869, pp. 144-46 (convictions); and *PP,* 1870, vol. 36, London Metro. Police Annual Report 1869, table 11, p. 22; and table 5, p. 18 (arrests and convictions).

41. Quoted in Augustine E. Costello, *Our Police Protectors: History of the New York Police from the Earliest Period to the Present Time* (New York, 1885), p. 114.

Notes to Chapter 5

1. Quotations from Michael Banton, *The Policeman in the Community* (New York, 1964), p. 106; Mayne to E. J. Stanley, August 25, 1834, Mepol 1/16, letter 25428; and T. A. Critchley, "The Idea of Policing in Britain: Success or Failure?" in *The Police We Deserve,* ed. J. C. Alderson and Philip John Stead (London, 1973), p. 26.

2. Charles Reith, *British Police and the Democratic Ideal* (London, 1943), pp. 50-51, 128-29.

3. For name-calling, see A Hypochondriac, *The Blue Devils; or the New*

Police: A Poem in Three Cantos (London, 1830), p. 16. The print is in the Guildhall library collection. Quotation from Humanitas, *A Letter to the Right Hon. Sir Robert Peel, Bart.... and Facts Demonstrative of his Intention to Subvert Public Liberty and Enslave the Country through the Espionage and Tyranny of the New Police* ... (London, [1835]), p. 33.

4. Quotations from W. H. Watts, *London Life at the Police-Courts* (London, 1864), p. 233; for public contempt, see Humanitas, *Letter,* p. 41.

5. For decline in complaints, see *PP,* 1834, vol. 16, Metro. Police, testimony of Rowan, p. 396, q. 6283; for lingering doubts, see Charles Reith, *A New Study of Police History* (Edinburgh, 1956), pp. 156–58.

6. Ralph Waldo Emerson, *English Traits* (Boston, 1857), p. 107; and "The Metropolitan Police and What Is Paid Them," *Chambers's Magazine* 41 (July 2, 1864): 424.

7. For Chadwick comments, see draft of unpublished "Thoughts on Municipal Police," 1830, in CP, box 2, p. 9; and Chadwick, "On the Consolidation of the Police Force and the Prevention of Crime," *Fraser's Magazine* 67 (January 1868): 16.

8. Quotations from Reith, *British Police,* p. 183; and Mayne to H. Fitzroy, September 29, 1853, Mepol 1/46, n.p. See similar statement, Commissioners to Home Office, January 6, 1835, Mepol 1/17, letter 27751; and specific examples, such as Rowan to R. Lindsay, October 1, 1830, Mepol 1/4, letter 2820; Commissioners to W. Johnson, September 19, 1835, Mepol 1/19, letter 32315; to H.O., July 20, 1836, Mepol 1/22, letter 37612; to H.O., October 29, 1836, Mepol 1/23, letter 39346, among many others. The conclusion on nature of complaints is from my examination of the Mepol letter books.

9. Peel quoted by Reith, *British Police,* p. 17; Patrick Colquhoun quotation from *A Treatise on the Police of the Metropolis,* 7th ed. (London, 1806), p. 523. Cf. Jeremy Bentham: "Liberty, which is one branch of security, ought to yield to *general security,* since it is not possible to make *any* laws but at the expense of liberty" (*Principles of the Civil Code,* quoted by Brian Harrison, *Drink and the Victorians: The Temperance Question in England, 1815-1872* [Pittsburgh, Pa., 1971], p. 202, original emphasis). Commentator's quotation from Frederic Hill, *Crime: Its Amount, Causes, and Remedies* (London, 1853), p. 154; theme of middle-class liberty discussed in Allan Silver, "The Demand for Order in Civil Society: A Review of Some Themes in the History of Urban Crime, Police, and Riot," in *The Police: Six Sociological essays,* ed. David J. Bordua (New York, 1967), pp. 8-15; and W. L. Burn, *The Age of Equipoise: A Study of the Mid-Victorian Generation* (New York, 1964), p. 194.

10. Quotations from Burn, *Equipoise,* pp. 83-84; W. Weir, "Some Features of London Life of the Last Century," in *London,* ed. Charles Knight, 6 vols. (London, 1842-44), 2: 345-46; [George Mainwaring], *Observations on the Present State of the Police of the Metropolis* (London, 1821), pp. 7-8; "The late Mr. Walker's" pamphlet, *The Original* (1835),

quoted in Hill, *Crime,* pp. 6-7; and *PP,* 1837-38, vol. 15, Police Offices, test. Rowan, pp. 184-85, q. 2102; see also *PP,* 1834, vol. 16, Metro. Police, test. K. Clark, pp. 286-87, qq. 4061-65; Rowan to Joseph Hume, M.P., n.d. 1838, Mepol 1/28, letter 49115; *The Great Metropolis,* 2 vols. (London, 1837), 2: 11; and James Grant, *Sketches in London* (London, 1st ed. 1838; 4th ed. 1850), p. 399.

11. Quotations from Charles Dickens, "The Sunday Screw," *Household Words* 1 (June 22, 1850): 291-92; *Illustrated London News* 18 (May 31, 1851): 501; ibid., June 28, 1851, p. 606; "The Police System of London," *Edinburgh Review* 96 (July 1852): 12 (also quoted in Silver, "Demand for Order," p. 5); and A. Wynter, "The Police and the Thieves," *Quarterly Review* 99 (June 1856): 173; see also Hill, *Crime,* pp. 3-4; and *Illustrated London News* 18, supplement (February 1, 1851): 86.

12. Gustave Doré and Blanchard Jerrold, *London, A Pilgrimage* (London, 1971; first pub. 1872), pp. 163-64, describes a later date's "chaff," which probably resembled that of twenty years earlier. For hostility, see PO, October 29, 1857, Mepol 7/19, p. 50; April 12, 1838, Mepol 7/5, fol. 311; and Geoffrey Best, *Mid-Victorian Britain, 1851-1875* (New York, 1971), p. 233.

13. Reith, *British Police,* p. 6; Geoffrey Gorer, *Exploring English Character* (New York, 1955), pp. 162-95; Best, *Mid-Victorian Britain,* pp. 228-33; Burn, *Equipoise,* p. 68; Trygve R. Tholfsen, "The Intellectual Origins of Mid-Victorian Stability," *Political Science Quarterly* 96 (March 1971): 57-91; and Roy Lewis and Angus Maude, *The English Middle Classes* (London, 1949), pp. 52-53.

14. Gareth Stedman Jones, *Outcast London: A Study in the Relationship between Classes in Victorian Society* (London, 1971), pp. 241-42.

15. Kellow Chesney, *The Victorian Underworld* (London, 1970), pp. 140-42; Best, *Mid-Victorian Britain,* p. 226; *Reynolds's Newspaper,* January 4, 1863, p. 4; *Lloyd's Weekly London Newspaper,* February 15, 1863, p. 6; and *Cornhill Magazine* 7 (January 1863): 79-81.

16. Quotations from *Lloyd's,* February 15, 1863, p. 6; and *St. Pancras Reporter and North London Advertiser,* January 17, 1863, p. 2; for leniency and punishment, see Burn, *Equipoise,* p. 156; and Chesney, *Victorian Underworld,* p. 143.

17. Charles Dickens, *The Uncommercial Traveller* (New York, n.d.; first pub. 1860 as a collection of earlier articles), pp. 373-81, at 377; "Our Police and Its Difficulties," *Saturday Review* 26 (November 14, 1868): 653; and *Weekly Dispatch,* February 16, 1868, p. 1, Tom Taylor, *The Ticket-of-Leave Man* (London, 1863), act 4, sc. 1, pp. 65-66; music-hall tune from "The Ticket-of-Leave Man, a Comic Medley," in *Diprose's Music-Hall Song-Book* (London, 1862), p. 28. Taylor's popular play was unusual in featuring a ticket-of-leave man who was at bottom honest. On plight of convict, see "Our Police," p. 653; J. J. Tobias, *Crime and Industrial Society in the Nineteenth Century* (London, 1967), pp. 56-57; and cf. Egon Bittner, *The Functions of the Police in Modern Society: A Review of*

Background Factors, Current Practices, and Possible Role Models (Washington, D.C., 1970), p. 118 and n. 159.

18. Burn, *Equipoise,* p. 191; and Edwin Chadwick, draft of unpublished "Suggestions with Relation to Police, and Secondary Punishments," 1831, in CP, box 2, pp. 1–3.

19. Burn, *Equipoise,* pp. 187–89, at 188.

20. "Judicial Statistics" published annually in *PP.* See esp. *PP,* 1870, vol. 63, "Judicial Statistics 1868–69," p. 10; for superintendents' quotation, see PO, December 21, 1836, Mepol 7/4, fol. 33.

21. Quotations from *Lloyd's,* May 10, 1868, p. 6; Henry Solly, *Destitute Poor and Criminal Classes: A Few Thoughts on How to Deal with the Unemployed Poor of London* (London, 1868), p. 9; and Custos, *The Police Force of the Metropolis in 1868* (London, 1868), p. 11; see also *Weekly Dispatch,* February 16, 1868, p. 1.

22. For poem, see *Punch* 55 (July–December 1868): 222. Orders requiring police action on all the subjects mentioned in it can indeed be found in the PO for 1868. See also *Times* (London), December 29, 1868, p. 6.

23. Quotations from *Reynolds's,* November 30, 1862, p. 4; January 17, 1869, p. 4; and February 9, 1868, p. 4; see also London *Daily News,* March 24, 1868, p. 4; and *Punch* 54 (January–June 1868): 63.

24. See Howard Jones, *Crime in a Changing Society* (Baltimore, Md., 1965), pp. 12–13; quotation from *Reynolds's,* October 25, 1863, p. 4.

25. Quotations from Custos, "Police Force," p. 23; Watts, *Police-Courts,* pp. 220–21; and *Reynolds's,* March 8, 1868, p. 4.

26. For Mayne, see "Our Police," p. 654; for recruitment problems, see *Times,* January 30, 1868, p. 6; *London Daily Telegraph,* February 21, 1865, quoted in Custos, "Police Force," p. 17; and *East London Observer and Tower Hamlets Chronicle,* January 11, 1868, p. 2.

27. For Henderson's changes, see *PP,* 1870, vol. 36, Metro. Police Annual Report 1869, pp. 1–4; for advocacy of local control, see *Daily News,* March 24, 1868, p. 4; and *Reynolds's,* January 17, 1869, p. 4.

28. Quotations from *Punch* 54 (January–June 1868): 63; *Times,* November 4, 1868, quoted in Custos, "Police Force," pp. 10–11; "Our Police," p. 654; and *Weekly Dispatch,* January 2, 1869, p. 9.

29. *Times,* December 29, 1868, p. 6; Burn, *Equipoise,* pp. 191–94; and Luke O. Pike, *A History of Crime in England, Illustrating the Changes of the Laws in the Progress of Civilization,* 2 vols. (London, 1876), 2: 660.

30. *Illustrated London News* 10 (March 13, 1847): 166; James Greenwood, *The Seven Curses of London* (London, 1869), pp. 193–95 (quotations); and Alan Harding, *A Social History of English Law* (Baltimore, Md., 1966), p. 366.

31. Tobias, *Crime and Industrial Society,* pp. 218–20.

32. "The Metropolitan Police and What Is Paid Them," p. 424.

33. Thomas Wright, *The Great Unwashed* (London, 1970; first pub. 1868), p. 5.

34. Quotations from Best, *Mid-Victorian Britain,* p. 92; Harrison, *Drink,* p. 135; Solly, "Destitute Poor," pp. 4-9, at 9; and Chesney, *Victorian Underworld,* chap. 2; on arrests of laborers and artisans, see CP, boxes 4, 16, ms. tables for July-December 1836 (also January-June with similar proportions) and for the full year 1876. These must have been prepared at Chadwick's request, for as far as I know such information was not made public during the period of my study.

35. *Reynolds's,* April 18, 1852, p. 8.

36. Poor man-rich man laws quotation from ibid., July 25, 1858, p. 9; lawyer's quotation from William Forsyth, "The Progress of Legal Reform," (1860) in *Essays Critical and Narrative* (London, 1874), p. 220; for "a more complete confidence" in the law as a source of increased orderliness, see *Illustrated London News* 18, supplement (February 1, 1851): 86; for the judgment that reforms made things easier for prosecutors, see Tobias, *Crime and Industrial Society,* pp. 223, 231; reforms of punishment and procedure are thoroughly discussed in William Holdsworth, *A History of English Law,* 16 vols. (London, 1909-65), vols. 13-15, ed. A. L. Goodhart and H. G. Hanbury; Leon Radzinowicz, *A History of English Criminal Law and Its Administration from 1750,* 4 vols. (London, 1948-68), vol. 4; and Tobias, *Crime and Industrial Society,* chaps. 11-12; for extension of magistrates' jurisdiction, see Hill, *Crime,* pp. 7-8; Tobias, *Crime and Industrial Society,* pp. 227-29; and J. Garwood, *The Million-Peopled City: or, One-half of the People of London Made Known to the Other Half* (London, 1853), pp. 5-6, who says that summary jurisdiction was extended to juveniles because juries balked at convicting them. The measure gave magistrates discretion to deal with juvenile delinquents as they saw fit, free from pressures of public sentiment. The theme of justices' harshness most often appears in *Reynolds's* (see, e.g., May 2, 1852, p. 8; August 17, 1862, p. 4; April 5, 1863, p. 4; and February 9, 1868, p. 4). Quotations from *Lloyd's,* July 5, 1863, p. 1; and Thomas Wright, *Our New Masters* (London, 1969; first pub. 1873), pp. 155-56.

37. The print is reproduced in Gerald Leinwand, *The Police* (New York, 1972), p. 131, without attribution or date. Cruikshank's signature is in the lower left-hand corner, and I have dated the print by clothing styles. Quotations from *PP,* 1834, vol. 16, Metro. Police, test. W. A. A. White, p. 126, q. 1822; "Metropolitan Police," p. 426; *Reynolds's,* October 25, 1863, p. 4; and Friedrich Engels, *The Condition of the Working Class in England,* trans. W. O. Henderson and W. H. Chaloner (Stanford, Calif., 1968; first pub. 1845), p. 318; see also Mrs. J. C. Byrne, *Undercurrents Overlooked,* 2 vols. (London, 1860), 1: 51, 54-55.

38. Commissioners to Mr. Jones, January 20, 1835, Mepol 1/16, letter 27957; and *Illustrated London News* 3 (December 23, 1843): 406.

39. *PP,* 1834, vol. 16, Metro. Police, test. Rowan, p. 11, qq. 165-67, at 166; see *PD,* 1830, n.s., vol. 25, col. 358; and "Police System of London" (1852), p. 9, for similar expressions; on police in poor districts, see Chesney,

Victorian Underworld, pp. 92-93; Byrne, *Undercurrents,* 1: 78-79; and James Greenwood, *The Wilds of London* (London, 1874), pp. 1, 56; quotations from Rowan to W. Hoskins, August 16, 1834, Mepol 1/16, letter 25294; and Commissioners to J. Rawlinson, Magistrate, January 30, 1839, Mepol 1/31, letter 54668; see also *East London Observer,* June 6, 1868, p. 5; July 4, 1868, p. 4; and December 5, 1868, p. 4.

40. My computations are based on the table, "Return to the House of Commons, nos. 24 and 138, sess. 1849," reproduced in Joseph Fletcher, "Statistical Account of the Police of the Metropolis," *Journal of the Statistical Society* 13 (August 1850): 240.

41. *PP,* 1870, vol. 36, Metro. Police Annual Report 1869, table 1, p. 14. The average number of patrolmen per square mile was 231. The numbers of policemen for 1848 included *all* ranks; those for 1869 include only *constables* (patrolmen). It is also important to remember that the whole patrol force was never on the streets at the same time. The effective strength at any given time might be half the figure given. On complaints from public, see Custos, "Police Force," p. 19; and *East London Observer,* December 5, 1868, p. 4.

42. Henry Mayhew, *London Labour and the London Poor,* 2d ed., 4 vols. (London, 1861-62), 1: 16, 22. Compare the similar complaints of ghetto blacks in today's American cities.

43. L. M. Thornton and W. E. Cockram, "The Policeman" (London, 1857). Since this was "first sung . . . at the Theatres Royal, Bath and Bristol," I assume it is aimed at a more substantial audience than working-class music-hall patrons.

44. For fines, see *Punch* 7 (July–December 1844): 243; and Wright, *New Masters,* pp. 155-56; for music-hall number, see C. P. Cove, "The Model Peeler," *Song-Book,* p. 50. Cove, whatever his real name, was something of a radical. On the same page of the collection is his "Not Just Yet," satirizing the establishment's promise of various reforms, but "not just yet."

45. Mrs. J. C. Byrne heard the following number in 1860: onto the stage strutted "a self-sufficient and red-nosed 'pleeceman,' wearing the orthodox livery, and ludicrously stiff in his movements, but wielding his badge of office [the club] with menacing vigour . . ., intimating that when [he] cannot succeed in coaxing a bonus out of the public [he threatens] them to the *refrain* of 'Now move on or I'll take you all up, if you don't act square.' " This was "highly to the taste" of the working-class audience (*Undercurrents,* 1: 256-57). Perjury and corruption are sung of in "Perpetual Motion" and in "The Victim from the Country" (*Song-Book,* pp. 29, 62). Quotations from Doré and Jerrold, *London,* p. 165; and *Daily News,* May 9, 1868, p. 4.

46. Quotations from Wright, *New Masters,* p. 153; and Engels, *Condition of the Working Class,* p. 318.

47. In 1890 Chadwick wrote that before the new police got under way,

"men who were mechanics in good position were asked why they did not have a watch to mark the time. 'Yes' was the reply 'and get my head broken by thieves.' They could hold in safety no personal property of any sort, and life would have been insecure. So with their families. They had no silver spoons, nor any other article of that kind. The possession of such property at that time endangered their lives" (CP, box 120, unsigned letter, July 2, 1890, quoted in Tobias, *Crime and Industrial Society,* p. 124). Thus, if Chadwick is right, respectable workers with a little property could be grateful to the police.

48. Peter Fryer, *Mrs. Grundy: Studies in English Prudery* (New York, 1964), pp. 95-107; *PP,* 1831-32, vol. 7, Sabbath, throughout; *PP,* 1847, vol. 9, Sunday Trading, throughout; and Charles Dickens, *Sunday under Three Heads: As It Is. As Sabbath Bills Would Make It. As It Might Be Made* (London, 1836), chap. 1.

49. Elie Halévy, *A History of the English People in the Nineteenth Century,* 4 vols. (New York, 1949), 4: 347-51; and Derek Beales, *From Castlereagh to Gladstone, 1815-1885* (New York, 1969), pp. 70-74.

50. Halévy, *History,* 3: 163, 4: 395-96; and Thomas McCrie, *Memoirs of Sir Andrew Agnew of Lochnaw, Bart.* (London, 1850), p. 308; Masterman quoted in Harrison, *Drink,* p. 223.

51. Marx denounced sabbatarians as "pious hypocrites," although he considered most Sunday labor exploitative—see *Capital,* 3 vols. (Moscow, 1954-59), 1: 264-65. He gives the Sunday question more extended treatment in *Marx and Engels on Britain* (Moscow, 1953), pp. 415 ff. Roebuck quotation in *PD,* 1868, 3d ser., vol. 190, col. 1857.

52. Brian Harrison, "Religion and Recreation in Nineteenth-Century England," *Past and Present* 38 (December 1967): 101. Until the late sixties the "Judicial Statistics" record less than ten prosecutions per year for violations of the law of Charles II in London. A sabbatarian crusade, carried on by citizens and parish authorities rather than the police, causes a jump to 377 prosecutions in 1867/68. They remain high through 1871. See *PP,* 1868-69, vol. 57, "Judicial Statistics," table 7, p. 28; *PP,* 1872, vol. 65, "Judicial Statistics," table 7, p. 28.

53. McCrie, *Agnew,* pp. 119-27, 271-73; Harrison, "Religion and Recreation," pp. 98-125; *PP,* 1833, vol. 3, Bills, n.p.; *Times,* April 1, 1833, p. 2; *Morning Chronicle,* April 4, 1833, p. 4; *Cosmopolite,* May 25, 1833, p. 47; *PD,* 1833, 3d ser., vol. 17, cols. 267-68, 1328-31, 1335; and Halévy, *History,* 3: 163, n. 3.

54. See, for example, Sunday Rest Association, *A Statement of the Sunday Question* (London, 1863); and A London Employer, *Sunday Trading in London* (London, 1856).

55. These arguments are distilled from speeches in Parliament, newspaper editorials, and testimony before Select Committees.

56. *Times,* April 3, 1833, p. 3; quotations from Dickens, *Sunday,* pp. 32-33; and Lord Taunton, *PD,* 1866, 3d ser., vol. 183, col. 1041.

57. Richard Mayne to Sir William Cintes, November 29, 1839, Mepol 1/45, n.p.; and Earl of St. Germans, *PD,* 1860, 3d ser., vol. 158, col. 550.

58. Quotations from *PP,* 1831-32, vol. 7, Sabbath, test. Superintendent Lowry, B (Westminster) Division, pp. 71-72, qq. 1009-27; Rowan to Frederick Byng, February 14, 1837, Mepol 1/45, n.p., original emphasis; Rowan to Sir Robert Peel, March 13, 1834, Mepol 1/14, letter 22683; and *PP,* 1850, vol. 19, Sunday Trading, test. Mayne, p. 127, q. 1515; see also Commissioners to Rev. Ward, May 20, 1830, Mepol 1/3, p. 109; to R. Lindsay, October 1, 1830, Mepol 1/4, letter 2820; to Rev. W. Ellis, July 13, 1838, Mepol 1/29, letter 50952; to Rev. Abdy, February 4, 1839, Mepol 1/31, letter 54726; and *PD,* 1860, 3d ser., vol. 157, col. 441; on preventing street cries, see PO, July 2, 1845, Mepol 7/11, fol. 16; and September 29, 1869, Mepol 7/31, p. 273 (at the height of the crusade by citizens and parish officials mentioned in note 52).

59. Quotation from *PP,* 1834, vol. 8, Drunkenness, test. George Wilson, p. 277, q. 3232; see also *PP,* 1831-32, vol. 7, Sabbath, test. Rowan, p. 55, q. 720; *PP,* 1834, vol. 16, Metro. Police, test. Mayne, p. 391, qq. 6250-51; *PP,* 1834, vol. 8, Drunkenness, test. Rowan, p. 26, q. 254; Commissioners to Vestry Clerk, St. Ann's Westminster, August 30, 1833, Mepol 1/13, letter 19687; on closing hours, see *PP,* 1835, vol. 3, Bills, n.p.; and *PP,* 1867-68, vol. 14, Sunday Closing, test. Mayne, p. 13, q. 224.

60. Quotation from Mayne to Joseph Hume, August 10, 1839, Mepol 1/45, n.p.; see also *PP,* 1850, vol. 18, Sale of Beer, test. Mayne, pp. 7-8, qq. 31-37; and Tobias, *Crime and Industrial Society,* pp. 197-98.

61. On evasion, see *PP,* 1867-68, vol. 14, Sunday Closing, test. Mayne, pp. 12, 15, qq. 203, 267; *PP,* 1847-48, vol. 16, Sale of Beer, test. Rowan, p. 4, qq. 7-11; PO, August 12, 1858, Mepol 7/19, p. 295; *PP,* 1852-53, vol. 37, Public Houses, test. Frederick Byng, Magistrate, pp. 528-29, qq. 9175-82; and Harrison, *Drink,* p. 53; quotation from *Illustrated London News* 3 (September 23, 1843): 198; for police misconduct, see *PP,* 1854, vol. 14, Sale of Beer, test. Robert Hutton, Magistrate, p. 86, qq. 1515-16; *PP,* 1867-68, vol. 14, Sunday Closing, test. Archbishop Manning, p. 98, qq. 2369-70; and Thomas Wright, *Some Habits and Customs of the Working Classes* (London, 1867), p. 226. Such charges are rare. Mayne said that the police "honestly discharge their duty. I have complaints sometimes made that they do not, but I have never found any reason to believe that they do relax" (*PP,* 1867-68, vol. 14, Sunday Closing, p. 4, q. 55). There was a breakdown of enforcement in 1845, which the commissioners moved to remedy (see PO, May 14, 1845, Mepol 7/11, fol. 10; May 17, 1845, ibid., fol. 11; and October 15, 1845, ibid., fol. 23).

62. PO, January 22, 1835, Mepol 7/3, pp. 168-69; see also PO, August 27, 1858, Mepol 7/19, p. 308.

63. For selection of men, see *PP,* 1834, vol. 16, Metro. Police, test. Rowan and Mayne, p. 391, qq. 6242-44; *PP,* 1867-68, vol. 14, Sunday Closing, test. Mayne, pp. 7-8, qq. 120-21; p. 16, q. 275 (quotation); and PO, February 18, 1864, Mepol 7/25, p. 59; quotation on reporting

violations from *PP*, 1852-53, vol. 37, Public Houses, test. Mayne, p. 3, qq. 39-40.

64. *PP*, 1854, vol. 14, Sale of Beer, test. Robert Hutton, Magistrate, p. 86, qq. 1515-16; and *PP*, 1847, vol. 9, Sunday Trading, test. Charles James, p. 22, q. 394; see also note 61 above.

65. On limited Sunday closing, see *PP*, 1854-55, vol. 10, Sale of Beer, test. Mayne, pp. 82-85, qq. 1075-1121; and test. G. C. Norton, p. 34, q. 443; quotation from F. H. F. Berkeley, *PD*, 1855, 3d ser., vol. 139, col. 183; see also Brian Harrison, "The Sunday Trading Riots of 1855," *Historical Journal* 8 (1965): 220.

66. *PP*, 1850, vol. 19, Sunday Trading, test. Mayne, p. 119, q. 1417; p. 121, q. 1441 (quotation). Grosvenor called Mayne his "most formidable opponent" (letter to *Times*, June 18, 1855, p. 10). An excellent analysis and description of the Hyde Park incident is in Harrison, "Riots," pp. 219-45. Quotations from *Times*, July 2, 1855, p. 8; and *Reynolds's*, May 6, 1855, p. 8. The *Morning Chronicle*, sympathetic to Grosvenor, said "There is one wrong which no high-spirited Englishman can endure—that of having good done to him against his will" (July 3, 1855, p. 4).

67. Harrison, "Riots," pp. 235-37; and *PP*, 1867-68, vol. 14, Sunday Closing, test. Mayne, p. 11, q. 187; p. 14, qq. 243-46; p. 3, qq. 38-41.

68. Quotations from *PP*, 1867-68, vol. 14, Sunday Closing, Report, p. iv; ibid., test. Mayne, p. 8, qq. 127-28; and Raymond Fosdick, *European Police Systems* (New York, 1915), p. 381.

69. After the 1855 Hyde Park disturbances, in which some of the police were clearly guilty of brutality, the proletarian newspapers were shocked. Said *Reynolds's:* "Many, if not most of the English people laboured under the belief that the sole object of police force was the protection of life and property; that commissioners, nor inspectors, nor constables, had nothing whatever to do with politics; that Whig and Tory, monarchist and republican, were all the same to them. We were all wrong in our estimate of the functions of the Metropolitan Police. They are . . . the political instruments of the minister of the day; and as for English rights and liberties . . . , that is all moonshine" (July 29, 1855, p. 8). *Lloyd's,* less radical, said, "Many a time we have endeavoured to advocate the rights of the force; many a time have we rendered our tribute of praise to the police, as a body of men of unquestionable worth; of men, scantily paid for work at once severe and delicate. As a body, we would still desire to respect and value them. Nevertheless, as a body they contain among the number . . . cowards and ruffians of the most brutal, the most savage temperament" (July 8, 1855, p. 6). After the month of July, such complaints disappear. One of the main reasons for the intensification of working-class criticism during the sixties, as during the thirties and forties, was the political ferment of the decade. Quotations from *PP*, 1854-55, vol. 10, Sale of Beer, test. Mayne, p. 86, q. 1138; and Chadwick, "Consolidation of the Police and Prevention of Crime," p. 12.

70. For assaults on policemen, see Greenwood, *Wilds*, 1: 56; and *PP*,

1870, vol. 36, Metro. Police Annual Report 1869, table 5, p. 18; for workers as leaders in the antagonism of the thirties, see *PD,* 1833, 3d ser., vol. 16, col. 1139; *PP,* 1833, Cold Bath Fields Meeting, test. Superintendent Baker, C (Marylebone) Division, p. 159, qq. 3914, 3917; and Grant, *Sketches,* p. 391.

71. Banton, *Policeman in the Community,* p. 180.

NOTES TO CHAPTER 6

1. *New York Herald,* April 21, 1857, p. 5; Charles MacKay, *Life and Liberty in America* (New York, 1859), pp. 28-29; and George Templeton Strong, *Diary,* ed. Allan Nevins and Milton H. Thomas, 4 vols. (New York, 1952), 2: 320; 4: 241.

2. According to Augustine E. Costello, George W. Matsell was the first to call the New York police "the finest" (see *Our Police Protectors: History of the New York Police from the Earliest Period to the Present Time* [New York, 1885], p. 102).

3. Junius Henri Browne, *The Great Metropolis: A Mirror of New York* (Hartford, Conn., 1869), p. 137, on firemen; p. 272, on slums; and p. 74, on volcano image. The "Points" improved because of increased police patrols, replacement of tenements by warehouses, and various charitable missionary projects. However, the area's lingering evil reputation distracted public attention from the growth of new slum districts during the later sixties. See James D. MacCabe, *The Secrets of the Great City: A Work Descriptive of the Virtues and the Vices, the Mysteries, Miseries, and Crimes of New York City* (Philadelphia, 1868), pp. 189-90; and Edward Crapsey, *The Netherside of New York: or, The Vice, Crime, and Poverty of the Great Metropolis* (New York, 1872), p. 155. Quotations from Samuel B. Halliday, *The Lost and Found: or, Life among the Poor* (New York, 1860), p. 332; and Charles Loring Brace, *The Dangerous Classes of New York, and Twenty Years' Work among Them* (New York, 1872), p. 29.

4. James W. Gerard, *London and New York: Their Crime and Police* (New York, 1853), pp. 9-10; and "Police," in *The New American Cyclopaedia,* ed. George Ripley and Charles Dana, 16 vols. (New York, 1860), 13: 445; quotation from Brace, *Dangerous Classes,* pp. 25-27.

5. Edward Crapsey estimated the number of professional criminals as 2,500 in the late sixties, in a Manhattan population of around 800,000 (*Netherside,* p. 24). Other figures range from 7,000 (Browne, *Great Metropolis,* p. 347) to 30,000 (Rev. H. W. Bellows, cited in Crapsey). Quotations from Crapsey, *Netherside,* p. 24; and Brace, *Dangerous Classes,* p. 31; on immigrants, see Crapsey, *Netherside,* p. 6; *New York City Board of Assistant Aldermen Documents,* 1842, vol. 19, no. 56, Police Report, p. 189; *SD,* 1858, vol. 2, no. 48, Police Report, p. 2; David Montgomery, *Beyond Equality: Labor and the Radical Republicans, 1862-1872* (New York, 1967), p. 37; David J. Rothman, *The Discovery of the Asylum: Social Order and Disorder in the New Republic* (Boston, 1971), pp. 161-72; and Gerard, *London and New York,* p. 8.

6. Quotation from Francis J. Grund, *Aristocracy in America, from the Sketch-Book of a German Nobleman* (New York, 1959; first pub. 1839), p. 51; see also James Harper (nativist mayor of New York), "To the Electors of the City and County of New York," 1844, Harper Papers, New-York Historical Society; and Joel Tyler Headley, *The Great Riots of New York, 1712-1873* (New York, 1873), pp. 66-68.

7. Crapsey, *Netherside,* p. 29; quotations from Browne, *Great Metropolis,* pp. 67, 71; and Brace, *Dangerous Classes,* p. 27; see also Herbert Asbury, *The Gangs of New York: An Informal History of the Underworld* (New York, 1928), chaps. 1, 6.

8. Quotations from *Herald,* March 25, 1856, p. 4; *AD,* 1866, vol. 3, no. 50, Annual Report, NYPA, 1865, pp. 161-62; and *New York Times,* April 21, 1867, p. 4.

9. For Anderson, see *Herald,* July 22, 1857, p. 1; quotations from ibid., July 27, p. 1; and July 28, p. 4. The *Times* predicted that Anderson's murder would dispel hostility toward the new force (July 23, 1857, p. 4).

10. *Herald,* November 11, 1858, p. 1; November 12, p. 5; and November 18, p. 1.

11. *Times,* November 18, 1858, p. 4. The absence of a hostile editorial in the *Herald,* usually critical of the police, illustrates the *Times's* point.

12. Ibid. (original emphasis); ibid., May 10, 1867, p. 4; see also James F. Richardson, *The New York Police: Colonial Times to 1901* (New York, 1970), pp. 157-58.

13. Rothman, *Discovery,* pp. 236-57; W. David Lewis, *From Newgate to Dannemora: The Rise of the Penitentiary in New York, 1796-1848* (Ithaca, N.Y., 1965), chap. 11. Reform was not totally abandoned, for "commutation" or cumulative reduction of prisoners' terms for good behavior, apparently a better regulated system than British ticket-of-leave, was instituted in the sixties (see *AD,* 1864, vol. 3, no. 65, NYPA, 1863, pp. 14-25; *AD,* 1867, vol. 3, no. 38, ibid., 1866, pp. 77-79).

14. See John B. McMaster, *History of the People of the United States, from the Revolution to the Civil War,* 8 vols. (New York, 1883-1913), 4: 541-46; 7: 150-51.

15. *Times,* November 18, 1858, p. 4.

16. Quotations from F. Byrdsall, *History of the Loco-Foco or Equal Rights Party* (New York, 1842), pp. 73, 88, 149, 165, found in Walter Hugins, *Jacksonian Democracy and the Working Class: A Study of the New York State Workingmen's Movement, 1828-1837* (Stanford, Calif., 1960), pp. 142-43; see also Edward Pessen, *Most Uncommon Jacksonians: Radical Leaders of the Early Labor Movement* (Albany, N.Y., 1967), p. 121; and Arthur M. Schlesinger, Jr., *The Age of Jackson* (Boston, 1945), pp. 329-33.

17. For Connolly, see Matthew P. Breen, *Thirty Years of New York Politics Up-to-Date* (New York, 1899), p. 519; for Dowling, see Matthew H. Smith, *Sunshine and Shadow in New York* (Hartford, Conn., 1868), p. 167; see also James D. Mac Cabe, Jr., *Lights and Shadows of New York Life: or, Sights and Sensations of the Great City* (New York, 1970; first pub. 1872), p.

239 (This book is a rewriting of *Secrets of the Great City,* with the author's name slightly changed for reasons unknown.); and Crapsey, *Netherside,* p. 28.

18. *Times,* March 24, 1855, p. 4; *New York Tribune,* July 28, 1845, p. 2; *AD,* 1849, vol. 6, no. 243, NYPA, 1848, pp. 160-61; *AD,* 1853, vol. 4, no. 108, ibid., 1852, p. 28; *AD,* 1869, vol. 4, no. 38, Metro. Police Annual Report 1868, pp. 7-8; and *AD,* 1870, vol. 2, no. 17, ibid., 1869, pp. 8-9.

19. Quotation from *Times,* December 11, 1855, p. 4; see also *SD,* 1856, vol. 2, no. 97, Police Investigation, testimony of John Gray, Warden of Tombs, p. 137; *AD,* 1863, vol. 2, no. 26, NYPA, 1862, p. 103; and *AD,* 1865, vol. 3, no. 62, ibid., 1864, pp. 119, 226.

20. For London, see *PP,* 1845, vol. 14, 8th Report, Criminal Law Commissioners, app. A, p. 242; for New York, see *AD,* 1849, vol. 6, no. 243, NYPA, 1848, pp. 160-61; *AD,* 1853, vol. 4, no. 108, ibid., 1852, pp. 27-28; *AD,* 1869, vol. 4, no. 38, Metro. Police Annual Report 1868, pp. 7-8; *AD,* 1870, vol. 2, no. 17, ibid., 1869, pp. 8-9; and *AD,* 1855, vol. 7, no. 150, Report of Select Committee on Code of Criminal Procedure, pp. 16-17; see also *SD,* 1869, vol. 2, no. 10, NYPA, 1868, p. 19.

21. *The Subterranean,* May 24, 1845, p. 2; June 21, p. 2; August 30, p. 2; and August 9, p. 2. The paper lasted only two years.

22. Quotation from *Herald,* December 22, 1860, p. 6; see also Mac-Cabe, *Secrets,* p. 190.

23. James F. Richardson, "The History of Police Protection in New York City, 1800-1870" (Ph.D. diss., New York University, 1961), p. 193; ms. Quarterly Reports of Police Captains, First, Second, Fourth, and Sixth wards, 1850-51, N.Y. City Municipal Archives; ms. Tenth Ward blotters, May 25-June 27; July 27-August 26, 1855; July 27-August 26, 1865, N.Y. City Municipal Archives. The figure for Irish-surname policemen in the ward (clearly including numerous second-generation Irish-Americans) is computed from lists in David T. Valentine, comp., *Manual of the Corporation of the City of New York,* 1855, 1856 (New York, 1856, 1857). Figures on complaints are rough calculations based on the surnames of officers and complainants in the Complaints against Policemen, 1845-54, CCP, boxes 3198-99; 3201-10. One hundred of the incidents were WASP-WASP, and 38 were Irish-surname officer and WASP-surname citizen. The small remainder involved German officers, and a few black citizens confronting policemen of various ethnic groups.

24. Richardson, *N.Y. Police,* p. 71.

25. On mobility, see Stephan Thernstrom, *Poverty and Progress: Social Mobility in a Nineteenth-Century City* (Cambridge, Mass., 1964); and Peter R. Knights, *The Plain People of Boston: A Study in City Growth, 1830-1860* (New York, 1971); on pay, see "Police," *New American Cyclopaedia,* 13: 445; and George R. Taylor, *The Transportation Revolution, 1815-1860* (New York, 1951), pp. 295-97; on makeup of force, see Applications, 1855, CCP, boxes 3209-10; for residence, family size, and ages of policemen,

see 1850, 1860 ms. Federal Census for wards 1, 4, 6, 10, 15 (microfilm, U.S. National Archives and Record Center); for age and marital status of arrestees, see *AD,* 1868, vol. 2, no. 20, Metro. Police Annual Report 1867, pp. 42-47, as well as the police arrest records generally; for London, see memo of 1850 on ages, Mepol 2/26, loose.

26. On Irish background, see George E. Berkley, *The Democratic Policeman* (Boston, 1969), pp. 60-61; on black police today, see Nicholas Alex, *Black in Blue: A Study of the Negro Policeman* (New York, 1969), throughout; on Irish policeman incident, see *Herald,* July 13, 1857, p. 1.

27. The annual reports of the New York Sabbath Committee, 1857-70, refer to the experiences of their British brethren. See also Timothy L. Smith, *Revivalism and Social Reform: American Protestantism on the Eve of the Civil War* (New York, 1957), p. 35.

28. For the 1813 law, see *BAD,* 1854, vol. 21, pt. 1, no. 12, pp. 250-52; for sabbatarians' fears, see NYSC, 1857, document 1, "The Sabbath in New York," pp. 7-8; and *Journal of Commerce,* June 5, 1859, quoted in NYSC, 1859, doc. 7, "Memorial Memoranda," p. 29.

29. Richardson, *N.Y. Police,* p. 48. The link of sabbatarians and nativists is clear in this comment on immigration: "The incursion of Goths and Vandals could hardly be more fatal to morals and religion. The whole atmosphere is tainted by its breath. Many parts of the city reek with its pollution" (NYSC, 1857, doc. 1, "The Sabbath in N.Y.," p. 8).

30. Of the thirty-eight men issuing the original call for a meeting which led to formation of the NYSC in 1857, fifteen were listed as worth $100,000 or more in Moses Beach, *The Wealth and Biography of the Wealthy Citizens of the City of New York,* 12th ed. (New York, 1855).

31. Lee Benson points out that differences between "puritans" and "non-puritans" transcended rural-urban boundaries and formed an important basis of party identification, most "puritans" being Whigs and most "non-puritans" being Democrats in the 1840s (see *The Concept of Jacksonian Democracy: New York as a Test Case* [New York, 1961], pp. 198-207).

32. On city council demand for enforcement, see *BAD,* 1854, vol. 21, pt. 1, no. 12, Report on Sabbath, pp. 250-52; on legal restrictions, see *N.Y. City Board of Councilmen Documents,* 1854, vol. 1, no. 30, Report of Corporation Counsel, pp. 572-74.

33. Quotations from *Times,* January 3, 1855, p. 4 (original emphasis); and *Herald,* January 22, 1855, p. 1; see also *Times,* January 22, 1855, p. 3; January 15, p. 4; January 29, p. 4; April 20, p. 1; *Herald,* March 6, 1855, p. 1; and Wood to Mr. Coleman of the Astor House, January 24, 1855, quoted in Donald McLeod, *Biography of Hon. Fernando Wood* (New York, 1856), pp. 254-55.

34. The law is printed in *BAD,* 1855, vol. 22, pp. 18-41; for temperance men's expectations of Wood and quotation, see *Times,* April 11, 1855, p. 4; on the nullification effort, see *Times,* April 19, 1855, p. 4; April 24, p. 4; July 4, p. 3; for Wood's instructions to the police, see McLeod,

Wood, pp. 266-70; for evasive actions, see *Times,* July 5, 1855, p. 1; July 6, p. 8; and *Herald,* July 5, p. 4; quotation from *Times,* July 7, p. 4.

35. The Court of Appeals (the state's highest) rejected the prohibition law as unconstitutional because its seizure provisions violated property rights (*Herald,* March 26, 1856, pp. 1, 4; *Times,* March 26, pp. 1, 4). The New Republican party had political motives for abandoning prohibition; it sought the votes of antislavery men who also opposed prohibition. Governor Myron Clark, who signed the 1855 bill, was denied renomination. See Eric Foner, *Free Soil, Free Labor, Free Men: The Ideology of the Republican Party before the Civil War* (New York, 1970), p. 241; see also NYSC, 1860, doc. 11, "Sunday Theatres," throughout; *Herald,* October 5, 1860, p. 6; and NYSC, 1861, doc. 15, "Civil Sabbath Restored," pp. 2-5; on the revival, see Smith, *Revivalism and Reform,* chap. 4, esp. pp. 63-66; and Arthur C. Cole, *The Irrepressible Conflict, 1850-1865* (New York, 1934), pp. 252-54.

36. NYSC, 1859, doc. 6, "A Year for the Sabbath," pp. 9-19; and ibid., 1867, doc. 34, "Tenth Year of the NYSC," pp. 4-9; Clifford S. Griffin, *Their Brothers' Keepers: Moral Stewardship in the United States, 1800-1865* (New Brunswick, N.J., 1960), pp. 237-39, briefly discusses the committee; on the Germans, see NYSC, 1865, doc. 30, "Eighth Year of the NYSC," p. 16. The NYSC in all their reports chronicle their activities among the Germans, but mention the Irish only once (1861, doc. 15, "Civil Sabbath," p. 14).

37. Accounts of the riot are in the *Herald,* July 13-15, 1857; and Richardson, *N.Y. Police,* p. 110; quotation from the *Herald,* July 15, p. 1; on German policemen, see *Staats-Zeitung,* July 14, *Demokrat,* July 14, translated in *Herald,* July 15, p. 8.

38. *AD,* 1859, vol. 2, no. 63, Metro. Police Annual Report 1858, p. 13; NYSC, 1859, doc. 7, "Memorial Memoranda," throughout; and ibid., 1859, doc. 8, "A German's Appeal to Germans on the Sunday Question," pp. 5-6, quoting resolutions of the commissioners.

39. *Herald,* July 4, 1859, p. 5; July 11, p. 1; July 18, p. 5; and July 25, p. 5.

40. Text of order in *Herald,* August 14, 1859, p. 3; see also August 15, p. 6; and July 18, p. 4.

41. *Herald,* July 18, 1859, p. 4; August 1, p. 5; NYSC, 1859, doc. 8, "A German's Appeal," pp. 7-8; and ibid., 1860, doc. 12, "Progress of the Sabbath Reform," p. 4. Regarding national drinking habits and disorder, a contemporary wrote: "The German may snore himself into insensibility in a deluge of lager beer, without doing dishonour to Faderland . . . ; but the Irishman, more impulsive, more mercurial, more excitable, will publish his indiscretion on the highway, and will himself identify his nationality with his folly" (see John Francis Maguire, *The Irish in America* [London, 1868], pp. 284-85). It was indeed the Irish who were most often arrested on intoxication and drunk and disorderly charges.

42. NYSC, 1861, doc. 15, "The Civil Sabbath Restored," pp. 5-9; and ibid., 1863, doc. 24, "Civil and Sacred Sabbath," pp. 5-7; quotation from *AD,* 1861, vol. 1, no. 27, Metro. Police Annual Report 1860, pp. 5-6.

43. *Times,* April 2, 1862, p. 4 (Brennan); April 18, 1862, p. 4 (McCunn); and May 4, 1862, p. 4.

44. *AD,* 1866, vol. 1, no. 12, Metro. Police Annual Report 1865, pp. 20-22; NYSC, 1866, doc. 31, "Ninth Year of the NYSC," p. 30; and ibid., 1865, doc. 30, "Eighth Year," pp. 12-13. The percentages are in the last-cited source, but the NYSC's closeness to the police probably makes them official figures.

45. NYSC, 1883, doc. 48, "Twenty-Fifth and Twenty-Sixth Years," pp. 3-4; and *AD,* 1867, vol. 8, no. 220, Metro. Police Annual Report 1866, pp. 15-17.

46. On opposition to excise act, see Richardson, *N.Y. Police,* pp. 154-55; Breen, *Thirty Years,* pp. 109-10; NYSC, 1867, doc. 34, "Tenth Year," pp. 15-18; *Herald,* June 5, 1866, p. 5; and *Times,* June 5, p. 4; on suspension of law, see *AD,* 1867, vol. 8, no. 220, Metro. Police Annual Report 1866, pp. 19-20, 74-77; for discussion of injunctions as a compromise, see the *New York World,* July 16, 1866, p. 5.

47. *World,* January 14, 1867, p. 1; January 21, p. 5; *Times,* July 15, 1867, p. 4; quotations from MacCabe, *Secrets,* p. 372; and *Times,* July 30, 1867, p. 4.

48. Richardson, *N.Y. Police,* pp. 155-56; and NYSC, 1871, doc. 38, "Thirteenth and Fourteenth Years," pp. 3-7. Source of quotation not identified.

49. Quotations from *Tribune,* July 19, 1867, p. 4; and *Times,* June 17, 1872, p. 4; see also NYSC, 1871, doc. 38, "Thirteenth and Fourteenth Years," pp. 6-7. The *Annual Report of the New York City Police Department,* 1872, p. 22, shows a 50 percent increase of Sunday arrests in the period April 1, 1870, to April 1, 1872, over the period November 1, 1868 to November 1, 1869, although average weekday arrests still exceeded Sunday arrests.

50. On state excise act, see NYSC, 1871, doc. 38, "Thirteenth and Fourteenth Years," pp. 6-7; quotation from Alexander Callow, Jr., *The Tweed Ring* (New York, 1966), pp. 192-94; on politics and enforcement, see Richardson, *N.Y. Police,* pp. 182-85, 251.

51. Thurman Arnold, *The Symbols of Government* (New York, 1962; first pub. 1935), pp. 149-59; quotation from Brace, *Dangerous Classes,* p. 72. Brace favored the legalization of Sunday beer and light wines.

NOTES TO EPILOGUE

1. William A. Westley, *Violence and the Police: A Sociological Study of Law, Custom, and Morality* (Cambridge, Mass., 1970), p. xiii, gives a succinct critique of professionalization.

2. *New York Times,* September 1, 1974, sec. 4, p. 6.

3. John R. Lambert, *Crime, Police, and Race Relations: A Study in Birmingham* (London, 1970), found the Irish to be the most violent group in that city.

4. *New York Times,* April 12, 1972, pp. 1, 12.

5. Ibid.

6. Anthony Burgess, review of *Blimey! Another Book about London,* by Donald Goddard, *N.Y. Times Book Review,* August 13, 1972, p. 5.

7. See *Red Weekly,* June 20, 1974, p. 1f, and *Workers' Press,* June 26, 1974, p. 11, quoting Lord Gardiner, former lord chancellor, for strong criticisms of police arbitrariness. These radical papers recall similar nineteenth-century criticisms of the police.

8. See Lord Gardiner's remarks just cited, and *New York Times,* August 7, 1972, pp. 1, 3.

GUIDE TO THE MOST IMPORTANT SOURCES

I. Unpublished Official Records

My account of the London police relies heavily on the manuscript Metropolitan Police Records in the Public Record Office. These, while not complete, provide details of both trivial and significant matters of official policy. The most important were Mepol 1, the commissioners' letter books from 1829 to 1861, and Mepol 7, the daily Police Orders, which are complete except for the decades of the forties and fifties. Starting in 1857–58 they are in printed (though not published) form instead of manuscript. Other useful records were Mepol 2, miscellaneous police reports, especially various official memoranda which do not appear elsewhere, and Mepol 4, more miscellany. The Home Office Records, HO 61, 64, and 65, were also useful, particularly HO 61, which was Home Office correspondence with the police commissioners. HO 64 was mainly copies of "seditious publications," mostly radical newspapers of the 1830s, but also including a printed silk handkerchief. Finally, an important semiofficial manuscript source was the Edwin Chadwick Papers in the library of University College, London. Chadwick had a lifelong interest in the police, and served as a member of the parliamentary commission which proposed a national constabulary force in 1839. The papers contain drafts of articles on the police and some official correspondence not available elsewhere.

Manuscript records are fragmentary for New York because the Police Department destroyed many volumes of orders and correspondence in 1914. Surviving material has nevertheless proved useful for my discussion of police-public relations and practices on the beat. Among the most interesting of the records in the Municipal Archives were the Complaints against Policemen, 1845-54, City Clerk Papers, boxes 3198-99, 3201-10. These contain routine departmental complaints such as sleeping on duty, but also citizen complaints of more serious infractions such as violence or arbitrary arrest. They are a treasure house of "human interest" stories, some grim and others delightful. Another human document is the diary of William Bell, a policeman who was "detailed" as inspector of pawnbrokers and junkshops.

Bell gives a somewhat laconic view of police work and New York's "low life" in 1850-51. This source is in the New-York Historical Society. More useful documents in the Municipal Archives were the Tenth Ward Blotters, May 25-August 27, 1855, July 27-August 26, 1856, and the Applications for Positions as Policemen, 1855, City Clerk Papers, box 3210. Finally, I used manuscript census returns to draw a social picture of policemen: 7th Census (1850) and 8th Census (1860), Wards 1, 2, 4, 6, 10, 15. These are on microfilm from the National Archives and Record Center, Washington, D.C.

II. PUBLISHED OFFICIAL RECORDS

London's Metropolitan Police unfortunately did not publish an annual report until 1870, but the *Parliamentary Papers* constituted an indispensable supplement to the manuscript records. Most of them were Select Committee investigations undertaken with an eye to framing bills. The testimony of the commissioners and other police and judicial officials often revealed the thinking behind policy decisions. While many of the investigations were partisan and there were numerous unasked questions, the testimony is a good guide to official and unofficial opinions. The most important of these investigations were *PP*, 1834, vol. 16, "Report from the Select Committee on the Police of the Metropolis"; *PP*, 1837-38, vol. 15, "Report from the Select Committee on Metropolis Police Offices"; *PP*, 1839, vol. 19, "First Report of the Commissioners Appointed to Inquire as to the Best Means of Establishing an Efficient Constabulary Force in the Counties of England and Wales"; *PP*, 1854-55, vol. 12, and *PP*, 1856, vol. 7, "Report from the Select Committee on Public Prosecutors"; and *PP*, 1867-68, vol. 14, "Special Report from the Select Committee on the Sale of Liquors on Sunday Bill." Other important *Parliamentary Papers* which were not investigations include *PP*, 1830, vol. 23, Accounts and Papers, "Returns Relating to the Metropolitan Police," which contained the full rules and regulations and selected police orders; *PP*, 1870, vol. 36, and *PP*, 1871, vol. 28, "Report of the Commissioner of Police of the Metropolis" for 1869 and 1870; and the annual "Returns of Criminal Offenders" and "Judicial Statistics," which provided useful statistical material. *Hansard's Parliamentary Debates* proved vital for legislators' opinions and the history of bills.

New York's published official documents are not as voluminous as London's, and many of the legislative investigations were more openly partisan than those across the Atlantic. However, testimony before committees goes a long way toward filling the gaps in manuscript records, and the publication of annual reports throughout the 1845-70 period gives a much fuller picture of some aspects of police work than was available for London. The two most important sets of documents were the *New York City Board of Aldermen Documents,* containing committee reports, mayors' messages, and the police reports up to 1857, and the *New York State Assembly* and *Senate Documents,* with investigations of the police and the annual reports after 1857. The latter also contained the annual secretary of state's report of criminal statistics and the semiofficial annual reports of the New York Prison Association. The most useful legislative investigations were *SD*, 1856, vol. 2, no. 97, "Report of the Joint Committee on Police Matters in the City and County of New-York, and County of Kings," which was the first of a long line of police investigations up to the Knapp Commission; and *SD*, 1861, vol. 2, no. 71, "Report of the Select Committee Appointed to Inquire into the Practice of Arrest, Detention, and Discharge of Persons by the Metropolitan Police Force." In 1846 and 1851 the New York City Municipal Police published its rules and regulations as *Rules and Regulations for Day and Night Police of the City of New-York; with Instructions as to the Legal Powers and Duties of Policemen.* The Metropolitan Police regulations appeared in 1860 as *Manual for the Government of the Police Force of the Metropolitan Police District of the State of New York,* available as *AD*, 1860, vol. 3, no. 88, pp. 86–110, or published separately in 1860 by Edmund Jones and G. T. Nesbitt, New York City. David T. Valentine, and later Joseph Shannon, comps., *Manual of the Corporation of the City of New York,* 1848–69, provided important lists of policemen's names and reprinted the state laws on police matters. Finally, although the New York Sabbath Committee was not an official organization, its reports and documents, collected in two volumes and published by the committee in 1868 and 1899, formed the backbone of my New York Sunday law discussion.

Reports of court cases were essential documents for both New York and London. For New York, the principal reports were *Howard's Practice Reports* and *Parker's Criminal Reports;* for London, *Cox's Criminal Cases* and *Dennison's Crown Cases Reserved.*

III. NEWSPAPERS

The London police commissioners revealed little about policies and practices to newspaper reporters and many of their official communications corrected journalistic inaccuracies in crime reporting. Newspapers did not give much of an inside view of the police, but provided editorials and important accounts of events. They were especially useful for reactions to Sunday laws, riots and demonstrations, and the "crime wave" of the late sixties. The *Times* (independent Tory) and the *Morning Chronicle* (Liberal) gave mainstream viewpoints, while *Reynolds's Newspaper* and *Lloyd's Weekly London Newspaper* articulated radical perspectives in the fifties and sixties. A few issues of early unstamped papers, *The Poor Man's Guardian* and *The Cosmopolite,* were also useful. *The Illustrated London News* provided some criticisms of the police from a liberal and sometimes radical standpoint. *Punch,* the humor magazine, was less hostile than satirical. *The Annual Register* provided accounts of riots and demonstrations from a conservative perspective.

New York newspapers were one of my most important sources; the completeness of journalistic coverage helped make up for the paucity of manuscript material. The police freely communicated many of their orders, and individual officers expressed their opinions to reporters. Although the accuracy of reporting is sometimes suspect, much valuable material would have been lost without journalistic interest in the police. The *Herald* (Democrat) and the *Times* (Whig-Republican) were most important for me. The *Herald* was known for lively reporting, which a cautious historian can still appreciate. The *Times,* more staid, covered some areas the other paper neglected and spoke up editorially much more often. Other useful papers were the *Commercial Advertiser, Journal of Commerce, The Subterranean, Tribune,* and *World. Harper's Weekly* said less about the police than I had hoped it would, but was sometimes good for comments and occasional cartoons on police and crime.

IV. CONTEMPORARY BOOKS, PAMPHLETS, AND ARTICLES ON POLICE,
THE ADMINISTRATION OF JUSTICE, AND CRIME

Mid-nineteenth-century Englishmen were fascinated by their new police system and the problem of crime, providing much important material for the historian. After Patrick Colquhoun's *A Treatise on the Police of the Metropolis,* 7th ed. (London: Printed for J. Mawman, 1806; first pub. 1797), commentators preferred to write pamphlets and articles on this subject instead of books. Fundamental articles on London's new police include "The Metropolitan Police and What Is Paid Them," *Chambers's Magazine* 41 (July 2, 1864): 423-26; "Our Police System," *The Dark Blue* 2 (February 1872): 692-700; "The Police System of London," *Edinburgh Review* 96 (July 1852): 1-33; Edwin Chadwick: "Preventive Police," *London Review* 1 (February 1829): 252 ff., and "On the Consolidation of the Police Force and the Prevention of Crime," *Fraser's Magazine* 67 (January 1868): 1-18; Harriet Martineau, "The Policeman: His Health," *Once a Week* 2 (June 2, 1860): 522-26; and A. Wynter, "The Police and the Thieves," *Quarterly Review* 99 (June 1856): 160-200. This last article and the Chadwick pieces were the most thoughtful.

A good idea of the pamphlets written principally in the 1820s advocating and anticipating a new police can be had from L. B. Allen, *Brief Considerations on the Present State of the Police of the Metropolis; with a Few Suggestions towards Its Improvement* (London: Printed for Joseph Butterfield and Son et al., 1821); [H. Grey Bennet], *Considerations on the Present State of the Police of the Metropolis* (London: Printed by R. and A. Taylor, 1822); and [George Mainwaring], *Observations on the Present State of the Police of the Metropolis* (London: Printed by William Clowes, 1821). Hostile early responses to the Metropolitan Police appear in Humanitas, *A Letter to the Right Hon. Sir Robert Peel, Bart., &c., &c., &c., on the Fatal and Ruinous Consequences of His Currency Bill, and Facts Demonstrative of his Intention to Subvert Public Liberty and Enslave the Country through the Espionage and Tyranny of the New Police ...* (London: W. Strange, [1835]); A Hypochondriac, *The Blue Devils; or the New Police: A Poem in*

Three Cantos (London: George Henderson, 1830); and G. C. Smith, *Weeding the New Police: or a Faithful & Fearless Investigation of the Modern Constabulary Force, Called the New Police for the Metropolis and Its Environs* . . . (London: T. A. Smith, 1830). Perhaps the most thoughtful analysis of the police force's difficulties in the late sixties is Custos, *The Police Force of the Metropolis in 1868* (London: William Ridgway, 1868).

A very useful type of contemporary literature which often touched significantly on the police in its accounts of crime and "low life" was the popular book of urban adventure, exploration, and exposé, written mostly by journalists. Some were sensationalistic, while others were of serious and lasting significance, such as the works of Henry Mayhew and Thomas Wright. All provided information about the police and their urban milieu not found elsewhere. Mrs. J. C. Byrne's *Undercurrents Overlooked*, 2 vols. (London: Richard Bentley, 1860), captures the genre's flavor. Other more or less useful works were Gustave Doré and Blanchard Jerrold, *London: A Pilgrimage* (Newton Abbot, England: David and Charles, 1971; first pub. 1872), best for the Doré illustrations; James Grant, *Sketches in London* (London: Thomas Tegg: 1st ed. 1838; 4th ed. 1850); James Greenwood: *The Seven Curses of London* (London: Stanley Rivers, 1869) and *The Wilds of London* (London: Chatto and Windus, 1874); Henry Mayhew, *London Labour and the London Poor: The Condition and Earnings of Those that Will Work, Cannot Work, and Will Not Work*, 2d ed., 4 vols. (London: Charles Griffin, 1861-62), vol. 4 with John Binny and Bracebridge Hemying; Henry Mayhew and John Binny, *The Criminal Prisons of London and Scenes of Prison Life* (London: Griffin, Bohn, 1862); W. H. Watts, *London Life at the Police-Courts* (London: Ward and Lock, 1864); [Thomas Wontner], *Old Bailey Experience* (London: James Fraser, 1833); and Thomas Wright's three important surveys of the working classes: *The Great Unwashed* (London: Frank Cass, 1970; first pub. 1868), *Our New Masters* (London: Frank Cass, 1969; first pub. 1873), and *Some Habits and Customs of the Working Classes* (London: Tinsley, 1867).

Another essential type of contemporary literature was the professional or scholarly treatise on crime, law, and the administration of justice. These works were both primary and secondary, revealing contemporary attitudes but also providing valuable historical information. Although not dealing directly with the administration of justice, Walter Bagehot's *The English Constitution* (New York, Doubleday, n.d.; first pub. 1867) shaped my thoughts about legitimation of power. He also reveals the establishment's view of the English political order before the reform of 1867. Works on crime and the administration of justice were Frederic Hill, *Crime: Its Amount, Causes, and Remedies* (London: John Murray, 1853); William Hoyle, *Crime in England and Wales in the Nineteenth Century: An Historical and Critical Retrospect* (London: Effingham, Wilson, 1876); Frederick W. Maitland, *Justice and Police* (London: Macmillan, 1885); Luke Owen Pike, *A History of Crime in England, Illustrating the Changes of the Laws in the*

Progress of Civilization, 2 vols. (London: Smith, Elder, 1876); and James Fitzjames Stephen, *A History of the Criminal Law of England,* 3 vols. (London: Macmillan, 1883). Two articles by William Forsyth, encountered accidentally, were most important: "Criminal Procedure in Scotland and England" (first pub. 1851) and "The Progress of Legal Reform" (first pub. 1860), both in *Essays Critical and Narrative* (London: Longmans, Green, 1874).

Finally, one must include Charles Dickens, not only for such novels as *Oliver Twist* and *Bleak House,* but also for articles on police work and the "Sunday question" which he published in his magazine, *Household Words.* Another novel which completely absorbed me in the British Museum reading room was Michael Sadleir's *Fanny by Gaslight* (London: Penguin, 1948), a grim tale of corruption and depravity set at the end of the period of my study. Sadleir is a careful historian as well as a good writer.

New Yorkers had less to say, or at least to write, about their police than did Londoners. One looks in vain for useful articles in popular magazines, although pieces like "The Judiciary of New York City," *North American Review* 105 (July 1867): 148-76, and "Municipal Government," *United States Magazine and Democratic Review* 25 (June 1849): 481-500 (on the Astor Place riot) were significant. Historians must rely more on the "lights and shadows" literature, journalistic explorations of the underworld which emphasize the striking contrasts of city life. This literature was as popular, if not more so, as its counterpart in London. The most important of these books was Edward Crapsey, *The Netherside of New York: or, The Vice, Crime, and Poverty of the Great Metropolis* (New York: Sheldon, 1872). Others included Junius Henri Browne, *The Great Metropolis: A Mirror of New York* (Hartford, Conn.: American Publishing, 1869); James Dabney MacCabe, *The Secrets of the Great City: A Work Descriptive of the Virtues and the Vices, the Mysteries, Miseries, and Crimes of New York City* (Philadelphia: National Publishing, 1868); and Matthew H. Smith, *Sunshine and Shadow in New York* (Hartford, Conn.: J. B. Burr and Hyde, 1868). Not strictly of this class, but bordering on it, is Charles Loring Brace, *The Dangerous Classes of New York, and Twenty Years' Work among Them* (New York: Wynkoop and Hollenbeck, 1872). Foreign travelers' accounts provided less information than I expected; they gave some background but did not dwell on the police at length. The most useful to me were James Fenimore Cooper's pseudo-travelogue, *Notions of the Americans, Picked up by a Travelling Batchelor,* 2 vols. (New York: Frederick A. Ungar, 1963; first pub. 1828); Frederika Bremer, *The Homes of the New World: Impressions of America,* 2 vols. (New York: Harper, 1853); James Dawson Burn, *Three Years among the Working-Classes in the United States during the War* (London: Smith, Elder, 1865); Charles MacKay, *Life and Liberty in America: or, Sketches of a Tour in the United States and Canada in 1857-58* (New York: Harper, 1859); and John Francis Maguire, *The Irish in America* (London: Longmans, Green, 1868).

Of materials directly related to the police, a unique and important document is James W. Gerard, *London and New York: Their Crime and Police* (New York: William C. Bryant, 1853), which influenced the police reform of 1853. George Washington Walling, *Recollections of a New York Chief of Police* (New York: Caxton, 1887), provided valuable information on police practices from a veteran. George S. McWatters, *Knots Untied: or, Ways and By-Ways in the Hidden Life of American Detectives* (Hartford, Conn.: J. B. Burr and Hyde, 1872), contained much old-fashioned melodrama but was only marginally useful. Although an unannotated scissors and paste compilation, Augustine E. Costello, *Our Police Protectors: History of the New York Police from the Earliest Period to the Present Time* (New York: Published for the Police Pension Fund, 1885), was the first history of an American police force and is useful as both a primary and a secondary source. Accounts of New York City's riots are David M. Barnes, *The Draft Riots in New York, July 1863: The Metropolitan Police, Their Honorable Record* (New York: Baker and Godwin, 1863); and Joel Tyler Headley, *The Great Riots of New York, 1712-1873* (New York: E. B. Treat, 1873); these reveal much about police practices and "respectable" citizens' attitudes.

I found some of Alexis de Tocqueville's thoughts regarding the impact of democracy on the administration of justice especially provocative, so *Democracy in America,* ed. Francis Bowen, 2d ed., 2 vols. (Cambridge, Mass.: Sever and Francis, 1863; first pub. 1835, 1840), was a major source. James Bryce, *The American Commonwealth,* 2 vols. (London: Macmillan, 1889); Francis Lieber, *On Civil Liberty and Self-Government,* enl. ed. in 1 vol. (Philadelphia: Lippincott, 1859; first pub. 1853); and Harriet Martineau, *Morals and Manners* (Philadelphia: Lea and Blanchard, 1838) shaped my conceptualization in lesser ways and provided information on the administration of justice.

V. MODERN HISTORIES OF POLICE, LAW, CRIME, AND SOCIAL CONDITIONS

Englishmen have long regarded the police as one of their nation's most important institutional developments. Consequently, they have produced a solid literature of police and legal history. Although supplanted by recent work, W. L. Melville Lee, *A History of the Police in England* (London: Methuen, 1901), is still useful although typically unsympathetic to political protest and reflective of upper- and middle-class faith in the police. The several works of Charles Reith, who has studied the police more thoroughly than anybody else, are the standard source. Reith, however valuable he is, should be read as a partisan of Colonel Rowan at the expense of Mayne, and as a conservative who dismisses all early criticism of the police as "bigotry and blindness." He does not pursue his subject much beyond the 1840s. See *The Police Idea: Its History and Evolution in England in the Eighteenth Century and After* (London: Oxford University Press, 1938); *British Police and the Democratic Ideal* (London: Oxford Unviersity Press,

1943); and *A New Study of Police History* (Edinburgh: Oliver and Boyd, 1956). Belton Cobb, *The First Detectives and the Early Career of Richard Mayne, Commissioner of Police* (London: Faber and Faber, 1957), is a reply to Reith which attempts to redress the balance in favor of Mayne. While useful, the book is unannotated and to me greatly overestimates Mayne's faith in detection as opposed to prevention. It should be read cautiously. T. A. Critchley, *A History of Police in England and Wales, 900-1966* (London: Constable, 1967), covers much ground since Anglo-Saxon days, but does not deal with the Metropolitan Police after the 1830s. He is especially strong for original work on country police forces during the nineteenth century. His *The Conquest of Violence: Order and Liberty in Britain* (New York: Schocken, 1970) is also useful for the study of efforts to cope with riots and demonstrations, but seems overoptimistic. A more scholarly work on the control of political disorder is Frederick Clare Mather, *Public Order in the Age of the Chartists* (Manchester: University of Manchester Press, 1959), the standard source but still in the tradition which sees demonstrators as "the mob." A widely accepted antidote to this tradition is George Rudé, *The Crowd in History, 1730-1848* (New York: Wiley, 1964), which has influenced my viewpoint. Returning to the general subject of police, Leon Radzinowicz, *A History of English Criminal Law and Its Administration from 1750,* 4 vols. (London: Stephens, 1948-68), is the most thorough and thoughtful treatment which places the police in the context of legal developments. Radzinowicz is indispensable, although like his predecessors he has not yet gone beyond the 1840s. Fortunately he is still at work. An old source, which is still useful because it does pay attention to the police after the 1850s, is J. F. Moylan, *Scotland Yard and the Metropolitan Police* (London: G. P. Putnam, 1929). Perhaps the most stimulating and provocative discussion of the demand for order and policing, although it does not always distinguish between the Metropolitan Police and the search for semimilitary policing of the industrial districts and countryside, is by an American: Allan Silver, "The Demand for Order in Civil Society: A Review of Some Themes in the History of Urban Crime, Police, and Riot," in *The Police: Six Sociological Essays,* ed. David J. Bordua (New York: Wiley, 1967). Along with a companion piece, "Social and Ideological Bases of British Elite Reactions to Domestic Crisis in 1829-1832," *Politics and Society* 2 (February 1971): 179-201, Silver's work on the police significantly influenced my thinking. Though often cited, J. L. Lyman, "The Metropolitan Police Act of 1829," *Journal of Criminal Law, Criminology and Police Science* 55 (March 1964): 141-54, is not especially important after reading the other sources. It is useful, however, as an introduction. Two articles by Robert D. Storch, though not used directly in this study, are essential reading for students of British police and working-class history. In "The Plague of the Blue Locusts: Police Reform and Popular Resistance in Northern England, 1840-1857," *International Review of Social History* 20 (1975): 61-90, and "The Policeman as Domestic Missionary: Urban Discipline and Popular Culture in Northern

England, 1850-1880," *Journal of Social History* 9 (Summer 1976): 481-509, Storch depicts continuing confict between police and workers during the nineteenth century in areas outside of London. His view contrasts with my picture of growing accommodation in London.

Along with Radzinowicz, Sir William Holdsworth's monumental *A History of English Law,* 16 vols. (London: Methuen, 1909-65), vols. 13-16 ed. A. L. Goodhart and H. G. Hanbury, provided the essential legal background. These more modern works, however, do not entirely supplant the Stephen and Pike volumes cited earlier. A scholarly and a popular study of nineteenth-century crime complement each other: J. J. Tobias, *Crime and Industrial Society in the Nineteenth Century* (London: Batsford, 1967), and Kellow Chesney, *The Victorian Underworld* (London: Temple Smith, 1970). Tobias provides valuable legal and social background as well as a careful if somewhat impressionistic discussion of crime and criminals. Chesney is lively, largely a distillation of popular nineteenth-century literature, but unfortunately is not annotated.

The development of English social history in the last twenty or thirty years produced books which were essential for placing the police in their social milieu. The most useful to me were Geoffrey Best, *Mid-Victorian Britain, 1851-1875* (New York: Schocken, 1971), provocatively chatty; W. L. Burn, *The Age of Equipoise: A Study of the Mid-Victorian Generation* (New York: W. W. Norton, 1964), especially good on attitudes toward crime; Asa Briggs, *The Making of Modern England, 1784-1867: The Age of Improvement* (New York: Harper, 1965), and *Victorian Cities* (New York: Harper, 1963), excellent respectively for political and urban background. Brian Harrison's works, *Drink and the Victorians: The Temperance Question in England, 1815-1872* (Pittsburgh, Pa.: University of Pittsburgh Press, 1971), "Religion and Recreation in Nineteenth-Century England," *Past and Present* 38 (December 1967): 98-125, and "The Sunday Trading Riots of 1855," *Historical Journal* 8 (1965): 219-45, provided the best treatments of drink, drunkenness, and the "Sunday question," although he does not deal extensively with the police response. Though covering a period later than my study, Gareth Stedman Jones, *Outcast London: A Study in the Relationship between Classes in Victorian Society* (London: Oxford University Press, 1971), provided valuable perspective on "respectable" views of the "dangerous classes" and led me to important sources. Francis Sheppard, *London 1808-1870: The Infernal Wen* (Berkeley, Calif.: University of California Press, 1971), was a thorough "urban biography." E. P. Thompson's classic, *The Making of the English Working Class* (New York: Vintage Books, 1963), stops just short of my period but provided essential perspective and a framework of analysis. A more general work, Karl Polanyi's *The Great Transformation* (New York: Rinehart, 1944), gave a unique economic insight into the demand for order.

When I first began research for this study there were no modern published histories of the New York or other American police forces. Events of the early and mid-1960s prompted historical interest in the police which has continued, though not as intensively, ever since. Roger Lane, *Policing the City: Boston, 1822-1885* (Cambridge, Mass.: Harvard University Press, 1967), was the first modern scholarly history of a police force. He places the police in their political and social context, although his Boston seems oddly conflict-free after the 1830s. James F. Richardson completed his Ph.D. dissertation, "The History of Police Protection in New York City, 1800-1870" (New York University) in 1961. It is fuller for my period than his book, *The New York Police: Colonial Times to 1901* (New York: Oxford University Press, 1970). I owe much to Richardson's source and interpretative leads, although I have taken a somewhat different tack. David R. Johnson, "The Search for an Urban Discipline: Police Reform as a Response to Crime in American Cities, 1800-1875" (Ph.D. diss., University of Chicago, 1972), and George A. Ketcham, "Municipal Police Reform: A Comparative Study of Law Enforcement in Cincinnati, Chicago, New Orleans, New York, and St. Louis, 1844-1877 (Ph.D. diss., University of Missouri, 1967), reveal the common patterns of police authority in American cities. A recent dissertation of particular importance, which I was not able to use in my research, is Allan E. Levett, "Centralization of City Police in the Nineteenth Century United States" (Ph.D. diss., University of Michigan, 1975). Levett moves beyond narrative history to place the police in a wider sociological context. His emphasis on fear of the "dangerous classes" as a motive for establishment of police forces parallels my own views. Selden D. Bacon, "The Early Development of American Municipal Police" (Ph.D. diss., Yale University, 1939), is a pioneer of scholarly treatment of the police. Two old books by Raymond B. Fosdick, *American Police Systems* (New York: Century, 1921) and *European Police Systems* (New York: Century, 1915), are still useful, despite their attribution of crime to immigration. Stephen F. Ginsberg, "The Police and Fire Protection in New York City, 1800-1850," *New York History* 52 (April 1971): 133-50, reminds us of the breadth of early notions of the police function. Thomas J. Fleming, "The Policeman's Lot," *American Heritage* 21 (February 1970): 5-17, 70-73, is a lively, nicely illustrated popular account, but it is full of small factual errors.

Richard Hofstadter and Michael Wallace, eds., *American Violence: A Documentary History* (New York: Knopf, 1970); Hugh D. Graham and Ted R. Gurr, eds., *Violence in America: Historical and Comparative Perspectives* (New York: New American Library, 1969); and David Grimsted, "Rioting in Its Jacksonian Setting," *American Historical Review* 77 (April 1972): 361-97, are among the most important treatments of a subject which has seized official, scholarly, and popular interest.

American legal historians have concentrated on constitutional law and the higher courts rather than the administration of justice on the lower levels. Studies of lower courts and police-judicial relations are needed. Unlike the situation for England, I did not find any useful works of legal history. Fortunately, however, the field does seem to be moving toward a more social orientation, so these gaps may be filled. Similarly, Americans have not yet produced as much solid work on the history of crime as the English. There is nothing comparable to Tobias's study or even to the old works for the period of my study. Herbert Asbury, *The Gangs of New York: An Informal History of the Underworld* (New York: Knopf, 1928), is quite informal but is frequently cited because it is the only book of its kind. Roger Lane, "Urbanization and Criminal Violence in the Nineteenth Century: Massachusetts as a Test Case," in *Violence in America,* ed. Graham and Gurr, is an important study of how improved policing influences the reporting of crime and arrest rates. David J. Rothman, *The Discovery of the Asylum: Social Order and Disorder in the New Republic* (Boston: Little, Brown, 1971), treats the establishment of and changes in prisons as parts of a broader trend toward institutionalization of deviants, but does not deal with the police. He does provide useful information about attitudes toward crime.

American urban and social historians seem to prefer quantitative studies of social mobility and demography over analysis of the power structure and class relationships. Important exceptions which were useful for my study were Samuel P. Hays, "Political Parties and the Community-Society Continuum," in *The American Party Systems,* ed. William N. Chambers and Walter D. Burnham (New York: Oxford University Press, 1968); Edward Pessen, "The Egalitarian Myth and the American Social Reality: Wealth, Mobility and Equality in the 'Era of the Common Man,'" *American Historical Review* 76 (October 1971): 989–1034; and Douglas T. Miller, *Jacksonian Aristocracy: Class and Democracy in New York, 1830–1860* (New York: Oxford University Press, 1967). Arthur C. Cole, *The Irrepressible Conflict, 1850–1865* (New York: Macmillan, 1934), a more old-fashioned work of social history, proved quite valuable for urban developments. General urban histories, like Charles N. Glaab and A. Theodore Brown, *A History of Urban America* (New York: Macmillan, 1967), gave useful background information. Oddly enough, New York lacks a comprehensive urban biography such as Sheppard's work on London. Richardson's dissertation and book on the police were very useful for describing the urban milieu.

VI. Sociological Studies of Authority, Police, and the Administration of Justice

While the British have produced the most and best police history, they have written little sociology. The image of the modern London police in the scholarly as well as the popular mind may rely too much on what the force was like in the past. However, one of the most useful sociological studies was British: Michael Banton, *The Policeman in the Community* (New York: Basic Books, 1964), a comparative study of the modern Edinburgh police and various American forces, which greatly influenced my conception of personal and impersonal authority. John R. Lambert, *Crime, Police, and Race Relations: A Study in Birmingham* (London: Oxford University Press,

1970); and J. C. Alderson and Philip John Stead, eds., *The Police We Deserve* (London: Wolfe, 1973), are among new books which indicate more thorough investigation of modern police problems. A suggestive but exaggerated English work is Geoffrey Gorer, *Exploring English Character* (New York: Criterion, 1955), which traces many English personality traits to the example of the bobby.

A number of American sociological studies were essential in shaping my thinking on broad themes and specific areas. The most important of these were Paul Chevigny, *Police Power: Police Abuses in New York City* (New York: Pantheon, 1969), in the best tradition of thoroughly informed polemic; Wayne R. LaFave, *Arrest: The Decision to Take a Suspect into Custody* (Boston: Little, Brown, 1965), a thorough study of the many ramifications of police discretion; Herbert L. Packer, *The Limits of the Criminal Sanction* (Stanford, Calif.: Stanford University Press, 1968), a philosophical and legal discussion of the definition of crime and the role of law in creating criminal actions; Jerome H. Skolnick, *Justice without Trial: Law Enforcement in Democratic Society* (New York: Wiley, 1966), an essential treatment of discretion which posits a conflict between the rule of law and the demand for order; William A. Westley, *Violence and the Police: A Sociological Study of Law, Custom, and Morality* (Cambridge, Mass.: M.I.T. Press, 1970), the most important analysis of police violence; and James Q. Wilson, *Varieties of Police Behavior: The Management of Law and Order in Eight Communities* (Cambridge, Mass.: Harvard University Press, 1968). Wilson develops a contrast between "watchman" and "legalistic" styles of police authority which significantly influenced my thinking, although the model does not perfectly fit the mid-nineteenth-century forces. Of less importance to me, but still valuable, were Nicholas Alex, *Black in Blue: A Study of the Negro Policeman* (New York: Appleton-Century-Crofts, 1969); Albert J. Reiss, Jr., *The Police and the Public* (New Haven, Conn.: Yale University Press, 1971); Arthur Niederhoffer, *Behind the Shield: The Police in Urban Society* (New York: Doubleday, Anchor Books, 1967); and Jonathan Rubinstein, *City Police* (New York: Farrar, Straus, and Giroux, 1974). James F. Richardson, *Urban Police in the United States* (Port Washington, N.Y.: Kennikat, 1974), places modern police problems and developments in the historical context.

Thurman Arnold, *The Symbols of Government* (New York: Harcourt, Brace, Harbinger Books, 1962; first pub. 1935) helped shape my thinking on the rule of law and discretionary power. Last, but perhaps most important, was Max Weber, *The Theory of Social and Economic Organization,* ed. A. M. Henderson and Talcott Parsons (New York: Free Press, 1964), and *On Law in Economy and Society,* ed. Max Rheinstein (Cambridge, Mass.: Harvard University Press, 1954). Weber is the starting point for anyone interested in the legitimation of power. While he does not have the last word, his opening remarks are essential.

INDEX

231

Riot squad, 22, 52
Robbers, station-house detention of, 61
Robbery: (London), convictions for, 88; increased reporting of, 113; (New York), low convictions for, 96
Roe, Sir Frederick A., 83
Roebuck, J. A., M. P.: quoted as antisabbatarian, 130
"Rookeries," 124-25
"Roughs," 120-21, 144
Rowan, Commissioner Sir Charles, 2, 39-40, 109, 124, 133
Royal Irish Constabulary, 1
Rule of law, 46-47, 102-3, 166, 169

Sabbatarianism (London): class basis of, 129; evangelical basis of, 129-30; moderation of, 132. *See also* Sabbatarians; Sunday laws
Sabbatarianism (New York): class basis of, 157; evangelical basis of, 157; and religious revival of 1857-58, 160. *See also* Sabbatarians; Sunday laws
Sabbatarians, and police: (London), 129-38; (New York), 156-66
Sailors, opposition to London police, 105
St. Giles, 5
Saloons, Sunday closing of, 161, 163
Scotland Yard. *See* Commissioners of Metropolitan Police (London)
Service functions of police, 107, 115-16, 128
Shaftesbury, Lord, 130
"Shoulder-hitters," 144
Slungshots, 53
Smoke Nuisances Act, 18
Society for the Promotion of the Due Observance of the Lord's Day, 131
Soldiers: opposition to London police, 105; in riot control, 14, 22-23
Solly, Henry: quoted on violence, 115
"Special constables," 9

"Spoils System," 29-32
Standing army, fear of police as, 4
Station-house discharge, 66-73
Stolen goods: and London police, 56, 86; receiving of, 88, 96
Stop-and-search, 55-57
Street vendors, antagonism toward London police, 105, 126
Sunday: among working classes in London, 129; disorder on, in London, 133-34; in New York, 164-65
Sunday laws: and London police, 132-38; and New York police, 158-66
Supreme Court (New York): and confessions, 77-78; and detention on suspicion, 60; (United States): and police, 46, 75, 169
Surveillance, police: of citizens, 4; of "ticket-of-leave men," 112, 119

Tallmadge, General Superintendent Frederick A., 52
Temperance reformers, 72, 73, 132
Thames police, 82
"Ticket-of-leave men," 112, 115, 119
Tocqueville, Alexis de: cited on uniforms, 36; quoted on discretionary power, 20
Tories, and London police, 12, 105
Traffic control, and London police, 105
Training of policemen (London), 41
Trial, police participation in: (London), 83-86; (New York), 95-96
Truncheon, 14 n 20; 48-49, 50, 51
Tweed Ring: and police, 18, 44; and Sunday laws, 165

Uniform, police: (London), 33-34; (New York), 34-37

Vagrancy, 54-55, 84, 93, 96
Vagrancy Act, 54-55
Varian, Mayor Isaac: quoted on police and citizens, 17
Vigilance committees, 140